S0-AFN-989

american education

An Introduction to Social and Political Aspects

Joel Spring

University of Cincinnati

Longman

New York and London

American Education

Longman Inc., New York

Associated companies, branches, and representatives
throughout the world.

Copyright © 1978 by Longman Inc.

All rights reserved. No part of this publication may be
reproduced, stored in a retrieval system, or transmitted
in any form or by any means, electronic, mechanical,
photocopying, recording, or otherwise, without the prior
permission of the publisher.
Second printing, September 1978
Developmental Editor: Nicole Benevento
Design: Pencils Portfolio, Inc.
Manufacturing and Production Supervisor: Louis Gaber
Composition: Maryland Linotype Composition Company, Inc.
Printing and Binding: The Maple Press

Library of Congress Cataloging in Publication Data

Spring, Joel H
American education.

(Educational policy, planning, and theory)
Index.
1. Educational sociology—United States.
2. Education and state—United States. 3. Educational
equalization—United States. I. Title.
LC191.S684 1978   370.19'3'0973   77–17608
ISBN 0–582–28020–6

MANUFACTURED IN THE UNITED STATES OF AMERICA

CONTENTS

INTRODUCTION

This text is intended for introductory courses in teacher education and as supplementary reading for courses in the social foundations of education. It was written with the conviction that a teacher's career involves more than being an educational technician. Actions within the public school, one of the major social and political institutions in modern society, affect society from the local community level to the level of national government policy. The issues involved in schooling range from control of the labor market to political socialization.

A teaching career therefore involves more than decisions about methods of instruction; it includes as well political, economic, and social decisions that affect the entire society. This textbook's purpose is to acquaint prospective teachers with the political context in which they will work and with the major social, economic, and political issues related to education.

Part 1 deals with the relationship between school and society. A discussion of the social, economic, and political purposes of schooling is designed to acquaint the reader with the major arguments for the support of public schooling. Following this discussion is a consideration of the central concern of educational policy in the 1960s and '70s: equality of opportunity and, specifically, equality of educational opportunity. This text treats these issues in relationship to social mobility, social-class differences, and desegregation. The concluding chapter of part 1 focuses on the relationship between a national youth policy and public schooling.

Part 2 introduces the reader to the structure of power in American education. Separate chapters deal with control of education at local, state, and national levels. These chapters are meant to make the reader aware of the realities when considering control in education. In addition, chapter 8 relates the history and goals of the National Education Association and the American Federation of Teachers, and provides a summary of their roles in the control of education. Chapters 9 and 10 deal with other major institutions that affect public schooling, including private foundations, Washington lobbyists, accrediting associations, and the courts. Chapter 10 also reviews court cases related to compulsion, religion, academic freedom, and school finances.

PART 1

THE
SCHOOL
AND
THE
SOCIAL
STRUCTURE

1

THE PURPOSES OF PUBLIC SCHOOLING

THE PUBLIC SCHOOL HAS BECOME ONE OF THE most central and controversial parts of society. Parents select housing in terms of available schooling; politicians are often forced to voice their opinions on school issues; racial and religious riots take place at the schoolhouse; some parents accuse schools of not being patriotic while others find them guilty of flag waving; some members of society argue that schools will end poverty and others contend that they maintain poverty.

One of the reasons for these developments is that the school has become the focus of the hopes of countless groups and individuals in society. One hundred and fifty years ago, the public school was seen as the key element in producing the citizen for the modern state. This was the view of the school that prevailed in both liberal and authoritarian societies. In addition, some nineteenth-century supporters of education argued that crime could be eliminated in a society only through the proper education of children. Thus, public education assumed the burden of moral and social training. In the twentieth century this impulse continued and expanded as schools adopted programs designed to end drug abuse and alcoholism, reduce traffic accidents, and improve community health. Economic arguments were also given to support the expansion of schooling. Some advocates of public schooling contended that mass education would increase the wealth of the entire community, eliminate poverty by giving all citizens job skills, and reduce tensions between the rich and the poor by providing equality of opportunity.

3

All the goals that have been given to public schooling have resulted in an institution that reflects both the hopes and frustrations of society. Crime and poverty have not been eliminated. Has the school failed, or are these impossible goals for this institution? Political corruption and complaints of an uneducated citizenry continue, and different groups in society argue that the school is not teaching the "correct" political doctrine. The frustration and tensions are heightened by a lack of consensus about social and political values. Some religious leaders claim the school should not be in the business of moral education, that the teaching of morality should be the province of the family and religious institutions. In Ohio in the mid-1970s some church leaders established their own "Christian" schools to combat the "godlessness" of the public institutions. In West Virginia riots and school shutdowns occurred as parents and other community members objected to the "un-American" and sacrilegious material in school textbooks.

Within this framework the different objectives of schooling should be discussed in terms of their contradictions and inherent problems. In this way one can understand why public schooling has become both the hope of modern society and the focus of conflict and tension.

The Political Purposes of Schooling

The most important political goal of public schooling in modern society is the education of the future citizen. This statement can mean different things depending on the nature of the political organization. For instance, in Nazi Germany in the 1930s schools were enlisted in a general campaign to produce a citizen who would believe in the racial superiority of the German people, support fascism, and be willing to die at the command of Hitler. Racial biology and fascist political doctrines were taught in the classroom; patriotic parades and singing took place in the school yard. The lesson learned from the experience of schools in Nazi Germany is that one must carefully evaluate the citizenship-training function of the public schools. Citizenship training is not necessarily good, nor can it exist apart from a general political philosophy.

In America early proposals for public systems of education reflected a variety of concerns about the establishment of a republican form of government. One of the major worries expressed immediately following the American Revolution was the source of future leadership for the new form of government. Since hereditary nobility and monarchy would no longer be the bases for leadership, there was a question about who would be the leaders of a republican government. Revolutionary leader Benjamin Rush proposed in the late eighteenth century the establishment of a national university and a requirement that all government officials must hold a degree from that institution. Rush argued that as one should not allow quacks to practice medicine, one should not allow quacks in politics. President George Washington proposed a national university before Congress as a means of training political leaders and creating a common national culture by bringing together within one institution students from all areas of the country.

One of the arguments against Washington's proposal for a national university as a training ground for political leadership was the charge of elitism. (Current criticism of reliance upon educational institutions as sources of political and social leadership makes the same charge.) Critics of Washington's proposal felt that a national university would be training leaders who would view themselves as being better and more important than the general public. These educated leaders would not necessarily represent the interests and welfare of the general public. The hereditary aristocracy might be replaced by an aristocracy of the educated. If only the rich have access to higher education, then the rich can use higher education as a means of perpetuating and supporting their social status.

One answer to the charge of elitism is the concept of a meritocracy. This idea permeates our existing educational institutions. A meritocracy is a social system where all members are given an equal chance to develop their abilities and rise in the social hierarchy. In a meritocracy the school is often viewed as the key institution for training and sorting citizens. One of the earliest and most elaborate proposals for a society based on the selectivity of education was Plato's *Republic*. In Plato's utopian proposal each generation was trained in music and gymnastics, and from each generation the most talented were selected for further education as guardians. The most talented guardians were educated to be philosopher-kings. An educational system functioning in this manner, Plato believed, would result in the wisdom of philosopher-kings ruling society.

One of the earliest proposals in the United States to create an educational system designed to select and promote talent into a social hierarchy was made by Thomas Jefferson in 1779 in a proposed *Bill for the More General Diffusion of Knowledge*. Jefferson's plan called for three years of free education for all free children. The most talented of these children were to be selected and educated at public expense at regional grammar schools. From this select group were to be chosen the most talented for further education. Thomas Jefferson wrote in *Notes on the State of Virginia*, "By this means twenty of the best geniuses will be raked from the rubbish annually, and be instructed, at the public expense. . . ."

The details of Jefferson's plan are not as important as the idea, which has become ingrained in American social thought, that schooling is the best means of identifying democratic leadership. This idea assumes that the educational system is fair in its judgments and that its basis for judgment has some relationship to the role for which students are being selected.

For instance, fairness of selection in education assumes that the individual is being judged solely on talent demonstrated in school and not on other social factors such as race, religion, dress, and social class. As will be discussed in later chapters, these factors have been related to performance in school. If, for instance, the educational institution tends to favor an individual from a particular religion or social class, then it would tend to select and promote that particular individual in school and, consequently, in the social hierarchy.

This situation could result in the creation of a democratic elitism in which certain groups were favored in school and the social power of their class was perpetuated through the school. For example, if all members of society were taught to believe that the school selected fairly and only those selected by the educational system could lead society, then all members of society would accept the social hierarchy perpetuated by the educational system. Acceptance of this situation might obscure other inequalities in society. For instance, if the educational system favored those with wealth, then all members of society might come to accept differences in wealth as differences in talent as determined by educational institutions.

Another debatable issue is the assumption of a relationship between talented performance in an educational institution and performance in a social role. There might not be any necessary relationship between the skills and attitudes required for good educational performance and those required for good occupational and social performance. The best medical doctor might not be the one who received the highest grades in medical school. The best politician might not be the one who received the highest grades in political science courses. Of course, this depends on what one means by the "best doctor" or the "best politician." The important question is whether or not one believes that the skills required to succeed in an educational institution are the best skills for a particular social role.

The differences between these approaches is reflected in the differences between Thomas Jefferson and Horace Mann, often called the father of American education. Jefferson proposed a very limited education for the general citizenry. The three years of free education that were to be provided to all children were to consist of training in reading, writing, and arithmetic with reading instruction being given in books on Greek, Roman, English, and American history. Jefferson did not believe that people needed to be educated to be good citizens. He believed in the guiding power of natural reason to lead the citizen to the correct political decisions. The political education of the citizen was to come from a free press where the citizen would judge between competing political ideas in newspapers. The only requirement was that the citizen know how to read.

Horace Mann, on the other hand, believed that a common political creed had to be instilled in all citizens. Without this political consensus a democratic society was doomed to political strife and chaos. Mann developed these ideas and his reputation as America's greatest educational leader while serving as secretary of the Massachusetts Board of Education between 1837 and 1848. Mann had begun his career as a lawyer; he dedicated his life to public schooling when, he claimed, he realized that schooling was the key to the reform of society.

Horace Mann lived during a period of great political tension and fear that the extension of suffrage would lead to violence and mob rule. Mann believed that political and social order could be maintained if all citizens accepted a common set of political values. These values were to be taught in a common public school and would provide a political consensus or framework in which democracy would function. The important thing for Mann was that all children in society would attend the same type of school. This was what was meant by "common." It was a school common to all children. Within the common school children of all religions and social classes were to share in a common education. Basic social disagreements were to vanish as rich and poor children, children whose parents were supporters of different political parties, mingled in the schoolroom.

Within the walls of the common schoolhouse were to be taught the basic principles of a republican form of government. Mann assumed that republican principles existed that members of all political parties could agree upon and that therefore could be taught without objection. In fact, he argued against the teaching of any politically controversial topic because of its potential for destroying the public school. The combination of common schooling and the teaching of a common political philosophy were to create the political consensus that would make it possible for a republican society to function. Political liberty would be possible, according to Mann's philosophy, because it would be restrained and controlled by the public school.

One of the many problems inherent in Mann's philosophy, and one that has plagued public schools in the United States since the nineteenth century, is the assumption of the existence of common republican principles upon which all citizens agree. Since the nineteenth century there have been continual pressures and controversies about the type of political philosophy to be taught in the public schools. Conservative political groups, such as the American Legion and the Daughters of the American Revolution, have throughout the twentieth century put pressure on local public schools to avoid teaching what these organizations consider "left-wing" ideas. On the other hand, liberal organizations and particularly labor unions have attempted to influence the schools to teach their particular political doctrines.

There has also existed a tradition of strong dissent to a public system of education teaching political doctrines. As far back as the late eighteenth century, English political theorist William Godwin warned against national systems of education because they could become a means by which those who controlled the government could control the minds of future citizens. Godwin wrote in 1793, "Their views as institutors of a system of education will not fail to be analogous to their views in their political capacity: the data upon which their instructions are founded."

Another problem with Horace Mann's vision of the democratic consensus built upon the common school is that the American public school has never been common to all children. All races, religions, and social classes have not mingled within a single common school. Racial segregation continues to exist in American public schools even after massive efforts at desegregation in the 1960s and '70s. A variety of religious groups, including the Amish and Catholics, have maintained a tradition of parochial schools in opposition to the secularism of the public schools. Children in wealthy suburbs attend private schools or public schools that are quite different from those in poorer school districts. Mann's dream of the common public school has never come into existence in the United States.

Horace Mann's hope to reduce tension between social groups in American society can be called a form of socialization. "Socialization" refers to the learning of habits and attitudes of social conduct. This learning primarily takes place in school through social interaction and not through the specific content of what is taught in the classroom. For instance, in the case of the common school, a reduction of tension between groups was to be primarily a result of the intermingling of students and not of textbook learning, class recitation, or lectures by the teacher.

It has been argued that socialization in the school is one of the most powerful means of political control. The very fact of having an entire generation within an institution where they are required to cooperate and obey rules is considered by some preparation to cooperate and obey the rules of the government. Johann Fichte in Prussia in the early nineteenth century asserted that schools would prepare the individual to serve the government and country by teaching obedience to the rules of the school and the development of a sense of loyalty to the school. He stated further that students would transfer their obedience to the laws of the school to obedience to the constitution of the country. More importantly, according to Fichte, interaction between students, as well as loyalty and service to the school and fellow students, would prepare the individual for service to the country. The school was a miniature community in which children learned to adjust their individuality to the requirements of the community. The real work of the school, Fichte said, was in shaping this adjustment. The well-ordered government required that the citizen go beyond mere obedience to the written constitution and laws. Fichte believed the child must be adjusted to see the government as something greater than the individual and must learn to sacrifice for the good of the social whole.

Fichte also advocated the teaching of patriotic songs, national history, and literature to increase the sense of dedication and patriotism to the state. This combination of socialization and patriotic teachings, he argued, would produce a citizen more willing and able to participate in the army and, consequently, would reduce the cost of national defense.

In the United States the combination of patriotic exercises and development of loyalty to the institution of the school began to appear in the 1890s. It was during this period of large immigration from Southern and Eastern Europe that the public schools became heavily involved in what were called "Americanization" programs. Americanization involved teaching the immigrant the laws, language, and customs of the United States. Quite naturally, this involved the teaching of American songs and customs. With the coming of World War I, the Pledge of Allegiance, the singing of patriotic songs, student government, and other patriotic exercises became a part of the American school. In addition, the development of extracurricular activities led to an emphasis on school spirit. The formation of football and basketball teams, with their accompanying trappings of cheerleaders and pep rallies, was supported with the idea that these activities improved school spirit and, consequently, service to society.

The involvement of the American public school in the teaching and development of patriotism has created problems for a democratic society with a variety of religious, ethnic, and political groups. Some religious groups object to pledging allegiance to the flag because it involves worship of a "graven image." The U.S. Supreme Court ruled in 1943 in *West Virginia State Board of Education* v. *Barnette* that expulsion of children of Jehovah's Witnesses for not saluting the flag was a violation of their constitutional rights of freedom of religion. Some teachers view patriotic exercises as contrary to the principles of a free society. In a later chapter on the rights of teachers (chapter 10) there is a lengthy discussion of the court cases dealing with academic freedom and loyalty oaths; conflict between patriotism and students' rights are also dealt with in this chapter.

Besides the question of the role of patriotism in a democratic society is the question of service to the country. Is it good in a democratic society to place service to society above service to oneself? Or should the individual demand that institutions in a democratic society be designed to serve the individual?

The problems inherent in using public schools as a means of political control in a democratic society are not easily resolved. One of the central questions is who or what group should determine the type of political teachings and political socialization in the schools? This question leads directly to the issue of who controls American education (discussed in later chapters). It may be that the attempt to use the school as a means of creating a political meritocracy or a political consensus or a sense of patriotism is contradictory to the ideals of political liberty.

The Social Purposes of Schooling

The hope of improving society through public schooling has almost become an article of American faith. Horace Mann believed it was the key to all social problems. He argued that past societies had experimented with different forms of government and laws in an attempt to stop crime and that they had all failed. The answer, Mann said, was in the proper training of young children so that they would not desire or perform criminal acts. Mann even suggested with a certain amount of utopian hope that America might see the day when the training of the schoolhouse would no longer make it necessary to enforce the law.

The idea of using the school as a means of social control was first explicitly stated by American sociologist Edward Ross in the 1890s. Ross referred to education as an inexpensive form of police. He divided social control into external and internal forms. Traditionally, he argued, internal forms of control had centered on the family, the church, and the community. The family and church had worked on the child to inculcate moral values and social responsibility to ensure social stability and cohesion. In modern society, Ross declared, the family and church were being replaced by the school as the most important institution for instilling internal values. Ross saw reliance on education as a means of control becoming characteristic of American society. More and more, the school was taking the place of the church and the family. "The ebb of religion is only half a fact," Ross wrote. "The other half is the high tide of education. While the priest is leaving the civil service, the schoolmaster is coming in. As the state shakes itself loose from the church, it reaches out for the school."

One of the things heard constantly throughout the twentieth century is that the family and religion are collapsing and thus the school must pick up the pieces. Whether or not these two institutions have in fact collapsed is debatable, but the argument has been used to justify the continued use of the school to solve problems.

The school has been used in a variety of ways in the twentieth century in attempts to solve social problems. For instance, the very act of requiring school attendance has been viewed as a means of reducing juvenile delinquency. The development of summer schools in the late nineteenth and early twentieth centuries was justified as a means of keeping youths off the streets. Once youths were off the streets it was hoped that the moral and social influence of the school would keep them from the future commitment of crime and the use of tobacco and alcohol. In later years the schools would assume the burden of eliminating traffic accidents through driver training; improving family life through courses in modern living and home economics; eliminating drug abuse, venereal disease, and a multitude of other social problems through health education.

For some twentieth-century Americans, the school became the symbol and hope for the good society. This hope is best illustrated by a story told to kindergarteners in the early part of the century about two children who bring a beautiful flower from their school class to their dirty and dark tenement apartment. The mother takes the flower and puts it in a glass of water near a dirty window. She decides the flower needs more light to expose its beauty. The mother proceeds to wash the window, which allows more light into the apartment and illuminates the dirty floors, walls, and furniture. The added light sends the mother scurrying around to clean up the now-exposed dirt. In the meantime the father, who is unable to keep a steady job because of a drinking problem, returns to the apartment and is amazed to find his grim dwelling transformed into a clean and tidy home. The transformation of the apartment results in the father wanting to spend more time at home and less time in the tavern. The father's drinking problem is solved; he is able to maintain a steady job, and the family lives happily ever after.

This story characterizes the hope that the moral influence of the school would reach out into the homes and neighborhoods of America. One unanswered question, and a question that is inherent also in the earlier discussion of political control is, whose moral and social values would permeate the American school? Horace Mann argued that there were certain moral values that all religious groups could agree upon and that these shared values would become the backbone of the moral teachings of the school. A variety of religious groups have disagreed with this idea from the time of Mann to the present. The largest single religious group to dissent and establish its own system of schools was the Catholic church. The argument of Catholic church leaders was that all education by its very goal of shaping behavior was religious and that it was impossible for a public institution to claim that it could satisfy the needs of all religious groups. Even if the public school eliminated all religious and moral teaching, this alternative could not be accepted because education would then become irreligious.

Of even more importance than the question of whose social and moral values should permeate the school is the question of whether or not the school should be involved in attempts at social reform or improvement. One reason why schools have gotten involved in so many social problems is because the school is the most available institution and the one least likely to affect other parts of the social system. For instance, alcoholism might be the product of boredom with monotonous types of work, deteriorating urban conditions, family traditions, or a variety of other factors in the social structure. To turn to the school to solve the problem of alcoholism through health classes is to say that the problem is one of individual training and not related to factors in the social structure. It is easier to give a health course than to change job conditions, improve urban environments, or manipulate family traditions. Of even greater importance is the fact that the school is less threatening than such direct changes. For instance, changing job conditions involves confronting the whole organization of industry and the conflicting interests of unions and business.

In other words, the school is often the safest and least controversial way of planning for social improvement. A politician in the state legislature or in the local community can call for social reform through the school and thereby give the appearance of doing good without antagonizing any community interests. From this standpoint it can be argued that reform through the school is the most conservative means of social reform.

This has been one of the charges made of the school's attempt to end poverty in America. In 1964 and 1965 the federal government under the leadership of President Lyndon B. Johnson launched a massive War on Poverty with the passage of the Economic Opportunity Act and the Elementary and Secondary Education Act. Both President Johnson and the congressional legislation placed primary emphasis upon the role of education in ending poverty. The theoretical support for government action came from the Council of Economic Advisers.

Within this theoretical framework education was seen as one element of a series of social factors that tended to reinforce the condition of being poor. For instance, an inadequate education restricted employment opportunities, which caused a low standard of living and consequently poor medical care, diet, housing, and education for the next generation. This model of poverty suggested that one could begin at any point in the set of causal relationships and move around the circle of poverty. The improvement of health conditions, for instance, would lead to less days lost from employment, which would mean more income. Better income would mean improved housing, medical care, diet, and education. These improved conditions would mean better jobs for those of the next generation.

The idea that the poor were locked into a circle of poverty led to the belief that a culture of poverty existed. Within this framework modern technological society had left the poor behind; and once they were caught in the circle of poverty, a culture of poverty developed that helped to perpetuate social conditions. The War on Poverty was to be a war to destroy a culture by attacking different social conditions. Government action was directed toward housing, diet, and health care; but greatest importance was given to education to begin the chain reaction that would end poverty.

The War on Poverty program included Head Start programs, special funding of programs in local schools for the culturally disadvantaged, job-training programs, bilingual education, minority education, and a host of other special programs. Head Start programs were based on the premise that children of the poor were culturally disadvantaged with regard to learning opportunities when compared to the children of the middle and upper classes. Head Start programs were therefore to provide early childhood education, which would give the poor a "head start" on schooling and allow them to compete on equal terms with other children. Job-training programs were based on the assumption that the cure for teen-age and adult unemployment was job training. Special reading programs were developed for the so-called culturally disadvantaged because it was argued that this was the most important reason for the failure of the poor in school. Bilingual and minority education programs were developed because it was argued that public education tended to discriminate against the culture of minority groups, which resulted in the failure of these groups in school. All these programs were to contribute to the ending of poverty in the United States.

More than a decade later, poverty had not ended in the United States, and serious doubts were expressed about the role of schooling in ending it. Some argued that the War on Poverty educational programs had never really been given a chance because of inadequate funding by the government and mismanagement by federal bureaucrats. Others insisted that better educational programs could be developed and that to do so would require more time and research. Still others felt that the school could accomplish nothing because of community and family influences on the child.

Of most importance for our discussion of the social purposes of schooling was the charge that emphasis upon education was one way of avoiding basic economic problems. The educational component of the War on Poverty assumed that if you educated the poor, they would be able to get jobs and achieve higher income levels. The one flaw in this thinking is that job training does not necessarily increase salaries. Society might always need people for menial tasks, and increased schooling might only result in educational inflation when the nature of jobs does not change but educational requirements are increased.

This became one of the problems of the early 1970s, when the labor market was flooded with college graduates and scholars with doctorates were driving taxicabs and cooking in small restaurants. In this situation the occupational structure did not expand to meet the increased educational training of the labor force. The response of educational institutions was to reorganize for more specific career training and call for more limited educational aspirations. The important lesson of this situation was that the nature of the labor market was more important in determining employment than was the amount of education available to the population. In terms of social reform it seemed to indicate that education alone would not solve the problems of poverty and that more direct changes had to be made in the organization of labor and the structure of the American economic system.

The dream of American education as the panacea for America's social ills continues to be plagued with the questions of whose social and moral values and goals should be in the schoolhouse, and is the panacea of education just a way of avoiding more direct and controversial approaches to social problems? These questions remain unanswered, but American educators still tend to share Horace Mann's hope that the school will be the heart and salvation of American society.

The Economic Purposes of Schooling

One of the most important arguments given for the support of mass public schooling has been that the growth of schooling will increase national wealth and advance technological development. The contribution of the school to economic growth has been seen as occurring in two distinct ways. One is the socialization of the future worker into the modern organization of industry. It is contended that the school, the first formal public organization encountered by the child, provides the preparation and training needed to deal with other complex social organizations. Within this argument the school is viewed as one of the important elements in the modernizing of underdeveloped countries from traditional agricultural societies to modern industrial societies. The second way the school is supposed to help economic growth is through the sorting and training of the labor force. By "sorting" is meant the identification of individual abilities and interests and the determination of the best type of individual training and future employment.

Let us first turn to a consideration of the role of the school in preparing the individual for the modern industrial world. One of the most extensive studies of this issue was conducted by a team of social scientists headed by Alex Inkeles and David Smith in rural and urban areas of Argentina, Chile, East Pakistan, India, Israel, and Nigeria. The general purpose of their study was to look closely at the interrelationship of social institutions and individual development in the making of the modern person. It was argued in the study that there is a difference between the type of individual existing in traditional agricultural societies and the type existing in modern industrial societies. Certain personality characteristics are required for individual participation in large-scale modern productive enterprises such as the factory and may be required for the efficient and effective operation of the organization. This particular study identified a list of characteristics of the modern person. The list included items such as openness to new experience, the readiness for social change, growth of opinion, planning, efficacy, sense of time, and the valuing of a technical skill.

The school, in relationship to what the authors called their scale of Overall Modernity, was found to be one of the major contributors to the making of the modern person. The study contended that in large-scale complex societies no single attribute of the person better predicts attitude, values, and behavior than the amount of schooling received by the individual. The authors stated that this relationship existed because of the school as a *social* organization and certain consequent learning that is incidental to the curriculum and formal instruction. In other words, the school modernizes through a number of processes other than formal instruction in academic subjects. The authors of the study identified these processes as generalization, exemplification, reward and punishment, and modeling.

The study declared that generalization was central to the development within the modern person of a sense of efficacy or belief that an individual can learn how to exert considerable control over the environment. The feeling that a person can advance his or her own goals, the authors found, was an important attribute of the modern person. In school persons developed this attitude when they generalized from a satisfying experience at one task or learning situation to a belief in attaining comparable success in other contexts. In other words, in school children learn to believe in their own ability to learn new things that will increase their competence to control their environments.

Exemplification was defined in the study as the incorporation within the individual of a motivational practice or general rule of a social organization. As examples of these characteristics the study gave the starting and stopping of schools at fixed times, the ordering of events within the school, and the planning of learning events. These situations, it was argued, incorporated within the individual the need for planning and maintaining a regular schedule. Put more simply, teaching a person to get to school on time is preparation for getting to work on time.

Reward, punishment, and modeling were considered as other methods used by the school to inculcate the general practices of social organizations. For instance, pupils are punished for being late, not getting their work done on time, and not obeying the general rules of the school. In modeling the child imitates the teachers or other officials of the school and adopts their behavioral patterns.

The idea of the school as socializer for an industrial society is found throughout the history of American education. One of the arguments given in the nineteenth century in support of marching, drill, and orderliness in schools was preparation for the coordination and orderliness required in the modern factory. Lining up for class as well as marching in and out of the cloakroom and to the blackboard were activities justified in terms of training for factory assembly lines.

In the 1970s the same desire to have the social organization of the school reflect the needs of the workplace were evident in a series of papers prepared by the Center for Economic Studies on the *Educational Requirements for Industrial Democracy*. These reports were part of a flood of literature that began to appear on the need to change the organization of the workplace. In part, this concern was caused by a 1972 report to the Department of Health, Education, and Welfare of the federal government that found that 43 percent of white-collar workers and 24 percent of blue-collar workers were dissatisfied with their jobs.

Proposals to eliminate dissatisfaction by changing work conditions all involved the problem of training workers to fit into the new organizations. The reports of the Center for Economic Studies attempt to match the changes required in work organization with changes in educational organization. For instance, allowing workers to choose their own work schedules, redesigning jobs to make them less burdensome, and increasing choices among job assignments and job rotation are linked by the reports to changes in the organization of schools that involve greater use of educational technology, differentiated staffing, and flexible school schedules.

Several important questions arise regarding the use of the school as the socialization agent for the workplace. Is it the proper role of the school to act purposely to instill certain attitudes and habits as preparation for future employment? Such socialization might create a static society in which the worker is prepared only for existing or known work organizations. More important, whose ideas on proper preparation for work should be included in the planned socialization of work? Employers will naturally suggest the development of work attitudes and habits that will maximize their profits, but these attitudes and habits might not be in the interest of the worker. At one time, a common tenet of the Protestant ethic was that hard, steady, and faithful performance of work would result in steady promotion and increase in salary. Labor unions contended that this was an ethic designed to persuade the worker not to fight through unionization and the strike for higher wages and better working conditions. Like the issues of political control and social reform, the issue of socialization for the workplace is concerned with whose values and attitudes will be instilled in the students.

Socialization of the future worker is one aspect of the other major economic purpose of the school, which is the training and sorting of the labor supply. The development of this purpose of schooling is directly related to the development of vocational education and vocational guidance. Vocational guidance as a function of schooling developed in the United States in the early part of the twentieth century as part of a general reform movement to create a more efficient society. It was argued that one of the most inefficient aspects of society was the distribution and selection of human resources. Strikes and worker dissatisfaction were seen as resulting from people being in jobs that did not interest them and for which they had no aptitude. In addition, human resources were not being fully developed to meet the needs of the labor market.

The early emphasis in vocational guidance, and certainly one of its lasting purposes, was the identification of student interests and abilities and the matching of those interests and abilities with an educational program that would lead to a suitable vocation. The vocational guidance counselor was envisioned as the link between school and industry. The counselor would determine the needs of industry in terms of where there were labor shortages and surpluses. This information would be used in the development of educational programs and the vocational counseling of students.

This general goal for vocational guidance counselors has never been achieved because of the difficulty of training enough people to staff all the junior and senior high schools in the country with expertise in labor-market analysis, work analysis, testing, educational programming, and psychology. Also, predicting the future needs of the labor market is very difficult and not easily used in educational programming. In addition, within the profession of counseling a tension has developed between counseling for improvement of psychological problems and interpersonal relations and counseling for vocations. During the depression of the 1930s counselors got more and more involved in student psychological problems as the job market retreated. During the 1950s the National Manpower Council and the Carnegie Corporation placed pressure on the federal government to support the training of guidance people that would emphasize vocational guidance and labor-market analysis. It was believed that guidance had to get out of therapy and back into manpower planning.

During the 1970s vocational guidance expanded its role in manpower planning and vocational training as it became part of career education. Career education was born in the early 1970s as a response to apparent dissatisfaction with the educational system and the large numbers of unemployed college graduates. Career education brought together vocational guidance and vocational education and attempted to resolve one of the major controversies in vocational education.

This traditional controversy has centered around the issue of whether vocational education should provide the future worker with a broad set of skills and knowledge or whether it should prepare the worker for a specific vocation. The controversy originated at the beginning of the twentieth century when unions were suspicious that vocational education would destroy apprenticeship programs. Unions worked hard both to assure their involvement in vocational education and to assure that vocational education should be training for broad sets of skills and not narrow specialization. In educational ranks there was controversy about whether vocational education should be located in specialized institutions or in a general high school. The National Education Association in 1918 supported the development of comprehensive high schools with college preparatory and vocational programs. It was felt that comprehensive high schools, with all types of students under one roof, would contribute to a sense of national community and that separate institutions would separate people and cause a breakdown of society.

During the late 1950s the role of vocational guidance in a comprehensive high school was reiterated in a widely circulated report by James Conant on *The American High School Today*. The 1959 report, written for the Carnegie Corporation, called for the consolidation of small high schools so that a greater variety of subjects could be offered within one comprehensive school. The courses of study within the school were to be more closely geared to the future vocational destination of the student. Conant argued that the heart of the school had to be the vocational guidance person, who would measure skills and interests and arrange an educational program that would provide the student with marketable skills. Educational administrators were to maintain contact with the local employment situation and assess educational needs in terms of the local labor market. Conant even made the recommendation, which never became a reality, that all high school graduates be given a wallet-size record of their subjects and grades, which could be presented to any employer on demand.

In 1971 and 1972, in response to unemployment problems and the supposed breakdown of American education, the Office of Education of the federal government began to initiate conferences and projects in career education. Like a fast-moving brush fire, career education entered the public schools of the United States. Within one year the Office of Education could claim the participation of 750,000 young people.

Career education places vocational guidance in the center of academic planning and learning. During the elementary and junior high school years, career education is to be a subject-matter field that will acquaint students with the world of work and the varieties of occupations available. After studying and preparing for an occupational choice in these early grades, the student upon entering high school is to begin preparing either for entry directly into an occupational career or into higher education. Career education as a subject-matter field means learning about all the different occupations available in the labor market and the types of interests and abilities associated with different occupations. In other words, career education or vocational guidance is something studied as a formal subject like science and arithmetic.

The process of acquainting the student with a variety of occupations supposedly answers the charge that vocational education at the public school level restricts future vocational choice by segregating students into one educational program. In addition, other school subjects are to be made more relevant because the student will supposedly be able to see the relationship between present learning and a future occupation.

One of the central questions of career education, as it is with the political and social purposes of schooling, is, should career education be a function of public schooling? For instance, one realistic problem is being able to acquaint the student with all possible occupations and at the same time teach the required subjects. The curriculum of the public school is extremely cluttered. It has been proposed that other subjects such as reading, writing, and social studies be taught using career-education material. This would mean that a child's contact with other literature including fiction, as well as with conflicting economic, political, and social ideas, would be greatly reduced.

It is also questionable whether social scientists have developed the necessary methods for accurately predicting future labor needs and rapidly organizing vocational-training material. Even if this were possible, is it desirable? Using the school as a key element in controlling the labor market assumes that the best economy is one that is planned and managed and that the existing economic system is the best. This assumption contradicts the traditional laissez-faire economics of the United States that the best economic system is one that is controlled by the natural forces of the free marketplace. On the other hand, critics of the existing economic system would argue that career education would be an educational system designed to maintain the power of the existing economic structure.

Also, career education does not change the nature of the labor market. It only eases the transition from school into the existing occupational structure. It does not mean that workers will receive higher pay or better working conditions. All career education can promise is the hope that less time will be spent in finding a job and that the entry-level job or first job will be related to an individual's interests and abilities. The danger is that career education will be viewed as a promise to solve basic economic problems in the United States.

Conclusion

The political, social, and economic purposes of schooling are the major reasons the public schools have received wide public support and have become one of the major social institutions of the twentieth century. In the United States the political reasons for supporting schooling have promised the establishment of a democratic community held together by a consensus of political values. Good education is supposed to be the backbone of good government. This promise has constantly encountered the problem of whose political values and ideas will guide the school. The reality of democratic politics is not consensus but a struggle for power. The social purposes of schooling have promised a society free from crime, poverty, and other social ills. The reliance upon the school has frequently been a method of avoiding confrontation with the basic issues. Education, as the hope of tomorrow for educating children, is one way of avoiding the problems of the present. The school as a socializer and sorter for the economy prepares students for an existing labor market and again avoids direct confrontation with the fact that it is the economic conditions surrounding the existing labor market that have caused unemployment.

One of the major questions asked throughout this chapter has been, who or what controls the educational system? The answer to this question determines the political, social, and economic values taught in the school system. It could be, for instance, that the school could become an instrument for control by some social class, economic group, or government institution. But even if a totalitarian power controlled an educational system, there would still be some hope. All learning carries with it the potential of learning things that are not prescribed in the curriculum. All modern societies need to educate people simply to maintain their present complex technologies. For a totalitarian system, the contradiction inherent in an educational system is that knowledge can lead one to question the existing system and seek fundamental changes.

EXERCISES

This chapter has focused on the major political, social, and economic purposes of education. Throughout the chapter questions have been raised about these purposes and the continuing problems they cause for public education in the United States. In a discussion group or in essay form present your ideas about the following issues:

1. Who or what group should determine the type of political teachings and political socialization in the public schools?

2. Should the public schools be used to create a political meritocracy?

3. What type of citizenship training should the public schools provide in a democratic society?

4. Who or what group should determine the moral and social values to be taught in the public schools?

5. What social problems do you think the schools are best able to solve?

6. What do you think should be the relationship between the school and social reform in a democratic society?

7. What do you think should be the relationship between the school and the economic system?

8. Should the focus of public schooling be on career education or should occupational choice and training be a direct function of the labor market?

Suggested Readings and Works Cited in Chapter

Conant, James. *The American High School Today.* New York: McGraw-Hill, 1959.

Major study of the conditions and goals of the American high school. This book had an important impact on shaping the future direction of the high school.

Cremin, Lawrence. *The Republic and the School.* New York: Teachers College Press, 1957.

A good selection of Horace Mann's writings taken from his reports to the Massachusetts Board of Education. A good introduction to the social and political purposes of American education.

Inkeles, Alex, and Smith, David. *Becoming Modern: Individual Change in Six Developing Countries.* Cambridge, Mass.: Harvard University Press, 1974.

Important study of modernization in underdeveloped countries and its relationship to social institutions including the school.

Katz, Michael. *The Irony of Early School Reform.* Boston: Beacon Press, 1968.

A very important study of the early relationship between social reform and education.

Lazerson, Marvin, and Grubb, W. Norton. *American Education and*

Vocationalism: A Documentary History 1870–1970. New York: Teachers College, 1974.

    A good collection of documents dealing with vocational education and the relationship between the school and the economy.

Lee, Gordon. *Crusade Against Ignorance: Thomas Jefferson on Education.* New York: Teachers College Press, 1961.

    Collection of statements by Jefferson about education and good introductory essay.

Levin, Henry. *Educational Requirements for Industrial Democracy: A Taxonomy of Educational Reforms for Changes in the Nature of Work.* Menlo Park, Calif.: Portola Institute, 1974.

    An attempt to change the methods of school socialization to meet the requirements of recent work reforms.

Perkinson, Henry. *The Imperfect Panacea: American Faith in Education, 1865–1965.* New York: Random House, 1968.

    A study of the attempts to use the school to solve major social problems in the United States.

Spring, Joel. *A Primer of Libertarian Education.* New York: Free Life Editions, 1975.

    First two chapters contain major criticisms of the social and political purposes of schooling.

2

THE SOCIAL STRUCTURE AND AMERICAN EDUCATION

Equality of Opportunity

FROM THE NINETEENTH CENTURY TO THE PRESENT AMERICA'S democratic ideology has sought a means of providing equal opportunity for everyone. "Equality of opportunity" means that all members of a society are given equal chances to enter any occupation or social class. This does not mean that everyone can choose any social position; rather, all have an equal chance to compete for any place in society. Ideally, equality of opportunity should result in a social system in which all members occupy their particular positions as a result of merit and not as a result of family wealth, heredity, or special cultural advantages.

Within the ideology of equality of opportunity an individual's life is viewed as a social race in which all members of society begin at the same starting line but finish the race in a different order. The most important thing is assuring that all have equal opportunity to run the social race. This means making sure that all begin at the same starting line and that the race is fair.

Education has often been viewed as the means of assuring that all members of society can begin at the same starting line. Within the common school, differences of social class and special advantages were supposed to disappear as everyone was given an equal chance to get an equal education. This was one of the reasons for the support of common schools in the nineteenth century. During the 1830s workingmen's parties advocated the establishment of public-supported common schools and the end of the public-supported pauper schools that had been the only free schools up to that time. It was asserted that with public schools for the poor and private schools for the middle class and rich, education reinforced social differences and doomed the children of the poor to a perpetual lower-class status. Only common schools could provide for equality of opportunity.

The most extreme statements came from one faction of the New York Workingman's party. This group argued that sending students to a common school would not in itself eliminate differences in social background, for the rich child would return from school to a home richly furnished and full of books, while the poor one would return to shanties that were barren of books and opportunities to learn. School, in the opinion of these workingmen, could never eliminate these differences. Their solution was that all children in New York should be removed from their families and placed in state boarding schools where they would all live in the same types of rooms, wear the same types of clothes, and eat the same food. In this milieu education would truly allow all members of society to begin the race on equal terms. This extreme solution to the problem did not receive wide support, and debates about it eventually led to the collapse of the New York Workingman's party.

One of the major problems regarding the equality-of-opportunity argument is deciding which part of a person's character is most important in the social race. During the twentieth century the most debated issue in this area has been that of IQ or native intelligence. In the early 1900s, French psychologist Alfred Binet developed a test designed to separate children with extremely low levels of intelligence from those with normal levels of intelligence. The assumption of the test was that an inherited level of intelligence existed and could be measured independently of environmental factors such as social class, housing conditions, and cultural advantages.

In the United States the movement to measure native intelligence spread rapidly because of its link to the ideology of equality of opportunity. The doctrine of native intelligence provided the premise that the role of the school was to eliminate all hindrances to the full development of individual intelligence. In other words, individuals would be given an equal chance to develop their particular level of intelligence. Identifying a particular characteristic such as intelligence and recognizing that all members of society would achieve different positions in the race because of differences in native intelligence seemed to give scientific certainty to equality of opportunity. The movement to measure intelligence allowed for equality of opportunity and at the same time justified a hierarchical social structure based on intelligence where all people were not equal. Within this framework democracy was viewed as a social system in which all people were given an equal chance to reach a level in society that corresponded to their level of intelligence.

The major problem in the link between attempts to measure native intelligence and equality of opportunity has been that levels of measured intelligence tend to be related to social class and race. That is, the poor and minority groups in the United States tend to get lower scores on intelligence tests than middle- and upper-class majority groups. This situation has resulted in the claim by some people that the measurement of intelligence discriminates against certain social classes and minority groups.

Discussions about the relationship between the measurement of intelligence and discrimination have centered around whether or not an inherited native intelligence exists and, if it does exist, whether or not it can be measured. For instance, those who believe that an inherited level of intelligence exists and is measurable by tests state that the differences in measured levels of intelligence accurately reflect the conditions of society. Alfred Binet contended that the reason the lower social classes did poorly on intelligence tests was because they did in fact have lower levels of intelligence and, moreover, that was why they were in the lower social class. More recently, psychologist Arthur Jensen has argued that existing tests accurately measure inherited intelligence and that difference in performance by certain racial and social groups are accurate. On the other hand, there have been those who believe in the existence of inherited intelligence but feel that the questions on existing tests reflect the cultural and social bias of the dominant middle class in the United States. The poor and certain racial groups perform poorly on existing tests because many of the test questions deal with things not familiar to these groups. Within this framework, the solution to the problem is the creation of an intelligence test that is free of any cultural bias.

Another approach to the problem is the complete rejection of the idea of inherited intelligence and the acceptance of the view that intelligence and·abilities are primarily a result of environment. This is the famous "nurture-nature" debate. Those who see nurture as being more important argue that differences in measured intelligence between social and racial groups primarily reflect differences in social conditions. The poor grow up in surroundings that are limited in terms of intellectual training: the absence of books and magazines in the home; poor housing, diet, and medical care; and lack of peer-group interest in learning all might account for poor performance on intelligence tests. This approach suggests that the school can act positively to overcome differences caused by social and cultural conditions.

Most recently, schools have tended to act from the premise that differences in backgrounds can be overcome in the schools. The argument for equality of opportunity has been placed in the context of the culture-of-poverty argument described in chapter 1. Through compensatory education and Head Start programs the schools have attempted to end poverty and provide equality of opportunity by trying to compensate for social conditions. Head Start and early childhood education programs are designed to counteract the supposedly poor learning opportunities of the children of the poor, and compensatory education is designed to provide special instruction in reading and other skills to offset cultural and economic disadvantages.

Of fundamental concern in current discussions is whether or not the school can make any contribution to equality of opportunity. One issue has been whether or not the school reproduces and reinforces the social-class structure of the United States. The other important issue concerns the degree of contribution the school makes to social mobility.

Social-class Differences in Education

One of the major criticisms of the public schools has been the apparent internal duplication of the social-class structure of society. This has been particularly true in the tracking and ability-grouping practices of the school. Tracking, primarily a practice of the high school, separates students into different curriculums such as college preparatory, vocational, and general. Ability grouping involves placing students in different classes on the basis of their abilities. These abilities are usually determined by a combination of teacher assessment of the student and standardized tests.

The pattern within American schools is for the social class of the students to parallel the levels of ability grouping and tracking. That is, the higher the social-class background of the students, the more likely it is that they will be in the better ability groups and/or a college-preparatory curriculum. Conversely, the lower the social-class status of the students, the more likely it is that they will be in the poorer ability groups and/or the vocational curriculum.

Studies have shown the existence of this condition in the American public schools from the 1920s to the present. One of the first major studies of social-class differences in relationship to adolescent culture and the high school was conducted in a small town in Indiana by a team of sociologists headed by A. B. Hollingshead. Their findings, which they titled *Elmtown's Youth*, can still be duplicated in a majority of high schools throughout the country.

The Hollingshead study divided the population of Elmtown into five social classes as shown in table 1. The tracks, or courses of study,

TABLE 1

Social Class in Elmtown

SOCIAL CLASS	
1	Upper class, wealth primarily a result of inheritance
2	Income from profession, family business, or as salaried excutive
3	Income from small businesses, farms, and wages from white-collar jobs in mines, mills, and public service
4	Income from blue-collar occupations in mills and mines
5	Income from unskilled, part-time labor and welfare

SOURCE: Summarized from chapter 5 of A. B. Hollingshead's *Elmtown's Youth* (New York: John Wiley, 1949).

at Elmtown's high school were college preparatory, general, and commercial. When the social-class origins in each track were determined, it was found that children from social classes 1 and 2 concentrated on college preparatory (64 percent) and ignored the commercial course. Class 3's were found mainly in the general course (51 percent), with 27 percent in college preparatory and 21 percent in commercial. Class 4's slipped down the hierarchical scale of curriculums; only 9 percent were in college preparatory, 58 percent in general, and 33 percent in commercial. Only 4 percent of class 5's were in the college-preparatory curriculum, while 38 percent were in commercial and 58 percent in general curricula.

Because the distribution of students in the various curricula of a school reflects social class does not in itself indicate a problem or that the school is responsible. Hollingshead found that social pressures from family and peer group contributed to the decision to enter a particular course of study. Upper-class parents tended to be more oriented to college while lower-class parents thought in terms of training for jobs within their own particular social class.

While pressures outside the school existed to support the differences in social classes, Hollingshead also found that the school, through a variety of methods, gave support to the differences in social class. Differences of response to a given educational situation tended to vary with the social class of the student. For instance, the parents of students were counseled differently according to social class. Although children from social classes 2 and 3 received better grades than lower-class children, parents of social classes 2 and 3 were more often called to school to discuss the work of their children. The parents of lower-class children, however, were more often called to school to discuss the behavior of their children. This situation was paradoxical because not only did lower-class children tend to receive lower grades, but they also tended to fail courses more often than children from the upper classes. Objectively, one would have assumed that if the school were acting free of social-class bias, parents of lower-class children would have received more counseling about school work than about behavior.

In the situation described by Hollingshead, problems related to children of the lower social class tend to be considered behavior problems in school while those related to the upper classes tend to be considered learning problems. Nothing so dramatically tells the story of institutional response to social class than the tale about the enforcement of the school lateness rule. Elmtown High School had adopted a new tardy rule, which the principal and superintendent intended to enforce with vigor. The first violator of the tardy rule was the son of a class 1 family, who arrived late to school in his father's Cadillac. The student was told by the principal to report for detention after school. When the student did not appear for detention after school, the principal phoned the father, who brought the student back to school. The superintendent, nervous about offending the father, greeted the boy at the school door and had him sit ten to fifteen minutes in his outer office before sending him home. The superintendent then called the father and explained the situation. The superintendent later stated that he did not want the boy to have to sit with the other students in the detention room.

The opposite response occurred the next day when a son of a class 4 family arrived late to school. The principal and superintendent made joking comments about the student's dress and statements about his father being a laborer at the local fertilizer plant. When school ended, the superintendent and principal roamed the halls, and when they saw the class 4 student trying to leave the building, the principal grabbed him and began to shout at him. The student broke from the grasp of the principal and ran through the halls, where he was eventually caught by the superintendent, who shook and slapped him three or four times. Eventually the principal and superintendent physically pushed the student out of school.

In the cases described above the school officials were able to identify the social-class origins of their students through personal contact within the local community. In larger educational systems social-class identification is often made through the dress of the student, the ethnic and racial background, the location of the home within the community, and informal discussions. For instance, a student might be referred to as coming from a particular section of town, which when mentioned is understood to be an area inhabited, say, by blue-collar workers in a local factory or executives in major industries. Ethnic names in large metropolitan areas can also cause a response with regard to the nature of the family or attitudes toward learning.

I noticed in a study that I have been conducting of an all-black suburban high school that dress is an extremely important factor in differentiating the social class of students. Lower-class black youths within this community tend to wear broad-brimmed hats. The wearing of these hats has become associated with a lack of interest in school, juvenile delinquency, and rowdiness in school. Middle-class black parents in this community, who are very concerned about the education of their children and about discipline in the school, have placed pressure on the school system to ban the wearing of these hats in the school. This has resulted in the inevitable struggle between adolescents trying to subvert the rulings and school officials trying to enforce community demands.

One important result of this situation is that teachers now tend to identify students who wear these hats as potential troublemakers who are not interested in learning and who will cause major behavior problems in the classroom. The teacher's immediate reaction on encountering a student with a broad-brimmed hat is to think of ways of controlling the student's behavior and not of improving his learning abilities.

The result of a situation of this type is to create certain expectations. Teachers and other school officials begin to expect certain students to act in certain ways. In its simplest form, this stereotyping results in students from middle- and upper-class families being expected to do well in school while children from lower-class backgrounds are expected to do poorly. Research findings suggest that one problem with such stereotyping is that students live up to expectations about them. If students are expected to do poorly, they do poorly; if expected to do well, they do well. This is referred to as the self-fulfilling prophecy.

The most famous study of the tendency to live up to expectations was Robert Rosenthal and Lenore Jacobson's *Pygmalion in the Classroom*. In the first part of the study a group of experimenters were given a random selection of rats and were told that certain groups of rats came from highly intelligent stock. Those rats labeled as coming from highly intelligent stock tended to perform better than the other rats even though they had been randomly grouped. The two psychologists tested their results in a school to see if teacher expectations would affect student performance. After giving students a standardized intelligence test, they gave teachers the names of students whom they called "late bloomers" and told teachers to expect a sudden spurt of learning from them. In fact, the names of these students had been selected at random from the class. A year later the intelligence tests were administered again, and the scores of the supposed "late bloomers" were compared to other children who had received scores similar to the supposed "late bloomers" on the original test. It was found that those students who had been identified to teachers as "late bloomers" made considerable gains in their intelligence test scores when compared to the group of students not designated as "late bloomers."

The principal inference of this study is that teacher expectations can play an important role in determining the educational achievement of the child. This might be a serious problem in the education of children of the poor and minority groups, where teachers develop expectations that these children will either fail or have a difficult time learning. Some educators, such as teacher and educational writer Miriam Wasserman, argue that teacher expectations are one of the major barriers to educational success for the poor and certain minority groups.

Wasserman, in her case study of the New York school system, *The School Fix, NYC, USA*, relates the issue of teacher expectations to what she calls the "guidance approach to teaching." The guidance approach means that the teacher tries to take into account the student's family background, social life, and problems outside school when planning instructional units. On the surface this sounds like good educational practice in relating teaching methods and materials to the background and needs of the student. In practice, Wasserman discovered the tendency to label all students from poverty areas as having learning problems, as not being interested in school, and as probably not succeeding in school. Teachers tended not to provide very challenging material to a student so labeled or explained their own failure to teach the student in terms of the student's background.

In further investigation of this problem, Wasserman interviewed students from poverty backgrounds who had been successful in school. She found that these students believed the major element in their successful educational career was having a teacher who was primarily interested in the student's learning and who emphasized and demanded high-quality work. These teachers had high expectations for their students, and these expectations were not influenced by the social-class backgrounds of the students.

The combination of the classification of students according to abilities and curriculum plus the expectations of teachers and other school officials all seem to contribute to the social-class divisions of the surrounding society being reflected in the placement and treatment of students in the school. In addition, it has been found that in terms of educational achievement the differences between children from different social classes becomes progressively greater from the first grade through high school.

Progressive differences between social-class groups were noted by Patricia Sexton in her major study of a large urban center, which she called Big City. Her study, *Education and Income*, divided the parents in Big City into income levels and compared these divisions with ability grouping, achievement scores, and tracking. She found a direct correlation between the income level of the parents and the child's performance on achievement tests and placement in ability groups and curriculum tracks. Children from lower-income levels tended to be placed in lower ability groups and noncollege preparatory tracks. In addition, she found lower-income groups receiving lower scores on standardized tests than children from parents in upper-income levels. This began occurring in the elementary grades with the differences between the scores of the children of upper- and lower-income groups increasing as the children went from elementary to secondary schools. Sexton's explanation of this result was that if a child did not achieve well in reading in the lower grades, this increasingly affected school work as the student moved through grades requiring increasing amounts of reading.

In addition to inequalities between groups within a school, Sexton found inequalities between schools within a large district. These inequalities were also related to the income level of the parents. She found that the money spent on schools and the quality of education offered varied in direct proportion to the income of families in the school's neighborhood. The differences were reflected in the quality and adequacy of school buildings, school and class overcrowding, quality of teaching staff, methods of testing and estimating pupil performance, quality of secondary curriculum, use of school buildings by the community, and other facilities and services.

The inequalities Sexton found between schools has become a major issue in the courts of the United States. Court cases have centered around the differences in school expenditures between school districts. School districts with a low-income population tend to spend less or have less to spend on schools than school districts with a high-income population. The legal issues involved are discussed in greater detail in chapter 10 on the courts and education. For present purposes, it is important to understand the extent of these differences in terms of social class.

Christopher Jencks, in his assessment of national data in the early 1970s, found that different individuals and groups received unequal shares of national educational resources. The conclusion given in Jencks' *Inequality* was that in terms of use of educational resources, working-class children spent 13 percent less time in school than white-collar children. But, Jencks argued, the differences in time people spent in school tend to be less than other differences in society.

In terms of inequalities in school expenditures, Jencks found that the children of the richest fifth of all families in the United States are in schools that spend about 20 percent more than the schools serving the poorest fifth. Now these differences in expenditures do not necessarily mean that the schools are guilty of promoting gross inequalities. For instance, Jencks contends that the inequalities in school expenditures are less than the inequalities in income in the United States. The top fifth of all families receive 800 to 1,000 percent more income than the bottom fifth. When this difference is compared to the only 20 percent difference in school expenditures, Jencks feels, the schools appear as a triumph of egalitarianism.

The differences in treatment, place in the school curriculum, and access to educational resources that were found between social classes do indicate unequal treatment between social groups but do not necessarily mean that education reinforces the existing social-class structure, according to Jencks. That is, just because these differences in schooling exist does not mean that because of them the children of low-income families will tend to enter lower-income careers or that children of high-income families will have the opposite experience.

In terms of the argument for equality of opportunity the most important questions that have to be asked are whether education is a major factor in determining future careers and social class, and whether unequal treatment in school of children from different social classes affects their future position in the social structure.

Social Mobility and Education

The key to understanding whether inequalities in education reinforce the social-class structure and whether education can contribute to equality of opportunity lies in the investigation of the relationship between schooling and social mobility. To understand the relationship between social mobility and schooling one must consider some of the problems inherent in describing social mobility as an entity. Mobility can cover a wide range of definitions including income, occupation, status, and political or social power. The son of the owner of the local construction company who becomes a university professor might be upwardly mobile in terms of status or prestige but not in terms of income. In a similar manner the son of a minister who becomes a small store owner might be upwardly mobile in terms of income but not in terms of status. Mobility also depends on the perspective of the person making the judgment. The son of a leading manufacturer who becomes a talented musician might be considered downwardly mobile in terms of status by his father and upwardly mobile by friends of the art.

Now in a society that prizes schooling, schooling will always provide a means for social mobility in terms of status. Some immigrant groups that came to the United States viewed the well-schooled person as having great status in society. They viewed the school as a means of mobility because it provided them with prestige in the community. The increased status given by schooling might exist independently of other indicators of mobility. The son of an immigrant store owner who completes college and becomes a high school teacher is mobile in terms of the prestige his father gives his diplomas and occupation but not necessarily in terms of income.

One of the problems in discussing the link between education and social mobility is the widespread acceptance of the idea that schooling contributes to social mobility. One of the reasons for the acceptance of this idea is that educational diplomas by themselves have become status indicators. More schooling, of course, can actually mean more status if the individual and society genuinely place great value in academic achievement, but the fact is, in our society, one can have many degrees and still be poor and socially ineffective.

Another problem in talking about schooling and mobility is distinguishing between mobility that results from structural changes in society and mobility related to educational achievement. For instance, occupational mobility is the most often discussed form of mobility. In most cases it is considered in terms of intergenerational mobility. That is, mobility is considered in terms of comparing current occupations with those jobs held by parents. Social mobility is measured in terms of the differences in occupations of parents and sons and daughters.

In the United States the link between schooling and occupational mobility has been directly conditioned by certain structural changes in American society. One might describe occupational mobility in a static society as two people exchanging occupational roles; that is, there exist only a set number of occupations in which the upward mobility of one person is dependent upon the downward mobility of another person. Ideally, the school as a selective mechanism would assure that this type of mobility took place in terms of merit and competency. But the United States has not been a static society in which mobility has been achieved on this basis. Significant structural changes have increased certain occupational areas and at the same time decreased the number of other occupations. The social mobility resulting from these changes in the social structure have often been credited to the school. Nevertheless, while the school has facilitated the flow of the population from one occupational area to another, it has not directly caused these changes.

The most significant structural changes in American society affecting social mobility have been the rapid rise in the number of white collar or business, government, and professional occupations and the rapid decline in the number of agricultural occupations. In 1900 farm workers, including owners and laborers, composed 37.5 percent of the labor force; by 1965 this number had declined to 5.8 percent. White-collar workers, on the other hand, represented 17.6 percent of the labor force in 1900 and 43.8 percent in 1965. White-collar workers included managers, sales personnel, professionals, and clerical help.

Schools, of course, provided the necessary education for those filling the expanded white-collar positions. Public belief in the relationship between mobility and schooling was reinforced by those who were able to move from the farm or factory into white-collar positions. They tended to see their new opportunities not in terms of the structural changes in American society, but in terms of their own effort through education to attain these new positions. Schooling did facilitate the structural changes, but the direct causes were outside the province of the school.

The importance of changes in the occupational structure on mobility rates was found by Seymour Lipset and Reinhard Bendix in their study of *Social Mobility in Industrial Society*, which involved a comparison of mobility rates in different industrial societies. The authors found little variation in mobility rates in industrialized countries as measured by shifts from manual to nonmanual occupations. This conclusion contradicted the widely held belief that there is greater opportunity for occupational mobility in the United States than in other countries.

Lipset and Bendix did find that in occupations where there were significant differences in mobility rates between industrial countries, these were related to differences in educational opportunity. High-ranking civil servants and professional occupations fall within this category. In both cases variation in mobility rates could be attributed to different educational opportunities. These variations are logical when one considers what the school is best able to do. In most countries, only through the school can one attain professional status. In the United States the high rate of mobility into professional ranks is a result of the expanded opportunities for higher education. It should be noted that, for many, upward mobility into professional ranks has been a result of changes in the occupational structure caused by the expansion of schooling. School has created a large professional class of professors, administrators, and other school officials. Access to these positions is only through the school.

One of the major conclusions of the Lipset and Bendix study was that schooling is a direct factor in mobility only for those occupations that can be reached exclusively through the school. In other areas, such as manual and white-collar jobs, the determining factor is changes in the occupational structure. In terms of mobility into political elites, Lipset and Bendix found that opportunity to enter the political elite through the electoral path was greater in Europe than in America. The reason, they asserted, was that in Europe labor and working-class political parties provide a means by which members of lower social classes can be elected to government positions.

Peter Blau and Otis Duncan arrived at similar conclusions in their study of *The American Occupational Structure*. They argued that mobility rates in the United States have been primarily affected by technological progress, immigration, and differential fertility rates. The substitution of manual work by machines made it possible for large numbers of workers to be engaged in white-collar work, thus fostering upward mobility. The millions of disadvantaged immigrants who moved into the lower ranks of the occupational hierarchy made it possible for the sons and daughters of men in these lower strata to move up to higher occupational levels. In addition, they contended, the relatively low birthrates of the white-collar class opened up other opportunities for upward mobility.

Like Lipset and Bendix, these authors found that structural changes in society are the primary causes of mobility. Their major disagreement is in comparing mobility rates between the United States and other industrial countries. Both studies found little difference between countries in mobility rates between manual and nonmanual occupations. But Blau and Duncan did find greater opportunity in the United States to move from the working class to the top occupational stratum of society. They asserted that this greater mobility between the extremes in American society has helped to foster America's continued belief in equality of opportunity and America as the land of opportunity.

While most studies agree that the rate of mobility is more dependent on technological changes and changes in the occupational structure than on education, there have been proposals to increase the rate of social mobility by changing the methods of measuring educational attainment. The most famous of these proposals has been made by Christopher Jencks in his previously cited work, *Inequality*. Jencks found, as others have, that the most important detriment to educational achievement is family background. This means that a person who comes from a family with a high income and high educational attainment, whose father has an occupation high on the occupational hierarchy such as professional or corporate executive, is more likely to receive more education and a more advanced educational diploma than a person from a low-income family whose father has a low-status occupation. Jencks also concluded that occupational status strongly related to educational attainment.

These conclusions suggest a certain rigidity being built into the social structure; family background determines education, which determines occupational status. Jencks has suggested that one way of breaking through this apparently self-perpetuating system is to measure educational attainment in terms of grades and test scores and not in terms of diplomas. In other words, educational attainment would be determined by a score on a standardized test or grades and not by diplomas earned at the end of four years of high school or college. Jencks found that family background is not as strongly related to test scores as it is to educational attainment. A child from a lower social class has a greater chance of achieving equal or better scores on a standardized test as compared to a child from an upper-class background than he or she has the chance of reaching the same level of educational attainment. Jencks found even less of a relationship between family background and grades received in school.

Based on these findings, Jencks argues that the rate of social mobility would increase if occupations were open to people on the basis of test scores or grades and not on the basis of educational credentials. For instance, if high-status occupations were open exclusively to people with high test scores and if all people with high test scores wanted to enter the highest-status occupations, then there would be greater social mobility. That is, there would be a greater chance of children ending up in social classes different from those of their parents. Children of high-status parents would have a greater chance of entering lower-status jobs, and children of lower-status parents would have a greater chance of entering higher-status occupations. The rate of mobility, according to Jencks, would be even higher if high-status occupations went exclusively to those students with high grades.

Inequality of Educational Opportunity and Equality of Opportunity

Do inequalities in educational opportunities directly affect equality of opportunity? It was shown in the first part of this chapter that sociologists and educators are in agreement about the existence of unequal educational opportunity. While they debate the extent of inequality, they agree that different social classes and (as will be discussed in the next chapter) racial groups receive unequal treatment in the public schools. There is also agreement that education is not a primary determiner of rates of mobility. That is, the amount of education provided in a society does not determine the amount of mobility. On the other hand, the level of educational achievement in the United States *is* related to occupational status, and the primary determiner of educational achievement is family background. Given these sets of findings, what is the effect of inequalities in education on equality of opportunity?

A major national study that looked at this question was a survey conducted at the request of the U.S. Congress as part of the 1964 Civil Rights Act. The survey was organized and planned by sociologist James Coleman and published as *Equality of Educational Opportunity*. This survey, known as the Coleman Report, was to become one of the most famous and controversial studies of American education.

Coleman and his group began the survey by outlining five approaches that could be taken in measuring inequality in educational opportunity. The first approach defined the problem in terms of the degree of racial segregation that existed in school systems. The second approach was in terms of inequality of resource inputs, items such as books, school facilities, and student-teacher ratios. The third approach was in terms of inequality of intangible resources, such as teacher morale.

The final two approaches to the problem of inequality asked broader questions of the meaning of inequality. The fourth approach measured the inequality of inputs in terms of their effectiveness for educational achievement. In other words, did differences in resources such as books, buildings, student-teacher ratios, and other school items have any effect on how well a student achieved? The fifth approach involved determination of whether or not inequality of output was evidence of inequality of opportunity.

Within the framework of these five approaches, the Coleman report asked some basic questions about the relationship between the school and the social structure. Of primary importance for school people was the question of what factors in schooling have the greatest effect upon educational achievement. This question was to be answered in the fourth approach, in which inequality of inputs were to be related to educational achievement. The major overall task of the report, of course, was to measure the extent of racial segregation and inequalities of resources as related to race and not social class. This aspect of the study will be discussed in more detail in the next chapter.

The Coleman Report found that in terms of school resources, white children as compared to minority children attended schools with smaller class sizes, with more science and language laboratories, with more books in the library, and with more opportunities for participating in college-preparatory and accelerated academic curriculums. The Coleman study then compared these differences in resources with student achievement. Student achievement in the report was determined by achievement tests. The report assumed about achievement tests that "what they measure are the skills which are among the most important in our society for getting a good job and moving up to a better one, and for full participation in an increasingly technical world." In terms of achievement scores, the Coleman Report found that, except for Oriental-Americans, all other minority groups scored significantly lower than whites and that the differences increased from the first through the twelfth grade.

When these differences in achievement were compared to school resources, it was found that "differences between schools account for only a small fraction of differences in achievement." The evidence for this finding included differences between the effect of school resources between white and minority students. The achievement of white students seemed to be less affected by the strengths or weaknesses of curricula and school facilities, while these did seem to have some effect on the achievement of minority students. Student achievement, however, was strongly related to the educational backgrounds and aspirations of the other students in school.

The conclusions of the Coleman Report led to a complex set of questions. It should be noted that the report did give strong support to the policy of school integration. Since the most important factor affecting achievement was pupil backgrounds, the report could conclude that "the analysis of school factors described . . . suggest that in the long run, integration should be expected to have a positive effect on Negro achievement." In general, the conclusions of the report seemed to suggest that the quality of school curricula and facilities bore little relationship to the question of equality of educational opportunity.

The conclusions of the Coleman Report startled those people who believed that schools would be the answer to the problems of poverty and could provide equality of opportunity. The study seemed to say that the school could do little in terms of teaching, curriculum development, and facilities to improve educational achievement and equalize opportunities for advancement in American society. The most important factors were peers and family background. This meant that the school could not play an important role in providing equality of opportunity. Schools could equalize educational opportunities by providing equal facilities, curricula, and quality teachers, but this would only solve the problem of the injustice of unequal treatment of different social classes and groups and not unequal opportunity.

This was also the major conclusion of Jencks' study *Inequality*. Jencks' study combined the data of the Coleman work with other major national studies. He concluded that equalizing the amount and quality of schooling would have only a minor effect on cognitive skills as measured by standardized tests. The major determiners of cognitive skills, he found, are a person's total environment and heredity. It should be mentioned that the tests used to measure cognitive skills have been criticized for cultural and social-class bias.

The study found that qualitative differences between high schools explain only a minor part of the variation in students' educational attainment. Jencks also concluded that school resources do not have any influence on students' educational attainments and that attending high school with bright, highly motivated classmates had both positive and negative effects on a student's chances of attending college. The one measurable factor that obviously influenced educational attainment was the curriculum to which a student is assigned.

Both the Jencks study and the Coleman Report suggest that inequalities in educational opportunity have very little effect on educational attainment and, consequently, upon intergenerational occupational mobility. This would mean that no matter how much a society equalized educational opportunities for all groups or provided superior educational opportunities for the poor and minority groups, there would be little or no change in the rate of upward occupational mobility. In other words, the schools cannot provide equality of opportunity.

Now it is possible to argue this particular problem from an entirely different perspective. Rather than asking what factors contribute to increased rates of social mobility, one can ask about the factors that contribute to intergenerational immobility. In other words, why isn't there more occupational mobility from parents to children in Western industrialized countries?

Economist Samuel Bowles contends that the school is one of the causes for occupational immobility. This argument completely reverses the idea of the school creating occupational mobility to the idea that the school has the opposite effect. Bowles, in constructing his thesis, accepts the findings that mobility rates are consistent throughout Western industrialized countries and that family background is one of the major factors in determining economic and social advancement. What Bowles argues is that the school is a medium through which family background is translated into occupational and income opportunities.

This translation occurs with regard to personality traits relevant to the work task; modes of self-presentation such as manner of speech and dress; ascriptive characteristics such as race, sex, and age; and the level and prestige of education. Bowles considers these four factors integral to the process of intergenerational immobility. It is these traits that emerge from the family background and are reinforced in the schools before entrance into the work force. Cognitive skills seem to have little significance in this process. Bowles asserts, and Christopher Jencks in *Inequality* agrees, that adult cognitive abilities have a minor influence on occupational success when considered independent of level of schooling and family background.

Bowles insists that the four factors of personality traits, self-presentation, ascriptive characteristics, and level of educational attainment are all significantly related to occupational success. They are also all related to the social class of the family. For instance, family background is directly related to level of educational attainment and the prestige of that attainment. In this particular case the economic level of the family is translated by the school into educational attainment. Children from low-income families do not attain as high a level of education as children from rich families. From this standpoint the school reinforces social stratification and contributes to intergenerational immobility. In terms of ascriptive characteristics such as race, the social advantages or disadvantages of a particular racial group are again translated by the school into levels of educational attainment.

Personality traits and self-presentation are, according to Bowles, important ingredients in occupational success. These characteristics are a direct product of child-rearing practices and reflect the social class of the family. Also, Bowles asserts, child-rearing patterns are directly related to the occupation of the head of the family. This argument is based on the work of Melvin Kohn in his study of *Class and Conformity: A Study of Values,* in which he found that middle-class parents are more likely to emphasize children's self-direction and working-class parents to emphasize conformity to external authority. By self-direction, Kohn meant internal standards of direction for behavior, while conformity meant externally imposed rules. Within this framework, working-class parents value obedience, neatness, and honesty; higher-status parents emphasize curiosity, self-control, and happiness. Even when racial and religious divisions are considered, Kohn found that social class still stands out as more important in determining child-rearing values.

There is, says Kohn, a direct relationship between the degree of occupational self-direction experienced by the head of the family and child-rearing values. In fact, he argues that this is the most important factor in determining child-rearing practices. The more self-direction experienced by the head of the family on the job, the more likely it is that child-rearing patterns will emphasize self-direction. Self-direction on the job is directly related to the social class of the family. Higher-status and higher-income jobs usually involve self-direction; lower-status and lower-income jobs tend to be more routine and require more conformity to imposed rules.

Child-rearing, Bowles declares, is important in developing personality traits related to entrance into the work force. Personalities evidencing a great deal of self-direction tend to have greater success in high-status occupations. The differences in child-rearing patterns, Bowles states, are reflected in the schools attended by different social classes. Schools with populations from lower-income families tend to be more authoritarian and to require more conformity than schools attended by children from higher-income families. This is often reflected in the differences between educationally innovative schools in high-income suburbs as opposed to low-income, inner-city schools. In some cases parents place pressure on local schools to be either more authoritarian or to allow more self-direction. The nature of this pressure tends to be related to the social class of the parents. The same pattern emerges in higher education, according to Bowles, when one compares the social relations of a community college with those of an elite four-year college. In this manner, Bowles argues, the child-rearing patterns of the family are translated through the medium of the school into the occupational structure. The school thus contributes to intergenerational immobility and limits equality of opportunity.

Conclusion

The debate about schooling and equality of opportunity has not ended in the United States. There is developing an educational literature that attempts to show that certain school practices such as teacher expectations and stereotyping of students can make a difference in educational achievement and, consequently, educational attainment. One criticism of the Coleman Report is that it measured only existing educational practices and did not take into account new educational methods that could be developed and could make a difference. This difference might eliminate inequality of educational opportunity and inequality of opportunity.

In addition, recent studies of underdeveloped countries have suggested that individual personality traits are not set for life and that education can make a difference in orienting an individual to the world of work. This was one of the significant findings of the six-nation study by Alex Inkeles and David Smith discussed in the last chapter. The effect of family background might not be immutable, and the school might make a difference in breaking patterns of child-rearing.

Whether or not the schools will ever contribute to increasing the rate of social mobility or increasing equality of opportunity is uncertain. One thing is certain: America will continue to hope and place faith in the social power of the school.

EXERCISES

1. One of the major issues discussed in this chapter was the relationship between social class and inequality of educational opportunity. Try and remember if this was a factor in your education. Can you remember social class being related to ability groups or different curricula?

2. Select a high school in your community and determine whether social class is related to the place of the student in the curriculum. Are there students at this school from particular social groups who are the major participants in extracurricular activities?

3. Make a chart tracing the major occupational changes in the last

several generations of your own family. Try and determine the major factors causing social mobility within your family.

4. In a group discussion or essay discuss whether or not you think the school should be used as an institution to foster equality of opportunity.

Suggested Readings and Works Cited in Chapter

Blau, Peter, and Otis, Duncan. *The American Occupational Structure.* New York: John Wiley, 1967.
     The classic study of mobility patterns in the United States and the effect of different social factors including education.

Bowles, Samuel. "Understanding Unequal Economic Opportunity." *American Economic Review* 63, no. 2 (May 1973): 346–56.
     Bowles argues that the schools reproduce and reinforce existing social-class differences.

Coleman, James. *Equality of Educational Opportunity.* Washington, D.C.: Government Printing Office, 1966.
     The famous "Coleman Report" dealing with the relationship between inequality of educational opportunity and student achievement.

Hollingshead, A. B. *Elmtown's Youth.* New York: John Wiley, 1949.
     The classic study of the effect of social class on adolescent life in a small town.

Jencks, Christopher. *Inequality.* New York: Harper & Row, 1972.
     A major study of the effect of the family and schooling on inequality in the United States.

Kohn, Melvin. *Class and Conformity: A Study of Values.* Homewood, Ill.: Dorsey, 1969.
     A study of the relationship between child-rearing methods and social class.

Lipset, Seymour, and Bendix, Reinhard. *Social Mobility in Industrial Society.* Berkeley: University of California Press, 1959.
     First major comparative study of social mobility in industrial countries.

Rosenthal, Robert, and Lenore, Jacobson. *Pygmalion in the Classroom.* New York: Holt, Rinehart & Winston, 1968.

This book argues that there is a relationship between student achievement and teachers' expectations.

Sexton, Patricia. *Education and Income.* New York: Viking, 1961.

A study of the relationship between family income and ability grouping, tracking, and achievement in a large city.

Wasserman, Miriam. *The School Fix: NYC, USA.* New York: Outerbridge & Dienstfrey, 1970.

First section of the book has case studies of students who did or did not make it successfully through the New York schools.

3

INEQUALITY OF EDUCATIONAL OPPORTUNITY AND RACE

THE DISCUSSION OF INEQUALITY OF EDUCATIONAL OPPORTUNITY IN the previous chapter focused on differences between social classes. When the factor of race is introduced, inequalities in educational opportunity take on another meaning. In terms of educational equality, the disparities between races are not differences of school expenditures or levels of educational attainment as much as they are differences of social class. For instance, Christopher Jencks in his work *Inequality* found that, although black children were more likely to live in poorly financed school districts than white children, this was primarily a result of more black children than white children living in the South, where less money is spent on education. Within either the North or the South, each racial group had the same chance of attending an affluent school. Of course, since blacks tend to receive lower incomes than whites, they would most often live in less-affluent school districts. What is important to remember is that social class is more important than race in determining equality of educational expenditure.

The same is true of the level of educational attainment. A 1976 analysis of national data by Robert Hauser and David Featherman found that disadvantages in schooling associated with southern birth, black skin, and Spanish origins have been declining; but disadvantages associated with poorly educated and low-status fathers persist. In fact, sociologists Alejandro Portes and Kenneth L. Wilson found that when blacks were compared to whites at the same socioeconomic level and mental ability, blacks outperformed whites at each stage of educational attainment. This means that not only is the gap between the educational attainment of blacks and whites closing, but when all other factors are equal, the black person will academically outperform the white person.

One reason for this situation is the high level of educational aspirations in the black community. Historically a great deal of the hope of the black community in the United States for upward mobility has centered on education. Following the close of the Civil War, the major debate between black leaders such as W. E. B. DuBois and Booker T. Washington was not over whether or not education should play the major role in the advancement of black people, but over what type of education would be best. In the twentieth century the major area of concern of the National Association for the Advancement of Colored People (NAACP) has been desegregation of the American schools and achieving equal educational opportunity for black children. Current sociological research has found that black educational aspirations when compared to white educational aspirations are higher within the same socioeconomic class.

The high educational aspirations of the black community in the United States have been a source of one of the great tragedies of American life. While educational aspirations and efforts have been high in the black community, this has not resulted in equal economic gains. One of the great burdens of being black or of having Spanish-American origins is that the economic value of each stage of educational attainment is less than it is for the majority white population. Peter Blau and Otis Duncan, in their study of *The American Occupational Structure* (discussed in chapter 2), found that education did not produce the same benefits for blacks as for whites in terms of occupational achievement or mobility. The difference between mean occupational status of whites and nonwhites increased with higher educational levels; their data showed that approximately the same amount of educational investment yielded considerably less in the form of superior occupational status or mobility to nonwhites than to whites. The burden of discrimination in the United States for nonwhites is that equal educational effort does not result in equal economic and social gains.

The other tragedy involved in the high educational aspirations of the black community has been the quality of education that has been provided. This tends to reflect institutional discrimination in terms of the quality of teaching, types of books, and resources available in the schools, and the tracking of black students into vocational and non-academic tracks.

Institutional racial discrimination occurs in the same form as it does with regard to social class. There is a tendency for white school-teachers and principals to have lower levels of expectations for black students than for white students. This is not necessarily an example of overt racism but is primarily a result of the cultural isolation of the white community from the black community and the lack of aware-ness by the white community of the high educational aspirations of the black parent and student. In addition to the problem of low levels of expectations of teachers, there is a tendency in large school systems for the younger and less experienced teachers to be placed in schools that are predominantly nonwhite.

The above forms of institutional discrimination and difficulties encountered by nonwhites in receiving a high-quality education is best illustrated by the following case study. The information provided here is from a community study that I conducted in 1976. This case study not only highlights forms of institutional discrimination, but also focuses on the problems that occur when the high educational aspirations of a nonwhite minority encounter the realities of the educational system.

Black Suburbia

This particular suburban community of about 40,000 people is on the border of a major midwestern industrial city. Prior to the 1960s the majority of the population was white, with incomes primarily in the lower middle and middle range. During the middle of the 1960s the population of the community began to shift rapidly from a ma-jority of white residents to a majority of black residents. This was dramatically reflected in school enrollments. In 1965 the percentage of black students enrolled in the school system was 10 percent. By 1970 the percentage of black students was 87 percent, and in 1974 it was 97 percent. By the middle of the 1970s the few remaining white children were in one elementary school in the more affluent section of the suburb.

The black population that moved into Black Suburbia was pri-marily in the middle-income range and very concerned about the quality of the educational system. When income figures from the 1960 and 1970 censuses for this suburban area are compared and 1960 dollars are adjusted to 1970 dollars, it is revealed that the black population moving into Black Suburbia in the 1960s had slightly higher incomes than the whites moving out of the community. The bulk of the black population moving into the area during this period were in what one would call the middle-income range and could be viewed as a group interested in upward mobility.

A study of the community in the late 1960s showed the mobility concerns and educational aspirations of the new black population. The study provided profiles of nine different social groups, including old and new white residents at different income and age levels and new black residents at different income and age levels. The study found that both middle-aged and young middle-class black residents had high expectations of upward mobility and believed that quality schools were a major element in a quality community. The population group labeled as "New, Middle-Aged, Black Middle-Class Residents" were described as earning more than $10,000 a year and as being employed as managers, proprietors, and professionals. This group was found to have an "extraordinarily high degree" of expectations for continuing upward mobility and a concern about the quality of schools. The same expectations and concerns were held by the "New, Young, Black Middle Class" who were described as earning between $6,000 and $9,000 per year and being employed as managers, proprietors, and professionals. (It should be remembered that the incomes quoted are in 1960 dollars, which were worth considerably more than the current dollar.)

The middle-aged and young black working class described in the study evidenced varying degrees of concern about the quality of schooling. For the middle-aged black working-class family, schools were not an important reason for moving to Black Suburbia. This group was described as being unskilled workers earning between $6,000 and $7,000 per year. On the other hand, the quality of schools was important to the young black working-class residents, who were earning between $5,000 and $9,000 per year and were employed primarily in skilled and semiskilled jobs.

During the early 1970s the high mobility and educational aspirations of the black residents who arrived in the 1960s were threatened by the rapid influx of a poor black population. The introduction of a large group of low-income black families was reflected in the percentages of children from welfare families in the school system. Between 1965 and 1970 the percentage of children from welfare families in Black Suburbia increased from 6 to 16 percent as the racial composition of the population changed. Between 1970 and 1973 the percentage of children from welfare families increased dramatically, from 16 to 51 percent. In other words, the migration of upwardly mobile middle-class blacks was followed by the rapid migration of welfare black families.

The educational aspirations of the early black migration were frustrated both by the response of the local school system to these new residents and by the later migration of poor blacks. One of the first things that happened was that educational expectations of the mainly white teachers and administrators in the school system began to be lowered. This seemed to be caused by the white school staff assuming that the blacks moving into the community were not interested in education and would create major problems in the school system. This assumption is most clearly shown when the educational expectations of elementary school principals are compared to the educational expectations of the black community.

In the early 1970s a survey by the local government of Black Suburbia included a question dealing with the level of educational aspirations. The survey asked parents how far they would like their son or daughter to progress in school. The response of the parents was that 73 percent and 71 percent respectively wanted their son or daughter to complete college. More importantly, when asked how far they actually believed their son or daughter would go in school, 60 percent and 62 percent respectively believed their children would complete college.

The contrast between the educational aspirations of the parents and the elementary school principals illustrates the problems and frustrations encountered by black residents. When I asked elementary school principals what percentage of the students in their schools they felt would go to college, the responses from three of the principals were 3 percent, 12 percent, and 10 percent. Two elementary school principals evaded the question and claimed it had nothing to do with their work in the elementary school, and one elementary principal gave a figure of 50 percent.

One of the important things about these responses is that the 50 percent figure was given by a new black elementary principal, who clearly was closer to understanding the values of the local community. All the other principals were white, and they had been principals in the school system before the racial change. The educational expectation levels of these principals were not only considerably below those of the community; they were also below those of the teachers. In a survey of elementary school teachers, teachers projected 29 percent of their students as graduating from college. Although this figure was still below that of the community, it was at least closer to community expectations than the principals' estimates. One of the reasons for this might be that the teaching staff had changed more than the elementary administrative staff, and there had been a recent effort by the school district to recruit black teachers.

Several examples can be used to show how the lower level of expectations of school staff was translated into practice. When I interviewed the head of the local community library, he informed me that in the years prior to the racial change, scholarly and professional journals were heavily used by high school students. This was not because the students read these journals for pleasure, but because teachers gave homework assignments in the journals. After the racial change, teachers stopped giving homework assignments in those types of advanced journals. In other words, the blacks who moved to the community because of its relatively high educational standards suddenly found those standards being lowered as their children entered the system.

The director of the local YMCA stated that a person who really wanted to know what was going on in the local school system should park his car outside the high school at closing time and count the number of students carrying books home from school. The director claimed that only a few students carried books, and this was another indication that teachers were no longer giving homework assignments and had given up trying to teach.

Complaints about teachers not teaching were echoed by students in the tenth and twelfth grades of the high school. A random sample of the tenth grade was interviewed and asked about their future plans and about any complaints about the school system. Fifty-eight percent of the students interviewed from the tenth grade had expectations of attending and graduating from college. The major complaint of the students was the quality of the teaching staff.

Twelfth-grade students were interviewed from a list of those students designated as the "best" by the school administration. Sixty percent of these students expressed concern and even bitterness about the teaching staff. The major complaint was that certain teachers made no effort to teach and wasted most class periods. One student stated that he had teachers who probably accomplished one day's worth of teaching out of every five days in the classroom. Another student stated that many teachers did not seem to care if students did the work or learned. There was no attempt to make students want to come to class. One student argued that teachers did not care because they were so upset at trying to control "rowdy" students.

The issue of "rowdy" students entered practically every discussion about the quality of education in the local high school. There seemed to be an underlying assumption in any conversation with a community member that the "rowdy" students came from low-income black families. This reflected a tension between the middle-class black who moved into the community in the 1960s and the low-income black who moved into the community in the 1970s. Low-income families represented a threat to the aspirations and status of the middle-class residents of Black Suburbia.

One example of this was a black member of the local school board who pounded the table and exclaimed that all he wanted was to live a middle-class existence and provide a home and future for his family. This, he stated, was why he had moved to the community. Now he felt those dreams were not being realized as crime increased in the community, and he feared that his children were not receiving an adequate education at the local school. He complained that every time his children left the house he worried that they would get involved with the "rowdy" youths of the community. Currently, he was sending his daughter to a private school, but his son went to the local high school. He worried constantly that his son would get in with the "wrong" group in the school.

This particular school board member led a group in the community that demanded a strict dress code. The reason for this was that those students identified as "rowdy" very often wore large hats and high-heeled shoes. The community members demanding the dress code saw it as a means of controlling and disciplining "rowdy" students. One result of this campaign was signs throughout the high school restricting the wearing of hats.

That the community related "rowdiness" with low-income background was evident from discussions with other community members. One leader of a community welfare organization claimed that "rowdy" juveniles were organized around natural street groupings with one street in rivalry with another street. These street groupings, he argued, were primarily based on economic differences, with kids from better streets putting down kids from poorer streets. The community social welfare worker saw "rowdy" juveniles as a product of poverty and characterized by a lack of a sense of direction, which led to an easy drifting into a life of stealing, drugs, and gambling. Another social welfare worker, who dealt directly with cases of juvenile delinquency, described middle-class youth in the community as walking a thin line where, at any time, pressures from this delinquent subculture could persuade the student to join the "rowdy" culture. This was very much the fear expressed by the school board member.

Students at the high school tended to see the "rowdy" student issue as one of the problems with the teaching staff. Teachers generalized from the misbehavior of a few students to all students. One of the common complaints of tenth graders was about the way teachers handled discipline problems. The majority of students felt that teachers were unable to control students in a just and fair manner. The problem was compounded, students believed, because teachers did not know how to control "rowdy" students and consequently acted mean toward all students.

The process of generalization from a few students to all students could have been one of the factors contributing to teachers in the school system not understanding or attempting to respond to the educational aspirations of the middle-class black community. The delinquent subculture might have reinforced existing stereotypes held by white teachers and administrators about the way black students acted and learned. This would have influenced the levels of teacher expectations, reflected in specific things such as not assigning homework or not expecting students to use the community library.

For the middle-class black who entered the community in the 1960s with high aspirations for mobility and quality education for their children, the school system became a source of frustration and disillusionment. Teachers did not provide the instruction they had hoped for, and additionally they came to fear that their children might enter a delinquent subculture. For the more-affluent black residents, the solution was a rejection of the public school and the transferral of their children into private schooling.

Black families and students who were not interested in college but hoped that the school could provide some form of immediate job training were also frustrated in attaining their goals as a direct result of racial discrimination. In the early 1970s the school system in Black Suburbia had built a new vocational high school directly connected to the traditional high school. The vocational school was the product of a state master plan for vocational education, which mandated the establishment of joint vocational school districts or individual vocational schools within each district. The problems of the vocational school in Black Suburbia were directly related to the discriminatory policies of the surrounding white suburban communities.

The story of Black Suburbia's vocational school came from the local superintendent and his staff, as well as a superintendent in the district next to Black Suburbia. After the resolution of the vocational school issue, these superintendents were no longer on speaking terms. It began when a meeting was called of all the superintendents in one suburban area of this metropolitan area to discuss the formation of a joint vocational school district as a method of complying with state requirements. The suburbs in this area were mostly white except for three integrated suburban communities and Black Suburbia. Before the actual meeting, the superintendents of the predominantly white suburbs agreed by telephone to form their own vocational district, which would exclude the three integrated school districts and Black Suburbia. When the four school superintendents representing the suburbs with sizable black populations arrived at the meeting, they found that all decisions had been made and that they would be forced to work together in establishing a separate vocational district.

There is no agreement on what happened after this meeting. The superintendent of Black Suburbia claimed that the three integrated suburbs were hesitant about working with his school district because the others represented communities with a higher-income population. Consequently, the superintendent of Black Suburbia was forced to build a vocational high school next to the one regular high school in the community. The superintendent of the adjoining integrated community claims the whole situation was a misunderstanding and that his community was willing to work on a joint vocational district.

The establishment of a separate vocational school in Black Suburbia had the effect of increasing the degree of segregation between white and black suburban schools. A joint vocational school covering the entire eastern area would have made a major contribution to school integration. The segregation of Black Suburbia's vocational school assured that its training programs would be inferior to the joint vocational school's programs because an all-black school faces major problems in establishing links with unions, which have traditionally excluded blacks, and with white businesses. Because it is difficult for an all-black school to establish these contacts, it is very hard to place students graduating from the vocational program.

This problem was highlighted in conversation with the head of the vocational high school. In his vocational-training programs he could claim the placement of only three welders in the last three years. The superintendent admitted conducting his own telephone survey to determine the problems in placement of the graduates in cosmetology. He found that only a few black graduates were able to get jobs in beauty parlors, and those jobs were at very low wages. Even those who got jobs found them lasting only a short time because beauty parlors depend upon a high turnover of personnel.

Another problem faced by the Black Suburbia school system is that it now has a vocational building that must be filled and a teaching staff that needs to protect its own jobs by attracting students. The size of the vocational school requires that almost half the students in the eleventh and twelfth grades enroll in its programs. In the tenth grade the students are shown through the school and given a choice between entering the vocational program the following year or continuing in an academic program. From the perspective of the staff of the vocational school, it is important to persuade students to enter their programs.

When the guidance counselor in the vocational school was asked what methods were used to persuade students to enter programs that could not promise jobs, his response was that they lied to the students. He justified this in terms of needing students to build good programs in the future and said that even though jobs would be difficult to find for the students, they would be receiving more useful training in the vocational program than in the traditional academic program. From his perspective, very few of the students in the secondary school were capable of going on to college.

A different interpretation was given by the black director of the local YWCA. She felt that the vocational school was keeping students from going to college. When she was asked the percentage of local high school students she felt would go on to college, she stated that before the vocational high school had been established, about 70 percent of the girls attending the YWCA planned on attending college. After the establishment of the vocational school, the number dropped to 30 or 40 percent. She argued quite strongly that if the community had been all-white, the vocational school would never have been built. It was, she felt, a racist institution designed primarily to give black students an inferior education. Another observer referred to the vocational program as "education for welfare."

The story of Black Suburbia highlights some fundamental problems encountered by minority groups in the United States. The expectations of teachers and school administrative staffs can be far below the aspirations of the minority group, which can cause a major decrease in the quality of education. In addition, the school staff can generalize from the behavioral problems of children from low-income families to all members of the minority group. In this case study students directly felt this process of generalization.

The problems encountered in the segregation of minority students are illustrated by the vocational education program. But even if a joint vocational district had been established that included students from Black Suburbia, there would have been no guarantee that other forms of discrimination, such as the school staff having lower expectations for blacks as opposed to whites, might not have occurred. Indeed, one would expect that, given the previous history of relationships between these school districts, there probably would have been discriminatory actions in a joint vocational district.

What the story of Black Suburbia represents is the struggle in the United States of minority groups to attain a quality education when faced with problems of segregation between schools and discriminatory actions within schools. The history of the black struggle in education has centered around the ending of segregation because segregated education can mean unequal education and a denial of access to all resources in a community. The difficulty of job placement from an all-black vocational school is only one example of the inherent inequality in segregated education.

Desegregation of American Schools

The historic 1954 Supreme Court school desegregation case, *Brown* v. *Board of Education of Topeka*, gave legal meaning to the idea that segregated education meant unequal education. Until 1954, segregated schools in the United States operated under a ruling given by the Supreme Court in 1895, *Plessy* v. *Ferguson*, that segregation did not create a badge of inferiority if segregated facilities were equal and the law was reasonable. The decision in both cases centered around the meaning of the Fourteenth Amendment to the Constitution. This amendment had been ratified in 1868, shortly after the close of the Civil War. One of its purposes was to extend the basic guarantees of the Bill of Rights into the areas of state and local government. The most important and controversial section of the Fourteenth Amendment stated, "No State shall make or enforce any law which shall abridge the privileges or immunities of citizens . . . nor . . . deprive any person of life, liberty, or property, without due process of law; nor deny to any person within its jurisdiction the equal protection of the laws."

The 1895 decision, *Plessy* v. *Ferguson*, involved Homer Plessy, who was one-eighth black and seven-eights white. He was arrested for refusing to ride in the colored coach of a train, as required by Louisiana state law. The Supreme Court's decision in this case, that segregated facilities could exist if they were equal, became known as the "separate but equal" doctrine.

The 1954 desegregation decision, *Brown* v. *Board of Education of Topeka,* overturned the "separate but equal" doctrine by arguing that on the basis of the findings of social science, segregated education was inherently unequal. This meant that even if school facilities, teachers, equipment, and all other physical conditions were equal between two racially segregated schools, the two schools would still be unequal because of the fact of racial segregation.

In 1955 the Supreme Court issued its Enforcement Decree for the desegregation of schools. One problem facing the Court was the lack of machinery for supervising and assuring the desegregation of schools. The Court resolved this problem by relying upon federal district courts as the determiners of equitable principles for desegregation. The Court argued that each local school district had its own set of problems with regard to how desegregation would affect the use of buildings, school transportation systems, and the determination of boundaries of school districts. These problems, it was felt, could best be handled on a local basis through the district courts.

The Enforcement Decree began the long and hard process of attempting to end inequality in American education as caused by racial segregation. It was and is an attempt to use the federal courts as a means of extending equality of educational opportunity to all Americans. One problem in enforcing the Supreme Court decision was the statement in the Enforcement Decree that the district courts should issue orders and decrees "as are necessary and proper to admit to public schools on a racially nondiscriminatory basis with all deliberate speed the parties to these cases." Many Americans in the 1950s and early 1960s felt that "all deliberate speed" had been interpreted by the district courts as meaning a snail's pace and were upset at the slow progress of school desegregation in the South.

In 1964 Congress took a significant step in the direction of speeding up school desegregation by passing the important Civil Rights Act. In terms of school desegregation, Title VI of the 1964 Civil Rights Act was most important because it provided a means for the federal government to force school desegregation. In its final form Title VI required the mandatory withholding of federal funds from institutions that practiced racial discrimination. Title VI stated that no person, because of race, color, or national origin, could be excluded from or denied the benefits of any program receiving federal financial assistance. It required all federal agencies to establish guidelines to implement this policy. Refusal by institutions or projects to follow these guidelines was to result in the "termination of or refusal to grant or to continue assistance under such program or activity."

Title VI of the 1964 Civil Rights Act was important for two reasons. First, it established a major precedent for federal control of American public schools by making explicit that the control of money would be one method used by the federal government to shape local school policies. (This aspect of the law will be discussed in more detail in chapter 7 on the control of American education.) Second, the law was important because it turned the federal Office of Education into a policing agency with the responsibility of determining whether or not school systems were segregated, and if they were, of doing something about the segregated conditions.

One result of Title VI was to speed up the process of school desegregation in the South, particularly after the passage of federal legislation in 1965 that increased the amount of money available to local schools from the federal government. In the late 1960s southern school districts rapidly began to submit school desegregation plans to the Office of Education.

With the passage of the 1964 Civil Rights Act it was possible to attack segregated school conditions either through the courts or through the threat of withholding federal educational funds. The pattern of enforcement that emerged in the 1960s was for the Office of Education to be relied upon in southern segregation situations and for the courts to be relied upon in segregation cases in the North. One reason for this was that in the South, it was more difficult to prosecute desegregation cases in district courts because the judges tended to share the prejudices of the local community. The enforcement of Title VI was effective in the South because local southern school districts needed the money. In the North the courts were more often used because of the nature of national politics. The first attempt to withhold money from a northern city ended in dismal failure. In 1965 the Office of Education announced that $32 million was being withheld from the Chicago public school system pending investigation. After the announcement by the Office of Education, Mayor Richard J. Daley, who represented one of the major political powers in the Democratic party, and congressional leaders from Illinois placed pressure on Democratic President Lyndon Johnson. When Johnson quickly let it be known that he wanted the funds to begin flowing to Chicago, the major thrust of Title VI was primarily directed at the South.

Prosecuting inequality in educational opportunity in the North as related to school segregation required a different approach from that used in the South. In the South, school segregation had existed by legislative acts that required the separation of the races. In the North there were no specific laws requiring separation of the races. But even without specific laws, racial segregation existed. In fact, the U.S. Commission on Civil Rights reported in 1967 that the level of racial separation in northern city schools was increasing: 75 percent of the black elementary students in cities attended schools that were nearly all-black, while 83 percent of the white students attended all-white schools. The trend in northern cities was toward increasing racial segregation.

Since actual laws requiring racial segregation did not exist in the North, it was necessary for those bringing complaints against northern school districts to prove that the patterns of racial segregation that existed were the result of purposeful action on the part of the school district. In other words, it had to be proved that school officials intended racial segregation to be a result of their educational policies.

The conditions required to prove segregation were explicitly outlined in 1974 in the Sixth Circuit Court of Appeals case, *Oliver* v. *Michigan State Board of Education*. The court stated, "A presumption of segregative purpose arises when plaintiffs establish that the natural, probable and foreseeable result of public officials' action or inaction was an increase or perpetuation of public school segregation." This did not mean that individual motives or prejudices were to be investigated but that the overall pattern of school actions had to be shown to increase racial segregation. In the language of the court this meant that "the question is whether a purposeful pattern of segregation has manifested itself over time, despite the fact that individual official actions, considered alone, may not have been taken for segregative purposes. . . ."

If a school district was found guilty of segregation, either in the North or South, it was required to submit a plan, or have a plan developed by an outside expert, for the desegregation of the school district. This was true both for court actions and actions taken by the Office of Education under Title VI of the 1964 Civil Rights Act. The usual procedure in court cases when the school district is found guilty of segregation is that the judge requests the development of a desegregation plan within a specified time period. The Office of Education, on the other hand, usually requires proof of some affirmative action to end segregation from educational institutions receiving federal money. During the 1960s the Office of Education required southern school districts to submit specific desegregation plans.

The most politically explosive and controversial aspect of both court actions and actions under Title VI have been desegregation plans. Some of these plans have required forced busing, which in some northern communities have resulted in riots, demonstrations, and the closing of schools. The issue of desegregation plans quickly became involved in local and national political campaigns, where candidates were forced to define their positions particularly about forced busing. Communities going through the process of desegregation without violence or major strife still had to use a large number of community relations experts to prepare the local population.

The development of desegregation plans began in the South. One of the major responses of southern school districts to the enforcement of Title VI was the development of freedom-of-choice plans. These plans allowed the students in any school system using the plan to choose any school to attend within the system. In the South this proved to be another method of maintaining segregation because of the tradition of white control and the harassment of black parents that forced them to choose all-black schools for their children. To counter this situation, the Office of Education began to establish racial quotas for desegregation plans. This meant that local school districts had to keep records of the degree of racial balance within their schools.

The issue of busing as a means of desegregation hit the national scene with full force in 1971 when the Supreme Court in *Swann* v. *Charlotte-Mecklenburg Board of Education* supported busing as a legitimate tool for bringing about the desegregation of school districts. The Court warned that "schools all or predominantly of one race in a district of mixed population will require close scrutiny to determine that school assignments are not part of state-enforced segregation." The implications of this decision were that segregation in northern urban school districts would come under close scrutiny of the courts and that busing would be considered a legitimate tool for implementing desegregation plans. Traditional arguments about the value of neighborhood schools could no longer be used to avoid integration. Also, school districts would be viewed as unitary systems, and wherever possible, racial integration within those districts must be achieved.

By 1972 presidential politics entered the picture directly when

President Richard Nixon sent a special message to Congress requesting a moratorium on student busing. Nixon's actions reflected the growing reaction of white parents in northern cities to the issue of forced busing. Some communities were able to accomplish desegregation with a minimum of problems; others, such as Boston, suffered a great deal of strife. During 1975 and 1976 the Boston public schools faced the problems of demonstrating parents, interracial fights between students, and clashes between community members and police.

What has often been lost in the rhetoric of politicians and the controversy surrounding busing is the essential issue that desegregation is an attempt to provide equal educational opportunity to all Americans. Not only in terms of the Supreme Court decision are segregated educational facilities inherently unequal, but also in terms of what has actually occurred in northern schools. As court cases have been prosecuted against northern school districts, it has become quite clear that past segregative practices resulted in unequal educational opportunity for minority groups.

The following case study of Cleveland, Ohio, demonstrates how past segregative practices resulted in inferior educational opportunity for blacks and how school officials are now attempting to end segregation. The material for the case study is taken directly from the decision issued by the U.S. District Court in 1976, which found the Cleveland Board of Education guilty of school segregation. Other documents include the appeals by the Cleveland Board of Education after the decision and the response of the NAACP to that appeal.

CLEVELAND, OHIO

The findings of the U.S. District Court against the Cleveland school district are examples of how segregated school practices are directly related to unequal educational opportunity.

Racial segregation had increased in Cleveland between 1940 and 1975. Table 2 gives the percentage of black students attending regular schools that were one-race schools in various years during that period. The chart shows the steady trend toward the concentration of black students in segregated schools in Cleveland, a trend that is not in itself proof of intentional segregation. What needs to be proved is that this pattern is a result of actions by school officials.

The most important issues are pupil assignment and school capacity. "Pupil assignment" refers to the way in which the school system sends students to different schools, either by drawing lines for school

TABLE 2

Percentage of Black Students in One-Race Schools

Year	Percent
1940	51.03
1950	58.08
1955	57.72
1960	76.03
1970	90.00
1975	91.75

districts or through special placement. Obviously pupil assignment is a key issue because the placement of students at different schools results in segregated or integrated conditions. What must be shown is whether or not the methods used by school officials in pupil assignment were affected by the race of the students.

The evidence used to prove the segregative intentions of pupil assignments by Cleveland school officials was school capacity. "School capacity" refers to the number of students a school building was designed to serve. It is assumed that a school district would attempt to assign students so that no building was either overcrowded or underutilized.

In the Cleveland decision the district court found that black pupils tended to be assigned to overcrowded schools despite the fact that some schools with a majority of white students had unused classrooms. This situation occurred in areas where district lines could have easily been redrawn to correct the problem. One example given in the court decision involved 13 elementary schools where the proportion of black students ranged from 95.4 to 100 percent. Only one of these schools had unused classrooms, and most schools were overcrowded. For instance, one school, designed to hold 980 pupils, had an enrollment of 1,350; another school, built to hold 945 students, had 1,446 pupils enrolled.

The court found that these 13 schools were surrounded by 12 other schools, all but 3 of which had proportional black enrollments substantially below the percentage of black students in the Cleveland public schools. Eight of the 12 surrounding-area schools had enrollments that were at least 200 students below their basic capacity; in all, these 12 schools had a total of 51 unused classrooms. The court reasoned that if school assignments had been made without consideration of race, then students would have been more evenly divided between schools. Situations such as this one resulted in the court's decision that school district lines had been drawn to maintain racial segregation.

In addition, the court found that pupil-assignment policy as related to special transfers was influenced by racial considerations. "Special transfers" could be granted to students when school officials determined some need for a student to change from one school to another. The court found that some school board employees placed a handwritten "W" on applications believed to be from white students. Thus special transfers were used to allow white students to attend predominantly white schools rather than their "neighborhood" schools, which happened to be predominantly black.

The court also found intentional racial segregation in terms of faculty assignment. The pattern it found was that as a school's black student enrollment increased, so too did the number of black faculty assigned to that school. One school employee, who had worked for the system for thirty-seven years, told the court, "Well, I don't know whether you want to call it policy or custom or understanding or whatever it is, but if you were black, you went to a school with a predominantly black enrollment."

The most important fact about the above patterns of intentional segregation is that it resulted in inferior education for black people in Cleveland. Overcrowding in black schools resulted in the establishment of "relay" between 1955 and 1961, in an effort to get twice the mileage out of a school day by teaching one group of students in the morning and another in the afternoon. The Court stated in its decision that "the instruction thus received was abbreviated, and therefore inferior, to that received by pupils not on relay classes and, in fact, fell far short of the minimal education standards set out by law." The court reported that the vast majority of the schools that employed relay classes had majority or predominantly black student enrollments.

The inferior education provided in overcrowded black schools, while classrooms in surrounding white schools remained empty, was one basis on which Ohio was found guilty of supporting racial segregation in the schools. The court ruled that, with regard to predominantly black schools, state officials had failed to fulfill their statutory obligation to enforce the minimum standards that the state had established for public schools throughout the state. During the periods when such minimum standards were not enforced, it was argued, "many of the schools in Cleveland which were identifiably black were demonstrably inferior to other schools in the Cleveland system and, therefore, unequal."

Specifically, the court found that the state board and the state superintendent expressly exempted Cleveland school officials from the requirement of providing at least five hours of classroom instruction per day in certain schools, the overwhelming majority of which were virtually all-black. The court stated, "the result was that in these schools, students were put on relay classes, that is they attended school for only three and a half hours per day, rather than five."

The examples given in the Cleveland case demonstrate some of the ways in which segregated education results in unequal education. Of importance and interest is the appeal of the Cleveland school system to the court's decision. The Cleveland Board of Education, while disputing some the findings of the court, has argued that while there might have been evidence of segregation in the past, the present school administration is dedicated to the integration of the school system. In other words, it is the intention of the existing administration to integrate and not segregate. The board also argued that massive busing was too expensive. The cost of buses and the operation of a massive transportation system would cause financial ruin to the school system.

In addition, the Cleveland school system has asserted that it is taking positive steps to end segregated conditions. One of these steps involves a variation of the southern freedom-of-choice plans. Magnet schools are established with specialized programs, which attract students from around the city. For instance, an aviation high school draws students from all areas of the city, and attempts are made there to maintain a racial balance.

The magnet-school concept began to sweep the nation in 1976. Milwaukee, Cleveland, and Cincinnati school systems, to name only a few, attempted to end segregation by creating specialized schools that would attract pupils from the entire city area and be used as a means of attaining racial balance. Some of the specialized programs have included the arts, particular teaching methods and curriculum such as Montessori, and specialized vocational training.

This method of dealing with segregation does not avoid the problem of transportation. Massive busing will still be needed to transport children from their neighborhoods to the magnet schools, but this will be done on the basis of parental choice and not through force. But magnet schools reduce the potential conflict over integration and supposedly provide improved educational facilities. In the case of Cleveland there is fear that the only way of dealing with busing without resulting violence is through voluntary selection of magnet schools.

Conclusion

A major problem that might result with the accomplishment of equal educational opportunity between races is increased inequality in educational opportunity between social classes. For instance, magnet schools might bring about racial balance but they also might result in a social-class stratification in particular schools. It is not beyond the realm of possibility that children of working-class parents, both white and black, might receive counseling that sends them to primarily vocational schools while upper-middle-class children are counseled to select academic programs. Thus the high aspirational levels of middle-class black parents might be satisfied, but with the danger of increased segregation between social classes.

This is a particularly important problem with regard to the relationship between education and social mobility discussed in the previous chapter. The high educational aspirations held by the black community are related to a belief that schooling is a means of social mobility. It is also true that segregated education has been a means of maintaining a stratified society by keeping black people separated from the career routes available to the majority population. Integrated education will be a means of moving the black population into the mainstream of occupational mobility in the United States. This could be one of the important consequences of integration.

On the other hand, as was discussed in chapter 2, receiving equal education does not guarantee social mobility, which is not directly related to the school but to the job market. In addition, there is some evidence that the school's role includes a combination of facilitating the movement of people into new occupations as they occur and maintaining stratification betweeen social classes. It is certainly a positive that poor black people receive equal education; but the same frustrations now felt by poor whites in using the school as a means of social mobility might well be shared by poor blacks as the middle-class black population reaps the rewards of integration.

One important consequence of school integration might be the stabilization of urban housing patterns and integrated neighborhoods. The quality of the schools often determines where people select housing. White parents, in particular, will choose one neighborhood over another because one area's school is all-white while another is all-black. This has been the pattern in northern urban areas. With integration of the schools, this factor is no longer important in selecting housing. Quality and price will become more important determiners of housing patterns than the quality and racial composition of the neighborhood school. School integration might contribute to the growth of more racially integrated neighborhoods as blacks achieve their dream of equal educational opportunity.

EXERCISES

1. To understand the aspirations and debates about education in the black community, read and compare Booker T. Washington's *Up From Slavery* and W. E. B. DuBois's *The Souls of Black Folk*.

2. Check with a local school district to find out how it has complied with Title VI of the 1964 Civil Rights Act.

3. Investigate a local school to determine the distribution of minority students in the curriculum and in ability groups.

4. Contact a local school system and find out the degree of faculty and student integration.

5. Conduct a small survey of students in a local school system to determine levels of educational aspirations.

Suggested Readings and Works Cited in Chapter

Blaustein, Albert P., and Ferguson, Clarence. *Desegregation and the Law: The Meaning and Effect of the School Segregation Cases.* New Brunswick, N.J.: Rutgers University Press, 1957.
 This is a good review and study of the major issues in early school desegregation cases.

Bullock, Henry. *A History of Negro Education in the South from 1619 to the Present.* New York: Praeger, 1970.
 This book won the Bancroft Award and is considered a pioneer work in the history of black education.

Hauser, Robert, and Featherman, David. "Equality of Schooling:

Trends and Prospects." *Sociology of Education* 49 (April 1976): 99–120.

This article argues that as the length of schooling has increased in the United States, it has become more evenly distributed. An important summary of research on educational opportunity.

Orfield, Gary. *The Reconstruction of Southern Education: The Schools and the 1964 Civil Rights Act.* New York: Wiley-Interscience, 1969.

A study of the desegregation of southern schools following the passage of the 1964 Civil Rights Act.

Portes, Alejandro, and Wilson, Kenneth. "Black-White differences in Educational Attainment." *American Sociological Review* 41 (June 1976): 414–31.

A good summary of studies dealing with black-white educational achievement and aspirations..

Spring, Joel. *The Sorting Machine: National Educational Policy Since 1945.* New York: McKay, 1976.

Chapters 4, 5, and 6 provide a history of the civil rights movement and school desegregation.

4

YOUTH
AND
THE
SOCIAL
STRUCTURE

THE ROLE OF YOUTH IN MODERN SOCIETY HAS been one of the major social and educational problems in the twentieth century. Concerns about youth have centered around unemployment and the development of a youth culture different from that of older people. In the twentieth century, young people—because of labor laws, unionization, and increased productivity—have slowly been displaced from the labor market. What can be done about youth if they are not able to be employed? One solution, in fact the main solution until the 1970s, was to increase the length of time spent in school. But now the fear is that youth has become too institutionalized, too segregated from the rest of society. Youth had developed its own culture, which is often antagonistic to adult culture. Other solutions must be found to the youth problem.

This chapter first discusses the development of youth culture in the United States in the twentieth century as a way of showing some of the traditional problems faced by youth. Later in the chapter, current proposals for solving the youth problem are discussed.

Youth Culture in the United States

Youth began to become marginal to the social and economic system before World War I. During the nineteenth century, young people found ready employment in agriculture and industry. In the factory, juvenile labor was welcomed as an important part of economic growth because it was energetic, dexterous, and cheap. Many parents were dependent upon their children's earnings.

During the early part of the twentieth century in the United States, there was a displacement of youth from its traditional economic roles. Improvements in farm technology and rural-to-urban migrations decreased the possibility of the young participating in farm labor. In 1900, 37.5 percent of the total labor force worked on farms. By 1910 this figure had decreased to 30.9 percent, and by 1930 to 21.2 percent. It has continued to decline.

Labor agitation, increased productivity, factory legislation, and technological advances that no longer required dexterity and flexibility all helped to displace the young worker from the factory. These changes in rural areas and in factories caused a decrease in the percentage of youth participating in the labor force. Between 1890 and 1900 the percentage of males between fourteen and nineteen years of age active in the labor force increased from 50 percent to 62 percent. After 1900 this figure began to decline, reaching 51.5 percent in 1920. This percentage, while it represents a slight increase over the 1890 figure, marks the beginning of a steadily declining participation not broken until the start of World War II.

One response to these changes was to seek further institutionalization of children and youth within the school. There was a general consensus that cramped city streets, lack of areas for play, and easy contacts with disreputable persons provided ideal conditions for producing juvenile delinquents and future criminals. Combined with this attitude was a feeling that the training in responsibility and industriousness characteristic of the small community and rural areas was lost in the city.

While problems associated with urban conditions were related to all age groups, there was an increasing concern about youthful sexuality. It was believed that the increasing marginality of youth to the economic structure meant that the sexual drives of youth could no longer be channeled through socially meaningful occupations. The romantic interpretation of youth emphasized that the solution of social problems and existence of the social structure depended on directing social-sexual instinctual developments into acceptable and useful channels.

G. Stanley Hall, America's pioneer developer of adolescent psychology, wrote in the introduction to his classic work *Adolescence* in 1904, "The whole future of life depends on how the new powers of adolescence now given suddenly and in profusion are husbanded and directed." Hall argued that social organizations should utilize the natural instincts of youth and "so direct intelligence and will as to secure the largest measure of social service, advance altruism and reduce selfishness, and thus advance the higher cosmic order." In a similar fashion, Jane Addams, a pioneer in social work, believed that the proper utilization of the sexual energies of youth could bring about the reform of society. She believed that the sexual energies of youth had to be recognized and used for the betterment of society. Parks, playgrounds, parades, education, and national ceremonies were to take the place of the cheap dance halls and movie houses that seduced youth.

During the 1920s, as the marginality of youth increased in importance, the sexuality of youth became a central issue in discussions of what was popularly defined as the growth of the generation gap. In this decade economic productivity in terms of output per man-hour in production increased by 27 percent. The increase in the amount a person could produce in a given time resulted from new technology and more efficient forms of corporate organization. The effect of increased productivity was not only more material abundance, but also a decreasing percentage of the population required in the work force. Increased productivity was reflected in the declining percentage of the male population between the ages of fourteen and nineteen years that belonged to the labor force; the 1920s saw a decline of ten percentage points, from 51.5 percent to 40.1 percent. Interestingly enough, this prosperity and increased productivity had little effect on the sixty-five-and-over age group in the labor force. This group decreased by only about 1.5 percentage points in the labor force, from 55.6 to 54 percent. The over-sixty-fives did not undergo significant displacement from the labor force until after World War II.

The increasing displacement of youth from the labor force brought increased school enrollment. Between 1900 and 1920 school attendance for those between the ages of five and seventeen increased from 78.7 percent to 83.9 percent, an increase of 5.2 percent. For the six-year period between 1920 and 1926 the percentage jumped another 6.5 percent to 90.4. College enrollment for those between the ages of eighteen and twenty-one followed the same pattern. In 1900, 4 percent of this group were in college; by 1920 the figure was 8.1 percent, and during the 1920s there was another 4.3 percent increase. The increase in the percentage of the population in these specified age groups enrolled in school and college more than equaled that of the previous twenty years.

The increase in productivity, affluence, and increased school attendance all contributed to what has been called the Flapper Era or the Jazz Age. A youth culture developed around new forms of dress, music, dance, codes of conduct, and technology. The flapper, jazz, modern dance, the new morality, and the automobile all became part of youth culture. Youth fads of the 1920s centered on the consumption of new products of technology. The automobile provided a form of mobility that had not existed for previous generations. Those concerned with the youth problem often traced the decline of morality, as well as the free spirit and rebellion against authority, to the automobile. Lengthy articles appeared in national magazines on the automobile and morality. Movie houses, different styles of clothing, new dances, and the gin mill stood alongside the automobile as symbols of youth culture.

To those who believed that the social order depended on properly controlling and directing social-sexual instincts, the new morality of the 1920s represented a direct threat to the foundations of civilization. But the frivolous style of life associated with youth in the 1920s came to an abrupt halt as the decade ended with the Great Depression. Unemployed youth became a central issue. Like other marginal groups—such as blacks—youth was often in the position of last hired and first fired. Lacking the seasoned skills of older workers, young workers found it increasingly difficult to obtain jobs during a time of high unemployment. The 1940 census revealed that by the end of the depression 35 percent of the unemployed were under age twenty-five, and only 22 percent of the total employed population was within that age range.

In response to the crises of the depression, the American Council on Education established the American Youth Commission to investigate the problems of young America. In 1937 the chairman of the council offered the following picture. Defining youth as between sixteen and twenty-four, he described a mythical town of Youngsville with a population of 200 youths. Within this town 76 youths had regular jobs, 40 went to school or college, 5 went to school part-time, 28 were married women, and 51 were out of work and out of school. Half of those who were out of work received federal aid.

One striking characteristic of youth reported during the depression was its lack of idealism and rebelliousness. One of the conditions that created this situation, different from the past, was that youth marginality in the 1930s was not accompanied by the affluence of the 1920s but by a desire for economic security. When the American

Youth Commission surveyed the young people of Maryland in the 1930s as a representative sample of all American youth, it was found that 57.7 percent of the youths surveyed named the lack of economic security as the major problem for young people in America.

The other important condition affecting youth during the depression was the cultural and social climate. *McCall's* magazine assigned Maxine Davis to travel around the country and report on the state of youth. Traveling four months and ten thousand miles through cities and backroads of America, she produced not only articles but also a book that labeled the youth of the depression as the "lost generation." She reported, "We never found revolt. We found nothing but a meek acceptance of the fate meted out to them, and a belief in a benign future based on nothing but wishful thinking." The major problem among the lost generation was the lack of economic security. The nature of the lost generation, Davis argued, was a product of the psychopathic period in which these young people grew up. Davis wrote,

---

Boys and girls who came of voting age in 1935 were born in 1914. Their earliest memories are of mob murder and war hysteria. Their next, the cynical reaction to war's sentimentality and war's futility. Their adolescence was divided between the crass materialism of the jazz 1920's and the shock of the economic collapse. In effect, they went to high school in limousines and washed dishes in college.

The problems and climate of opinion during the depression resulted in the federal government's becoming directly involved in the youth problem with the establishment of the National Youth Administration and Civilian Conservation Corps. The National Youth Administration was established in 1935 to provide relief for youths in school. Initially the program began with providing a monthly allotment to high school and college students whose families were on relief and comparable aids for older youths who were out of school. Schools were to develop work projects in which young people could render some form of service for the money they received. The National Youth Administration set an important precedent, for it established some form of financial assistance linked to schooling as a solution to the youth problem. In later years this would be more fully developed in government scholarship and loan programs.

The most important and significant of the government's youth programs in terms of later development was the Civilian Conservation Corps (CCC). The first CCC camp opened in 1933 to provide conservation and work relief. The basic principle of the CCC was that unemployment could be dealt with by government hiring of youth to perform conservation work. Youths who signed up for the CCC were housed in camps around the country.

The CCC became a major effort at social and educational reconstruction. The camps planned group educational work designed to change social attitudes and provide vocational training. It was even advocated that the CCC become universal and compulsory for all youths reaching the age of eighteen; it would include military, civic, and vocational training. As a universal and compulsory institution it would solve the problem of youth unemployment by removing one million youths annually from the labor market.

Although the CCC never became a universal youth program, it did establish a model for future proposals to deal with the youth problem, including universal military training, selective service, job corps camps, and national service. The CCC program itself was abandoned with the beginning of World War II. The war provided a temporary solution to both the youth problem and the depression. War industries and the armed forces solved the economic problems and absorbed the young. Youth's marginality to the occupational structure no longer was a factor, and the young were reintegrated into the mainstreams of social and economic activity in the United States.

The proportion of those between the ages of fourteen and nineteen involved in the labor force increased from 44 percent in 1940 to 69.2 percent in 1944. The 1944 figure even exceeded the previous high, 62 percent in 1900. With more places available in the occupational structure, there was a corresponding decrease in school enrollments. During the depression, school and college enrollments had climbed from 89.7 percent in 1930 to 94.1 percent in 1940 for those members of the population between the ages of five and seventeen, and from 12.4 percent in 1930 to 15.6 percent in 1940 for those between eighteen and twenty-one. Increases in school enrollment during the depression reflected the displacement of the young from the occupational structure; decreases in school enrollment during World War II indicated their reentry into it. Enrollments for those between five and seventeen steadily declined during the war until 1944, when 89 percent of that age group was in high school. College attendance for those between eighteen and twenty-one declined to 11.9 percent in 1946.

Following World War II, youth was called the "beat generation." Jack Kerouac provided the label in 1950 simply by saying, "You know, this really is a beat generation." Cellon Holmes, an author and friend of Kerouac, defined the meaning of the beat generation in a 1952 *New York Times Magazine* article entitled "This Is the Beat Generation." He called it a generation beat from the depression, the war, and the feeling that the postwar peace was only as secure as the next headline. "More than mere weariness," Holmes wrote, "it implies the feeling of having been used, of being raw. It involves a sort of nakedness of mind, and, ultimately, of soul; a feeling of being reduced to the bedrock of consciousness. In short, it means being undramatically pushed up against the wall." The new generation, said Holmes, lived in a world of shattered ideals and accepted the mud in the moral currents: "They were brought up in these ruins and no longer notice them. They drink to 'come down' or 'get high' not to illustrate anything. Their excursions into drugs or promiscuity come out of curiosity, not disillusionment."

After the precedents established during the depression, the federal government immediately became involved in the youth problem after World War II. President Harry Truman advocated universal military service for all American youth. He was very explicit that the program would involve more than military training. It was, he argued, a method of establishing a national system of health examinations, remedial training in basic educational skills, and vocational guidance. In addition, there were also concerns about the nation having enough scientists, engineers, and technicians to maintain the military superiority of the United States. What this meant was that more youths needed to be persuaded to attend college and receive advanced training.

The compromise between the desire to provide universal military service and the need for trained manpower was the Universal Military Training and Service Act of 1951. This act provided a system of selective deferments which allowed male youth after high school either to be drafted into military service or to be deferred to go on to college or into a job of value to the national security. In other words, the youth problem was to be solved by youths either going to college or into the military.

The military draft and deferment system did help to solve some of the youth problems that began to occur after the end of World War

II. Following World War II, the involvement of males between fourteen and nineteen in the labor force decreased slowly. It did not approximate the 1920 figure until about 1953, when 50 percent of that group participated. The fact that young people could not still find employment after 1945 spread alarm among some educators; they launched a back-to-school campaign in the years immediately following the war.

During the spring of 1949 unemployment of both adults and young people increased considerably. The marginality of youth was again apparent; the general unemployment rate was 5 percent, but for those between sixteen and nineteen years of age it was around 14 percent. Changes in the job market were again reflected in school enrollment figures. In 1946 the percentage of those between the ages of five and seventeen enrolled in school was 90.3. In 1948 the percentage dropped to 89.5 and by 1950 it increased to 92.6. After 1950 this percentage steadily increased, except for a slight drop between 1958 and 1960, until it reached 97.1 percent in 1965. College enrollments followed the same pattern. Enrollment in higher education for those between eighteen and twenty-one increased to 22.1 percent in 1947, reached 31.2 percent in 1956, and by 1965 was 43.9 percent.

Economic and social conditions were ripening in the mid-1950s for a repeat of the generation gap of the 1920s, although on a more massive scale. During and after World War II productivity increased. By 1955 it had more than doubled the 1929 figure. Increased output per man-hour required increased consumption and displacement of portions of the population from production, but not from consumption. Locked in school, middle- and upper-middle-class youths could consume the excesses of technological production without contributing to its further increase.

The post-World War II child grew up in the richest abundance of technology and mass consumption the world had ever known. As the beat generation moved out of the colleges and universities and achieved its goal of economic security, it was replaced by the children of postwar economic affluence. Almost 50 percent of this generation was to be delayed from entering the occupational structure by continued education after high school. The combination of extended dependency, consumer exploitation, and the sharing of a common social life helped to create the youth culture of the 1960s.

The youth culture of the 1960s was characterized by involvement in civil rights campaigns, antiwar activity, and development of a "hippie culture." The combination of affluence and marginality to the productive structure again set the stage for the return of youthful romanticism and idealism. Locked in institutions of higher learning, youth's only important social functions were preparation for future entrance into the occupational structure, and present and future consumption of technology's products. As a social group freed from concern with working, youth could define its social importance in terms of humanitarian crusades. Youth again accepted the labels of idealism and romanticism and joined with blacks in the early 1960s in a massive civil rights campaign. During the middle and late years of the decade, young people defined their social role by participating in civil rights campaigns, battles against pollution, political campaigns, and a variety of other social projects.

It is important to recognize that not all youths participated in the affluence and college life of the 1960s. Minority youths in particular suffered from the problem of being both out of school and out of a job. In 1960, 1961, and 1962 the unemployment rate for white males aged eighteen and nineteen was 13.5, 15.1, and 12.7. For nonwhite males in this age category, it was 25.1, 23.9, and 21.8 percent. These unemployment rates represented a striking increase over previous figures. For instance, in 1948 the unemployment rate for white males was 8.3 percent, and for nonwhite males 7.6 percent.

Unemployed youth was a major concern of the federal government in the early 1960s. The eventual response of the government was Title I of the Economic Opportunity Act of 1964, which established the Job Corps. The Job Corps was to be a unique combination of approaches to the youth problem. First, it attacked unemployment among young people by providing urban and rural residential training centers. Youths enrolled in these centers would essentially be removed from the labor market. One of the activities of the Job Corps in rural residential centers was to be "conserving, developing and managing the public natural resources of the Nation." This idea was a carry-over from the Civilian Conservation Corps of the 1930s and had also provided the major thrust for solving youth unemployment in the bills for a Youth Conservation Corps submitted to Congress in 1959, 1961, and 1963. The Conservation Corps was retained within the Job Corps as a means of winning support for the legislation from conservationists in Congress. Title I specifically stated that at least 40 percent of the Job Corps enrollees had to be assigned to camps doing conservation work. Besides aiding the problem of youth unemployment, the Job Corps was to attack poverty by providing residential centers, vocational training, and remedial education.

In addition to the Job Corps, Title I of the Economic Opportunity Act provided work-training and work-study programs. The work-training programs were to be an extension of the public-service-employment approach to solving unemployment among youth. The training programs were to be conducted by local public institutions or nonprofit organizations. The law stated that the purpose of the programs was "to provide useful work experience opportunities for unemployed young men and young women . . . so that their employability may be increased or their education resumed." The purpose of the work itself would be to perform some "service in the public interest that would not otherwise be provided." Like the Jobs Corps, this section of the law reflected the continuing idea of youth being mobilized for some form of national service.

In a sense these provisions for youth in the Economic Opportunity Act of 1964 could be viewed as one section of a three-part national attempt to provide activity for youth: one part was higher education; another was selective service; for those who could not make it to college or were rejected by the armed forces, there was the Job Corps. In fact, major support for the youth programs came from a report issued in 1964 by the President's Task Force on Manpower Legislation, which claimed that the high rejection rate of draftees by the armed forces was related to poverty.

By the end of the 1960s the various methods that had been developed for handling the youth problem began to encounter serious problems. First, the social activity of students in college escalated from protest of the Vietnam war to campus riots and deaths. This created a national concern about law and order on campus and raised serious doubts in the minds of many national leaders about the wisdom of channeling such a large proportion of youth into college. Second, the very specific device of the Selective Service System as a means of channeling youth into college was widely protested. Third, because of the increased number of college students, "educational inflation" began to take place.

Educational inflation was something that no one had expected. It occurs when the level of education of the population begins to go beyond the educational requirements of the job market. When this occurs, the educational credentials required for jobs begins to increase beyond what is actually required for the job. For instance, a job in the 1950s that required only a high school diploma might by the early 1970s be employing people with college degrees, even though there was no significant change in the job's activities.

The federal government's response to the breakdown of the youth policies of the 1950s and 1960s was to eliminate selective service and establish a voluntary armed forces. In addition, new plans emerged for the solution of the youth problem. The group given this responsibility was the 1972 Panel on Youth of the President's Science Advisory Committee.

Report of the Panel on Youth

The report of the Panel on Youth was publicly issued in 1974 as *Youth: Transition to Adulthood* and is popularly called "Coleman II." James Coleman, the major author of *Equality of Educational Opportunity* (cited in the previous chapter), was chairman of the Panel on Youth.

The report described seven major issues with regard to the role of youth in modern industrial society. The first major issue was the segregation of youth from adults versus the integration of youth with adults. The report argued that during the last century youth has become segregated from the rest of the adult population as increasing numbers of youths have extended their years of education. Adult contacts have tended to be confined to parents and teachers. The report asserted that some of the benefits of this segregation are protection from the harsh work activities of adults and possible corruption from unfit adults. Nevertheless, the concern about protection of youth from work, according to the report, is not as important today as it was in the past. The harsh labor that children needed to be protected from in the past has vanished from the workplace, and an elaborate set of laws have been developed to protect youth from exploitation. Other benefits of age segregation, as given in the report, are the benefits to adults in having an institution such as the school to take care of their children while they work or perform other adult functions. In addition, the report felt that extreme age segregation, in which youth lived in a community composed entirely of other young people, might allow youth to fill roles currently occupied by adults, such as construction, purchasing, cooking, and the like.

In opposition to the segregation of youth from adults, age integration would allow youth to learn from the incidental experience occurring as a result of direct contact with a variety of adults during the course of a day. It was asserted that this type of incidental learning is a major means of transmitting skills, culture, ideas, and information.

Age integration, the report argued, would also benefit adults by lessening social conflict between the two age groups and enlivening the adult environment by the presence of young people. The concern expressed in the report about social conflict between youth and adults reflected the general concern about student demonstrations and the conflict that had occurred in the 1960s. It was in the context of these events that the report emphasized the importance of age integration to both the world of the young and the adult world, arguing that the benefits of age integration outweighed those of age segregation.

A similar conclusion was reached with regard to the second major issue, that of age segregation among youth. (What was meant in this case by "age segregation" was the separation of high school students from college students and the separation that occurs between youths in different grades in school.) The report indicated that the benefits of age integration among youth were more important than the benefits of age segregation. The primary benefits of age segregation were administrative, the report argued. Dividing students in a school by age was an easy way to reduce the unfair advantages of older children over younger children. On the other hand, benefits of age integration among youth include the experiences young people gain through contact with others outside their age group. Older children in relationship to younger children learn a sense of responsibility about their actions, as well as learn to interact with younger children. Older children can also be an effective source of learning for younger age groups. For these reasons, the report felt that age groups should be integrated.

The third major issue of the report of the Panel on Youth was directly related to the issue of age segregation. The issue was that of grouping youths according to the stage of development rather than by chronological age groupings. The report did not adopt a particular method for grouping youths, but did suggest that American education needed to get away from the one-year chronological age grouping. The report admitted that there was no certainty in terms of present knowledge about what type of grouping might be most beneficial.

The fourth issue dealt with in the report was the difference between activity for self-development and productive activity such as work. It was contended that neglect of self-development, such as education, results in an unskilled adult who is unable to deal with the complex modern world; neglect of productive activity results in youth being overly idealistic and romantic and without a clear sense of the workings of the world.

The ideal, the youth panel felt, was to blend the two sets of experiences. They gave examples of four alternative ways in which the combination of self-development and productive activity were presently occurring in education. One alternative was in the form "continuing education" on a part-time basis, where persons employed in full-time jobs attend school part-time, usually at night schools. Another alternative given was Sweden's "recurrent education," where the individual alternates between full-time work and full-time education. The pattern implies full-time work before entering the university. To a certain extent this pattern has developed also in the United States, where students drop out of college for a couple of years and engage in full-time occupations before returning to school. The third alternative the panel discussed was "career education," which shifts the central focus of education to the study of occupations and relates the subject matter of the school to future occupations. The fourth alternative was "learning at work," which could range from cooperative education, where a student spends half a day at work and the other half at school, to educational programs that would exist at the place of employment.

The fifth major issue defined by the youth panel was role segmentation versus community. At one extreme of this issue young people would be in a role-segmented society like that of the larger society; at the other extreme they would be in a youth community. The panel felt that the most beneficial resolution of this issue would be a variety of institutions, each covering a different portion of youth's activities. In this manner youth would have the benefits of a sense of community within an institution and at the same time experience a variety of roles in different institutions.

The sixth major issue related to the youth problem was the scope of formal schooling. The issue in this case was one of the extent to which nonacademic content should be introduced in the school. It should be recognized that since the nineteenth century the American school has increased the scope of its activities to include such things as drivers' training, home economics, drug education, and a host of other activities that would be considered nonacademic. From the viewpoint of the panel, the continuing trend to expand the scope of the school should end. The panel believed that the benefits of incorporating nonacademic activities in the school were far fewer than the benefits of incorporating them in outside organizations. The position taken by the panel on this issue might mark the beginning of a reduction of the social functions of the American school.

The last and extremely important issue was that of the legal status and rights of youth. The panel described the issue as being between laws that are protective and those that are constraining. For instance, child labor and school attendance laws protect youth from some of the harmful effects of work and assure that youth will have the opportunity to attend school. On the other hand, these laws are constraining because they hold young people in environments that might be harmful and unproductive. For instance, it might be harmful to some youths to keep them from leaving school when that setting does not provide the things needed by the individual. What the panel felt needed to be done was to develop laws that would assure the rights of the young person with some degree of self-determination, and at the same time protect youth from exploitation.

CONCRETE PROPOSALS OF THE REPORT

The 1972 Panel on Youth of the President's Science Advisory Committee proposed concrete ways in which the issues raised by its report could be resolved. The actual proposals represented some basic shifts in thinking about social policy for youth. Some of these policy statements elicited strong criticism, which resulted in further elaboration of concerns about the role of youth in modern society.

In response to the problem of the introduction of youth to work roles, one proposal was for the expansion of work-study programs to include both vocational and preparatory students. The Panel on Youth suggested that two alternative models be tested. The first would involve alternation between periods of full-time schooling and full-time work. The second model would involve half-time schooling and half-time work occurring at the same time.

The major part of the criticism resulting from these proposals for expanded work-study programs centered around the lack of educational value of most occupations in modern society. It was argued that most workplaces are boring and that the majority of people do not work because they enjoy it or because it is meaningful. Most jobs in an industrial society, it was asserted, are hard and tedious and tend to require little learning or provide few chances for intellectual stimulation. In addition, it was suggested that massive costs and logistical problems in placing students would make it impossible to include all American youth in a work-study program. Even if this were possible, there would probably be objections from adult workers, who would perceive themselves as competing with young people for job opportunities in a time of employment scarcity.

There was also concern that early introduction to work roles would generate a great deal of criticism from parents of all social classes. Lower- or working-class parents would object to the work experience because they would see it as relegating their children to the very life experiences they are trying to escape. Lower- or working-class parents might view work-study programs as reducing possibilities of using the school as a means of upward mobility. Middle- and upper-middle-class parents would probably object because there would be little evidence to convince them that learning what a shoe salesman or plumber does during the day will improve performance on college-entrance examinations. These parents would probably consider work-study a hindrance to their children's opportunities to attend college.

Similar objections were raised to the Panel on Youth's proposal that work organizations incorporate youth into their organizational structures. According to this proposal, young people rather than finishing high school would enter a work organization, where they would spend a part of their time working and another part at self-instruction. Self-instruction would be possible through the use of televised or videotaped teaching. It was argued by the panel that with televised instruction, a classroom full of students is no longer necessary and scheduling could be fitted to a work schedule.

An additional criticism was that the Panel on Youth overemphasized the importance of the school in the socialization of youth and assumed that life in the school was not reflective of the "real world." These criticisms were strongly voiced by educators, who tended to view the criticisms of the panel concerning the increased institutionalization of youth as direct criticisms of the work of the school. Educators tended to view it as a positive that the school protected youth from the world of work and provided an opportunity for youth to concentrate upon learning.

The concern of professional educators about reducing the role of the school and increasing the role of the workplace in the lives of youth is understandable and reflects one of the traditional tensions in the evolution of national youth policy in the twentieth century. During the 1930s educators were very critical of federal policies such as the Civilian Conservation Corps, which removed part of the responsibility for the education of youth from the public schools. Both child labor laws and compulsory schooling laws were considered ways of protecting young people from the exploitation and harshness of the work world. For public school people, the recommendations of the Panel on Youth were a direct threat to their own interests in extending and improving schooling.

Another highly criticized proposal of the panel was for a dual minimum wage that would be lower for youth than for adult workers. It was contended that a flat minimum wage rate constricts the number of jobs available to the young because of their lack of experience and low productivity when compared to experienced and mature workers. It was also felt that a lower minimum wage for youth would provide an incentive for employers to provide general training through work. One of the major dissents to this proposal came from a member of the panel who pointed out that a dual minimum wage would allow employers to pay young workers a lower wage than adults for the same job. This would result in loss of employment for adult workers. It could also establish a precedent for providing a subminimal wage to other underemployed groups such as blacks or women.

One interesting and important proposal of the Panel on Youth that did not result in any major criticisms was the development of a voucher system for youths who did not attend college. Under the present system of school finance, a person receives full benefit of the money spent on education only by continuing in school through college. The Panel on Youth felt that this system financially discriminates against those who are not interested in continuing their education within formal educational structures. With a voucher system, all youths at age sixteen would receive an educational voucher worth a certain number of dollars that could be used for attending a formal educational institution or acquiring a wide range of skills.

Two important features of the proposed voucher system were that choice about use would be left to the individual youth and that the voucher could be used at any time during the life of the individual. This last feature would introduce a great deal of age flexibility into the educational system. People would be able to postpone their education until their later years and would be able to interrupt it at any stage. A voucher system would also revolutionize the present method of financing schools by placing the responsibility for the final spending of the educational dollar in the hands of the student.

The Family, the Workplace, and the School

In November of 1976 the Interagency Forum on Youth Participation met in Washington, D.C., with James Coleman, the original leader of the Panel on Youth, delivering the opening remarks. Coleman argued that the authority of the family had been steadily declining and that other institutions would have to assume the responsibility of child rearing. Coleman called for the state to assume the role of wise parents.

Coleman's remarks immediately sparked the reaction among other participants that there was no proof that the family was declining. Since the organization of the family had undergone constant change through history, to speak of its decline did not make historical sense. In fact it was stated by one participant that the family in the twentieth century had slowly been *extending* its role in child rearing. As the amount of time spent in schooling in the twentieth century has increased, so has the length of time youth is dependent upon the family. Consequently, it can be argued that the institutionalization of youth has resulted in strengthening the role of the family in child rearing.

The issue of the decline of the family has been one of the continuing concerns in the twentieth century and is directly related to the development of a national youth policy. Since the late nineteenth century, educators and other social leaders have been complaining that the family is collapsing and suggesting that the school or some other institution must therefore assume the functions of the family. The issue with regard to youth policy is whether policy should be planned that will strengthen the family in terms of its control over youth, on the one hand, or increase the independence of youth from the family, on the other.

For instance, any policy that might increase the length of time youth spends in educational institutions might increase or maintain the authority of the family over youth. That is, youths attending school might continue to be dependent upon their families for basic shelter and food. In fact, a policy could be developed that would determine the age at which youth would be able to be independent of the family. Basic scholarships and jobs that would not make youth financially independent could be provided up to the age of twenty-one. After that age, assistance could be provided that would make it possible to leave the family. The age at which independence would be considered desirable could be varied.

In contrast, one could decrease the role of the family in the rearing of youth by establishing some form of national policy that would allow youth to become independent of the family at an early age. A massive public works project that would hire youth at an age of thirteen or fourteen and would provide enough income to allow young people to live away from home would reduce the number of years they spent under the care of the family. Scholarships, boarding schools, and youth communities could be other means by which the length of time youth spent in the family could be reduced.

The important point is that any form of national youth policy will have a direct effect upon the nature of the American family. In the same manner a national youth policy will have a direct effect on the role of the school. Current complaints are being made about the extended role of the school over youth and the lack of contact of youth with the world of work. The difficulty and questionable value of integrating youth into the work world might lead to reversal of this concern, however, and attention might be focused instead upon extending the role of the school.

The family, the school, and the workplace have been continuing elements in the dialogue about the place of youth in the modern industrial world. The development of a workable policy that would provide some final solution to the youth problem appears impossible at this stage of development. Indeed, the problem might be inherent in the economic organization of modern industrial society, and any policy that deals only with youth might leave untouched the basic economic causes of the problem.

EXERCISES

1. Youth culture has changed rapidly in the twentieth century. In a discussion group or in an essay discuss the current state of youth culture in terms of consumption patterns, music, political ideas, and social life. Does this youth culture vary according to social class and race?

2. Contact the local state employment office in your community and find out the current unemployment figures for youth. Inquire about the different types of youth programs available in your community.

3. In a discussion group or in an essay describe what you think should be the national youth policy in the United States. Consider the following factors in the formulation of your youth policy:

   a. the role of the school
   b. the role of the family
   c. the role of the workplace
   d. economic independence for youth
   e. national youth service

Suggested Readings and Works Cited in Chapter

Aries, Philippe. *Centuries of Childhood: A Social History of Family Life*. New York: Vintage, 1962.

A history of the changing concepts of childhood and their relationship to the structure of the family. Important in understanding how educational policy can affect the structure of the family.

Coleman, James, et al. *Youth: Transition to Adulthood*. Chicago: University of Chicago Press, 1974.

This is the report of the Panel on Youth of the President's Science Advisory Committee. The report contains sections on the history of youth, major issues and recommendations.

Davis, Maxine. *The Lost Generation*. New York: Macmillan, 1936.

The book that gave the name of the lost generation to the youth of the 1930s.

Holmes, Cellon. "This Is the Beat Generation," *New York Times Magazine*, 16 November 1952, p. 10.

The first article to define the beat generation.

Krug, Edward. *The Shaping of the American High School 1920–1941*. Madison, Wisc.: University of Wisconsin Press, 1972.

Chapter 12 of this history details the struggle between the government and educators for the control of youth in the 1930s.

Spring, Joel. "Youth Culture in the United States." In *Roots of Crisis* by Clarence Karier, Paul Violas, and Joel Spring. Chicago: Rand McNally, 1973.

A history of youth culture in the twentieth century.

PART 2

POWER AND CONTROL IN AMERICAN EDUCATION

5

POWER AND CONTROL IN THE LOCAL SCHOOL DISTRICT

TWO OF THE MAJOR ISSUES RELATED TO THE control of American education in local school districts have been the representativeness of the members of the local boards of education and the actual amount of power wielded by boards of education in relation to the professional staffs of schools. The issue of representativeness concerns whether or not the membership on boards of education should reflect the social composition of the local population. The question of the power relationship between boards of education and professional staffs of schools deals with the consideration of what educational matters should be controlled by boards of education and what educational matters should be controlled by school administrators and teachers.

To understand the importance of these issues, one must first consider the organization of education at the local level in the United States. In most American communities some form of appointed or elected board of education has the responsibility of representing public opinion in school matters. Whether or not the board is appointed or elected and how it is appointed or elected will vary from community to community. In general, boards of education formulate educational policy, which is then administered by the school staff. In the local school district the superintendent of schools has the responsibility for administering educational policy and advising the board on the needs of the local school system.

The central office staff is usually composed of an administrative staff, which deals with the overall organization of the school system's curriculum, financial matters, personnel policies, and any programs that affect all schools within a district. In terms of the control of local education, the central office staff is very important because it often controls the lines of communication between the building principals and teachers and the superintendent. Building principals have the responsibility of administering school policy within their particular elementary or secondary school.

The reader should be cautioned that this description of organization in the local district is a gross oversimplification of the actual lines of power and communication that exist within each district. For instance, teachers often deal directly with the board of education when they are organized into a local association for the purpose of collective bargaining for wages and work conditions. One of the purposes of the following sections of this chapter is to help the reader understand the complicated nature of these relationships.

The first two sections of this chapter deal with the social composition of boards of education, the political world in which they function, and the extent of their governing power over schools. The third section deals with the internal relationships between members of the school staff. The fourth and final sections deal with the issue of the relationship between the board of education and the professional staff with regard to control of educational policy.

The Social Composition and Political World of Boards of Education

A traditional criticism of boards of education in the twentieth century has been their elite membership. By "elite" is meant that the membership is primarily drawn from the professional and business groups in the local community. This situation is not as true in rural communities, where there is often heavy representation from the farm community. Most boards of education in the United States tend to be composed of white male professional or business persons. The representation from this group on boards of education tends to be out of proportion to their actual numbers in comparison with the rest of the population. In other words, the membership of boards of education in the United States tends not to reflect the social composition of the local community.

This situation with regard to local school districts is reflected in national statistics. L. Harmon Zeigler and M. Kent Jennings reported in their study *Governing American Schools: Political Interaction in Local School Districts* (a national survey of the social composition of boards of education conducted in the early 1970s) a major lack of representativeness of board members in comparison to the general population with regard to the social and economic characteristics of sex, education, income and occupation. Table 3 provides a summary of some of their findings.

A close examination of table 3 indicates that a disproportionate

TABLE 3

A Summary of the Social and Economic Comparison between Board Members and the General Public

CHARACTERISTICS	GENERAL PUBLIC %	BOARD MEMBERS %
Sex:		
Males	48	90
Females	52	10
Education:		
Less than 12 grades	41	7
12 grades	32	22
1–4 years of college	23	47
Graduate and professional school	4	25
Income:		
Under $7,500	56	10
$7,500–$19,999	39	54
$20,000 and over	6	36
Occupation:		
Professional and technical	16	34
Managers, officials, and proprietors	14	32
Farmers	5	13
Clerical and sales	11	9
Craftsmen and foremen	19	8
Operatives	16	2
Service and laborers	11	2
Other	8	—

SOURCE: L. Harmon Zeigler and M. Kent Jennings, *Governing American Schools* (North Scituate, Mass.: Duxbury, 1974).

number of board members are male, have college educations, are in the upper-income groups, and have high-status occupations. For some educators, this social composition of boards of education is a positive asset to the local school district. Joseph M. Cronin in his history *The Control of Urban Schools* found that educators during the early part of the twentieth century believed it was important to have successful and well-educated men on the school board because this social group was more knowledgeable and more interested in education. In fact, the whole trend toward centralization and the reduction in size of urban school boards in the early part of the twentieth century was premised on the idea of limiting public participation in school affairs to the social leaders of the community. Opposition to this trend came from organized labor, which felt if board membership was drawn from only one sector of the community, this would result in particular political and economic views dominating the school policy.

Zeigler and Jennings also found in their *Governing American Schools* that the major route to either election or appointment to a school board was participation in civic-business clubs such as the Chamber of Commerce, Kiwanis Club, Rotary, and other luncheon-service clubs. In addition, an active role in local educational organizations such as the PTA and Citizens Advisory Committees often preceded election or appointment to school boards.

Knowledge of the social and economic background of board members and their route to boards of education is important for an understanding of the linkage between boards of education and the formal and informal power structure of the local community. In most communities in the United States school board elections are nonpartisan and usually separate from other political campaigns. One consequence of the nonpartisan nature of most school board elections is their separation from formal ties with established political parties. In other words, activity within a political party such as a local Democratic or Republican organization is not usually a route to board membership.

This situation means that board membership tends to be more closely related to the informal power structure of the local community than to political parties. Of course, local political parties often have the same ties to the local informal power structure. In the case of board members, however, there is greater reliance upon the local informal power structure as opposed to the formal structure of political parties and local government. This is reflected in the importance of civic-business clubs and educational organizations as routes to board membership. It is also reflected in board members' statements about the types of encouragement they received. While in most elections to government positions support of a political party is very important, this is not the case with school board members. Zeigler and Jennings found that nearly a quarter of their national sample of board members claimed that no individual or group requested them to run for the board. Twenty-nine percent of board members claimed encouragement to run for the board from other board members, and 21 percent received requests from formal citizen groups. Only 13 percent claimed they were requested to become members of the board by governmental and political figures. The remainder of board members stated they were requested to run for the board by friends and professional school personnel.

What all this means is that understanding the informal power structure of a local community is extremely important for understanding the politics and policies of local boards of education. The nature of the informal power structure varies from community to community. Michael Y. Nunnery and Ralph B. Kimbrough in their *Politics, Power, Polls, and School Elections* have defined several different types of power structures that can exist within local communities and can have a direct effect upon the local schools. They argue that understanding the nature of the local power structure is important for understanding both the politics of the board of education and the type of community support and methods to be used in gaining support for educational policies.

Nunnery and Kimbrough argue that there are four basic types of local power structures, ranging from monopolistic systems to ones characterized by democratic pluralism. In a community with a monopolistic power structure there is very often a single group of businessmen, professionals, and politicians who control the community. Sometimes this occurs in one-industry towns or in rural areas governed by groups of large landowners. Within a monopolistic system a few top influentials make the major decisions for the community. These systems are characterized by very little conflict and confrontation. Another somewhat closed type of system is the multigroup and noncompetitive power structure. In this power structure, although there are rival groups within the structure seeking their own economic advantage, there is still general agreement about the basic policies within the local community. For instance, leaders of the different groups within this power structure might compete for such things as school contracts for building and insurance but still agree upon general educational policy.

Another type of power structure that affects board of education politics is one characterized by competition between elite groups. This very often occurs when a community is undergoing some type of social change, such as a rural community rapidly changing into a suburban community. In this particular case, major competition is seen between established and newer elite groups over questions such as zoning, planning, industrialism, and education. There are very often differences of opinion between elite groups about basic school policy. For instance, a traditional rural community might place less emphasis upon preparation for college than a new elite associated with suburban development. Although strong conflict exists between competing elite groups in this structure, there is still little general citizen participation in the power structure.

The fourth type of power structure is one characterized by democratic pluralism, where the system is continually open to new persons and groups gaining positions of power. Very often, the people who are influential in the community decision-making process change depending upon the issue being considered. For instance, people who are influential in the educational decision-making process might be different from those involved in other community affairs. Within this structure there is a great deal of citizen participation.

Nunnery and Kimbrough believe that for a school administrator to work effectively, it is essential to understand the type of power structure within the local community. It is equally true that to understand the politics of the local school board and its policies one must understand the power structure that is responsible for their election or appointment to the board. One of the difficulties in doing this is being able to generalize from one community to another. No two communities are necessarily alike in terms of their power structure and the informal network that leads to board membership. Each community must be studied to determine its particular type of power structure.

Nunnery and Kimbrough have suggested some methods that school administrators can use to determine the nature of the local power structure. These methods are also valuable to the student and local citizen in coming to understand the political and social forces behind the school board. Nunnery and Kimbrough recommend the following procedure. First, a person should become acquainted with the variety of literature on community power structures as a basis for interpreting any data gathered. Second, a person should become acquainted with the leaders in different areas of the community. Nunnery and Kimbrough recommend beginning with the heads of the local chamber of commerce, women's clubs, unions, churches, political parties, newspapers, radio and television stations. In addition, prominent attorneys, physicians, and bankers should be contacted.

In discussions with these persons questions should be asked about important issues, problems, and decisions; notes should be taken with regard to the names most frequently mentioned. Discussion should also be encouraged with regard to whom the community leaders think are the most influential people in the community. From these conversations a person can begin piecing together an outline of the relationships between those people considered the most influential in the community. Next, one should check the membership lists of local boards of directors of financial institutions, community groups, and the chamber of commerce. With this information a person should be able to outline the informal power structure of the community. After this is done, the results can be tested through participation in community activities to observe the degree of citizen participation and the importance of the power structure in the decision-making process.

The same methods recommended by Nunnery and Kimbrough can be directly applied to a study of the membership of the local board of education. Interviews with current and former board members can reveal why they got involved in the board activities and their relationship to the general community power structure. Of extreme importance in this regard are the informal contacts. One can determine both through membership lists in organizations and direct questions whether or not a great deal of informal contact takes place between board members or other members of the local power structure. Very often decisions about school issues and school board participation are made at informal social gatherings and parties in homes and in social clubs. This is true both for economic elite groups such as businessmen and professionals and for social interest groups such as racial and ethnic organizations.

While the linkage between the school board and the community power structure is important for understanding the actions of board members, it is also important for understanding the linkages between the board and the school administration. It is essential for the superintendent of schools, in terms of being effective and for job protection, to have a cooperative and friendly board of education. For this reason, school administrators tend to favor school board members with a successful business or professional background.

Zeigler and Jennings found in *Governing American Schools* that school board members from lower social economic groups tended to become more involved in administrative detail in their relationship to the superintendent. This means they sought a greater involvement in the day-to-day workings of the school system. On the other hand, board members from higher social and economic groups tended to be more involved in consideration of overall educational policy. From the standpoint of the superintendent, board member involvement in administrative details can restrict and hinder the actions of the administrative staff. In most cases the superintendent would rather have board members restrict their activity to educational policy.

The above finding supports the argument given in the early part of the twentieth century that board membership should be restricted to the successful and educated because of their greater interest in educational policy. But this does not mean that lower-status board members are not interested in educational policy. What it does mean is they have a greater interest in the actual control of the educational system. In fact, higher-status board members gave more importance to the opinion of the superintendent, as compared to lower-status board members; consequently, there was less conflict between higher-status board members and the superintendent than between lower-status board members and the superintendent. This might be because the superintendent and higher-status board members tend to share the same social world. They often attend the same social gatherings and belong to the same civic-service clubs and other social organizations. This situation might result in the superintendent and board members sharing the same views about the components of a good educational program and other social and economic policies.

The major objection to the elitist composition of American school boards is that they do not reflect the interests and opinions of all members of the community. Basic disagreements can occur between social groups in our society over educational policy. For instance, higher-status groups in a community might give strong support to a vocational program for lower-status children, whereas lower-status groups might disapprove of this type of program because they want a college-preparatory program for their children as a means of providing upward mobility. Which group is right in this case is not important in terms of this discussion. What is important is that fundamental differences between social groups can exist over educational policy. Because of the social composition of school boards and their linkage to the informal power structures of local communities, however, these differences are not being reflected in the debates between school board members.

The Governing Power of Boards of Education

The discussion of elite membership of boards of education might seem meaningless when one begins to consider the actual authority of school boards. Although boards of education are supposed to be important mechanisms for achieving local control of the schools, most board members today feel they have very little real power over the schools and what little power they have is being rapidly eroded by other areas of government and other organizations.

During the 1970s a flood of articles began to appear in educational magazines about the lost authority of boards of education in the United States. Lee K. Davis, a member and former chairperson of the Orange County School Board in Florida, summarized this point of view in an article titled "The School Board's Struggle to Survive" in the November 1976 issue of *Educational Leadership*. Among the things listed by Davis as causing the erosion of school board authority are increased state and federal involvement in education policy, increased regulation from court decisions, and the unionization of teachers. For instance, Davis cited the example of his own school district, the thirty-second largest in the United States, where the majority of time-consuming educational issues were initiated outside the local system.

Court decisions regarding desegregation, student rights, teacher rights, and corporal punishment have forced school boards to devote a great deal of attention to complying with these court orders. State legislatures and the federal government have increasingly become involved in matters concerning school curriculums and, consequently, have limited part of the control of school boards over these issues. State legislatures are mandating specific programs such as vocational education, sex education, and social studies courses, as well as those in other areas of the curriculum. In addition, financial pressures have forced local school districts to seek more and more federal money. Most money from the federal government is "categorical," which means that it is designated for use in particular programs and in compliance with federal guidelines. Like state-mandated curriculums, federal guidelines have all restricted the power of the local board of education to control the local school curriculum.

Teacher unionization has restricted the power of boards to control personnel matters. In the past, boards of education had the final voice in the quality of types of teachers that were to be hired in the local district. Boards also had greater control over the issues of salary and retention. Today in many districts around the country, this power is shared with teacher organizations, which function as collective-bargaining units. Highly detailed contracts are negotiated between teacher organizations and boards with regard to salaries and work conditions. In addition, many teacher organizations are demanding greater control of educational policy and the curriculum.

All these conditions have led to a general feeling of despair among board members around the country that the authority of boards of education has rapidly been eroded. To put this situation in perspective, one must consider how school boards have traditionally functioned in the twentieth century.

Most educational literature seems to agree that school boards have been most active and involved when there is some crisis within the schools and community. In most such cases, board members tend to rely heavily upon the actions and opinions of the local school administrative staff. Situations that are most likely to make school boards the center of political activity are major changes in the social composition of the local population or some particular school controversy dealing with sex or religion.

Examples of major school board activity resulting from population shifts can be found in a number of community studies. Herbert Gans's study of Levittown provides one example of a new population coming into conflict with the local power structure and school administration. Levittown was a planned community that was built in what had been a rural area. As the new residents moved into this new community from nearby urban areas they began to demand improved college-preparatory programs and the introduction of what were considered more educationally advanced programs. When new residents began to participate in elections to the school board, their candidates began to place direct pressure for change upon the rather traditional rural school administration that had previously existed in the area.

The community of "Robertsdale" described in Laurence Iannaccone and Frank W. Lutz's *Politics, Power and Policy: The Governing of Local School Districts* is another example of studies of heightened school board involvement and activity. "Robertsdale" is about a school controversy in a growing suburban community where a new power structure begins to come in conflict with an already existing structure. In this case the school superintendent had direct connections to the existing informal power structure and was forced to resign after the incumbents to the board lost in the election.

Along with changes in the social composition of the local population, controversies dealing with sex, religion, and politics can spark increased school board activity and involvement in the schools. Controversies of this type are very difficult to predict. Sometimes such a controversy begins with only a few people in a community objecting to books being used in classes or made available to students in the libraries. During the 1950s members of so-called patriotic organizations stood watch in many communities to assure that books considered "communistic" did not enter the school system. Many communities and school systems were torn apart during that period by attacks from such vigilante-type groups. Sex education and books with sexual content can create similar conflicts. The novels of the well-known writer Kurt Vonnegut were removed from the shelves of school libraries and reading lists for English classes in some communities in the early 1970s because of pressure from local groups. One school system in North Dakota burned Vonnegut's books in the school furnace.

The most famous school controversy of the early 1970s took place in Kanawha County, West Virginia, in September 1974, when protestors appeared at the schools demanding their closure because of alleged dirty, anti-God, anti-American textbooks. Local coal miners struck in sympathy with the protest. The miners' strike and spreading school boycott resulted in a $2 million loss, the shooting of two men, firings on school buses, and the bombing of elementary schools. It required state troopers and the FBI to restore order to the school system.

In some ways these examples illustrate the lack of involvement and control of most school matters by local boards of education. Textbook and library selections are usually determined by the school administrative staff or teacher committee. They become major concerns of the community and school board only when a local person or group protests their contents. School book controversies are not common to all school systems; in fact, when one considers the number of school systems in the United States, they are rare. The content of books is certainly an important part of education, and in most communities the control of textbooks is largely in the hands of the professional staff. The increased involvement and activity of boards during periods of population change also highlights the lack of activity when these conditions are not present.

The important point about these examples is that the erosion of school board authority is not simply a product of the 1970s but has been a problem for some time. In the 1960s James Koerner wrote a book called *Who Controls American Education?* in which he argued that the control of American education had been taken over by the professional educator. At the local level this meant that the majority of control was held by the school staff, with the board of education just rubber-stamping the decisions made by the administrative staff. Only situations like those described above sparked board involvement in the actual control of the schools.

If the real control of local education is in the hands of the administrative staff, then the discussion of the elite membership of boards of education is largely academic. The combination of local administrative power, state and federal regulation, and court decisions might have destroyed any pretense of local control of education as supposedly represented in boards of education. To understand the interrelationships between board and administrative control of local educational issues, we must next look at the political world of the local superintendent and administrative staff.

The Political World of the School Administrative Staff

In the November 1976 issue of *Educational Leadership*, Lee Hansen, an associate superintendent for the Ann Arbor Public Schools, Michigan, predicted the imminent rise of what he called the "political superintendent." Hansen argued that such an individual would be a politician first and an educator second. The important qualities of the political superintendent were to be communication skills, ability to manage public opinion, ability to use the informal power structure, and ability to create an atmosphere of openness and trust.

Lee Hansen based his prediction of the political superintendent upon what he viewed as the collapse of the traditional political world of the superintendent. Hansen argued that superintendents back in the 1960s could feel fairly confident of their ability to collect, control, and use power. During this period community power structures were relatively dominant and stable; coalitions of support were easy to assemble and maintain; and a basic faith in education and educators still existed. Since the 1960s there has been a steady collapse of the power base of most superintendents. Like boards of education, superintendents are finding more and more of their areas of decision making being assumed by state and federal governments. State aid formulas, mandated programs, and educational standards have taken away many of the decisions that would have traditionally been made by the administrative staff. In addition, federal programs have turned superintendents into administrators of programs that they did not initiate and whose basic design they did not participate in.

On the local level, the modern superintendent has had to contend with more competitive community power structures. In many communities monopolistic power structures have changed and are being replaced by ones of democratic pluralism, in which there are ideological splits between liberals and conservatives, as well as pressures from organized minority groups and community groups lobbying for special programs. In addition, teacher unionization and organized student rights groups have made it difficult for superintendents to deal in areas where they have traditionally had a lot of control.

The growth in democratic pluralism in local community power structures is an extremely important factor in changing superintendents' actions within local communities. As mentioned, the traditional political world of the superintendent was most often centered around a fairly stable and clearly defined informal power structure. To both attain and remain in the position of superintendent, an individual had to be accepted by the local power structure. Most superintendents joined the local chamber of commerce or other civic-service organizations and mixed informally with members of the community elite. Once established within a community, a superintendent often participated informally in the selection of local candidates for school board elections. An astute superintendent would build a power base by creating a loyal community following through organizations like the PTA and winning the loyalty of the community elite through formal and informal contacts.

In both the traditional and emerging political world of superintendents their actions in relationship to the power structure are conditioned by their own aspirations. Ernest House in *The Politics of Educational Innovation* has described two types of aspirations that are characteristic of superintendents. One type of superintendent aspires to remain within the community as long as possible and eventually plans to retire from the position. This type of superintendent House calls "place bound." The other type of superintendent views his current position as one step to another and better superintendent's position. This type of superintendent House calls "career bound" and characterizes this superintendent's actions as primarily directed toward gaining recognition outside the local community as a means of attracting other job offers.

These two types of superintendents have differing relationships with the local power structure. Both are dependent upon its support for initial appointment to the position. After acquiring the job, the "place bound" superintendent is concerned about acquiring a loyal following from members of the community and establishing support from the local power structure. The "career bound" superintendent, on the other hand, is more interested in winning recognition either at the state or national level. The "career bound" superintendent tends to show less loyalty to desires of the local power structure and spends less energy on building a following within the local community.

The relationship between the superintendent and the local power structure is important in determining the relationship between the school board and superintendent. In situations where the school board is directly linked to a monopolistic power structure and a "place bound" superintendent has close ties and support from the local structure, there will probably be little conflict between the board and the superintendent. In this type of situation the board will probably give more and more of its prerogatives and authority to the superintendent. On the surface, it would appear in this situation that the superintendent and administrative staff really run the schools while the board has a diminished role. In reality, the superintendent is given increased authority as long as his actions and decisions are congruent with the desires and educational goals of the monopolistic power structure.

The opposite situation prevails when there is a "career bound" superintendent and a power structure characterized by democratic pluralism. This is very often the situation today in large and medium-sized cities. In these situations there tends to be more conflict between the board and superintendent and more school board involvement in school affairs. Superintendents might find themselves dealing with both the traditional community power structure and new pressure groups representing the demands of racial and ethnic minorities, women's groups, and other groups representing specific demands on the schools. It is for these situations that Lee Hansen has called for the training of a political superintendent who is able to build a power base on the demands of these often conflicting groups.

The relationship with the community is only one aspect of the political world of the superintendent. The other is with the central office staff of the local school system, which includes the assistant superintendents, a financial officer, record keepers for the school system, and the directors of special programs. This group is supposed to help the superintendent run the school system. This group also can exercise a great deal of control over the superintendent and school policy.

A study by Joseph McGivney and James Haught titled "The Politics of Education: A View from the Perspective of the Central Office Staff" argues that one of the inherent goals of the administrative staff is to maintain control over the educational system. Techniques used by the staff to maintain their power include controlling communication between groups attempting to place pressure upon the school system. In addition, the central office staff has a central role as gate-keepers of information flow between building principals and school staff, and the superintendent and the board of education. Members of the central office staff hold meetings with principals, teachers, and students. In turn they hold meetings with the superintendent and school board committees in which they convey information and concerns from the rest of the school system. This gatekeeping function can be very important in influencing educational policy.

McGivney and Haught found that through the control of information the central office staff had a major effect on the decision-making process of the board of education. Boards of education seldom reject proposals that come from the central office. Proposals from outside groups that are contrary to the desires of the central office staff are often intercepted by the staff before they reach the board. One technique the central office staff can use against outside groups is to question their information base and their sincerity.

Ernest House has argued in *The Politics of Educational Innovation* that the gatekeeping functions of the central office staff are pivotal to any attempts to change or introduce new programs into a local school system. The staff controls the flow of information to teachers about the program and the flow of information from the system to outside sources. House found in one case that the central office staff tended to manipulate information. In a special educational program for gifted children, the central staff of a local district did not tell one-third of the teachers that they had been listed as teachers of the gifted in a proposal to the state. Teachers also only received information from the state office when the central office staff had informally approved the information.

House has described the central office staff as the type of elite governing group that can be found within any organization. There is some debate about whether the superintendent or central office staff is more influential. In terms of introducing change into the educational system, it was found that the values of the inner circle elite were more important than those of the director and staff in predicting innovation. In other words, the attitudes of the central office staff tend to be more important than the attitudes of the superintendent or teachers in influencing educational policy within a school system.

The central office staff cannot, of course, function independently of the power of superintendent. A new superintendent will attempt to organize a staff that will reflect his or her policies. But total staff change is not usually possible when a new superintendent begins, and there are usually many members of the central office staff who maintain their positions through a successive number of superintendents. These long-term staff members very often exercise a great deal of power within a school district.

The combination of the power of the central office staff and the superintendent has led writers such as James Koerner to argue in *Who Controls American Education?* that the real control of the school is in the hands of the professional educators who occupy those positions. Most decisions in a school district are turned over to the expertise of these professional groups. The role of the school board in most cases is to place its stamp of approval on decisions recommended by the superintendent and the central office staff. In these situations it can be argued that local public control of education has been replaced by local professional control of education.

On the other hand, the position can be taken that the real power in a local school district is actually in the hands of the informal power structure, which remains silent as long as the professional staff pursues policies that it approves. The approval of the informal power structure can be indicated through silence or informal communication with the administrative staff. Informal communication can take place at social gatherings or at functions of civic-service organizations such as the chamber of commerce. It also can be the case that the informal power structure will choose a superintendent who will reflect their values and goals for the educational system. In turn, the superintendent will select and organize the school staff to reflect those values. In this situation, indirect control of the educational system by the local power structure is achieved by turning control of the school over to a "friendly" professional staff.

It can also be argued that the expertise of the school staff can have an influence upon the board members and the informal power structure. That is, the superintendent and central office staff can attempt to control the educational opinions of the local power structure. One way of understanding this situation is to look at the relationships between superintendents and boards of education.

The Superintendent and the Board of Education

Zeigler and Jennings in their previously mentioned study, *Governing American Schools*, tried to measure in their national survey the types of methods a superintendent might use to control and influence the local board. They argued that there are specific ways in which this can be done. One way is through gatekeeping, or control of information received by the board. According to this argument, the superintendent is ideally situated to select the information that he or she wants the board to hear. In addition, superintendents can convince boards that most issues require technical expertise and should be decided upon the basis of advice from the school staff.

Zeigler and Jennings attempted to measure the degree of gatekeeping in superintendent and board relationships in the United States by determining the degree of control of agenda setting at board meetings by superintendents. Agenda setting is a very important political function at board of education meetings because it determines what will be discussed and in what order. In some situations a member of the board or board committee might have responsibility for determining the agenda. In other cases it might be the superintendent, or the superintendent and a board member. If the superintendent determines the agenda, it means that he or she has a great deal of power as a gatekeeper of issues to appear before the board.

The findings in the Zeigler and Jennings national survey were that in 70 percent of the school districts in the United States the superintendent had the primary responsibility setting the agenda, and in two-thirds of the districts they were solely responsible for agenda setting. Zeigler and Jennings felt that these findings indicated that superintendents did occupy powerful gatekeeping positions and had the potential power to strongly influence board members.

The other measurement that Zeigler and Jennings made was to ask board members to name their four most important sources of educational information of a technical or professional nature. The purpose was to determine how much control superintendents had over the information received by the board. They found that in over half the districts the proportion of information received from the superintendent was over 30 percent. Even though this indicated that a sizable amount of information passed through the hands of the superintendent to board members, it was not enough to support the argument for the gatekeeping function of superintendents with regard to educational information. Determination of the agenda was more important.

Another attempt made by the same team to measure the influence of superintendents over board members was to look at the number of hours per week a superintendent was in contact with board members. The median number of hours they found was less than four per week, with one-third of districts having superintendents that spent more than five hours per week with board members. Zeigler and Jennings compared these findings with the level of board opposition to superintendent. They found that there tends to be more interaction between board members and superintendents when there is greater conflict between them. This finding supports the argument that boards become more active and involved in school affairs during periods of conflict.

Important differences highlighted by the national study of Zeigler and Jennings are among urban, suburban, and small-town school boards and superintendents. For instance, Zeigler and Jennings were interested in the role that indoctrination of new board members plays in superintendents' gaining and maintaining power. They found that superintendents in small towns who socialize with their new board members have a reasonable chance of winning future battles with the board. On the other hand, early socialization with and indoctrination of board members by the superintendent has little effect in suburban and urban areas and, in fact, it is more associated with board victories in these areas.

In terms of building community political support, 31 percent of city superintendents, 29 percent of suburban superintendents, and 28 percent of small-town superintendents sought private political support by talking to local influentials, trying to involve specific groups in school activities, and gaining a place in a local organization. Urban areas, as opposed to suburban and small town, tend to be more conducive to superintendents' achieving potential political support from the community, with Zeigler and Jennings arguing that superintendent interaction with influential leaders of the community discourages the board from opposing the superintendent. This is not true in suburban districts, however, where private support seeking is associated with high probability of board victory. In the case of suburban districts, the seeking of private support by the superintendent might be a sign of loss of board support, which requires the superintendent to seek other help. In small towns, the seeking of private support by the superintendent is slightly related to decreasing the possibility of board victory over the superintendent in any controversy.

The differences between urban, suburban, and small-town districts in terms of the superintendent's use of private support against the school board is related to the power structure of the particular community. The study by Zeigler and Jennings is not helpful in this regard because they did not relate the political activities of the superintendent to particular types of community power structures. But one can assume, for instance, that in urban areas characterized by a high degree of democratic pluralism, private support seeking would be very important to a superintendent faced with a board that reflects a lot of different groups and attitudes within the community. It would be essential for superintendents in these situations to build their own political power base and support system to protect themselves from the potential hostility of the board. On the other hand, in communities where the board of education represents a monopolistic power structure, support from private sources is the same thing as support from the board. In these situations the superintendent cannot use the support of private sources against the board because the board represents those private sources. Of course, the situation could arise where a superintendent might try to organize community support to defeat control by the monopolistic power structure.

In summary, one cannot say with certainty whether the superintendent and the professional staff wield more power over the local school district than does the elected board of education. Interconnections of power and support are too close to confirm any particular conclusion. Superintendents can use gatekeeping, agenda setting, indoctrination of new board members, and private and community support to enhance their power. But it is hard to determine whether a superintendent's strength is derived from these activities or from the silent support of the local power structure, which is given because the superintendent pursues educational policies supported by these groups.

Local Control in American Education

Any statement about local control in American education must recognize the almost general agreement about the steady erosion of power in local school districts to state and federal governments and to national public and private organizations. The next series of chapters deals with these groups and their influence on local school curriculum, school organization, and student and teacher activities. In many respects, as will be shown, the United States has a national system of education with some variation at the state and local level.

The variation at the local level is still enough to give importance to consideration of the political power of superintendents and boards of education. The board and school staff can determine the degree of freedom of political expression that will take place within the school and the quality and variety of educational programs that will be offered. The actions of the local district can affect the types of options that are made available to a student and the degree of emphasis placed on vocational and academic programs. The board and superintendent can create a tone within a school system that will either attract or repel certain types of teachers and other staff members. For instance, a school district noted for lack of toleration of nonconservative political views will not attract particular types of teachers. Local boards also still have power with regard to local financial support of the schools and spendings. In one community, the board and superintendent might agree that money should be spent for new construction and expansion of the athletic program. In another community, money might be given for support of special fine arts programs. In contrast, another board might decide it is more important to reduce taxes and therefore support the reduction of spending in certain areas.

Increasingly, the major governing roles of local boards and school administrative staffs are as interpreters and administrators of educational policies dictated at the state and federal levels. This is still a very important function. For instance, the board and administrative staffs can have a lot of influence on the execution of something like a desegration order from the courts or the federal Office of Education. In some communities desegregation has been accomplished with a great deal of success because of the cooperation of the school board; in other communities the exact opposite has occurred.

All these continuing functions of boards of education and superintendents still depend on the political structure of the local community. One national generalization that can be made about members of boards of education is that they tend to be drawn from the upper social and economic groups within a community. What this means in terms of a local district depends upon the power structure within that community. The variation in power structures between communities requires that each community be studied separately to learn its particular organization. Techniques such as those described earlier in the chapter can be used by any person interested in finding out about the nature of power in their local community.

The division of power and control between the board and administrative staff will also vary from community to community. A person can look closely at the gatekeeping, agenda setting, and political activities of the local superintendent to determine the extent and nature of the power within a particular community. One good measure of the division of responsibility between the superintendent and board is the number of times the board and its committees meet and the range of topics discussed and acted upon. One can assume that a school board that talks only about taxes and construction and not about curriculum and teaching has relinquished most of those concerns to the administrative staff.

Another important way of determining the relationship between the superintendent and the board is to investigate how superintendents have been selected within a particular community and how people are able to get elected or appointed to the local board. Usually, some formal board committee structure is responsible for searching and reviewing potential candidates for a superintendent's position. What one needs to investigate is the informal power structure that plays a major role in the selection. The best way of asking the question is, which people does a candidate for the superintendent's position have to please to get the position? One technique for finding this out is to look at the formal and informal contacts each candidate for the position has to make during the interview process. For instance, does each candidate meet with certain business and civic groups? Why do some groups interview candidates and not others? In communities characterized by democratic pluralism there will usually be a large number of groups and individuals involved in the interviewing process.

Methods of election or appointment to the board of education will usually depend on the nature of the community power structure. For instance, in communities characterized by a monopolistic power structure there will usually be one organization or informal group of community influentials responsible for most candidates for the school board. On the other hand, in a community with democratic pluralism there will be a lot of competing groups trying to get their particular candidates on the board. One gauge of the community power structure and its relationship to the school board is often the degree of competition surrounding board elections or appointments.

Any analysis of the educational politics in a community must include the role of the central office staff. This is one of the most difficult areas for determining the extent of power by a person outside of the school system. In some school districts the central office might be just a place where older teachers from within the system are placed when it becomes difficult for them to teach or they encounter problems within the school system. Sometimes superintendents will remove people from principalships and place them in the central office as a method of opening up the position for some other person. When the central office staff is composed of persons who have been placed there for these reasons, then it can be a sign of a very weak political force. But this can be deceptive because even under these conditions many members of the central office staff might have held their positions under a number of different superintendents and can exercise a great deal of power because of knowledge and community support received as a result of length of time in the position.

On the other hand, the central office staff might be composed of people brought in from outside the school system because of their expertise. When this occurs the superintendent very often relies upon the expertise and opinions of the staff. This situation enhances the gatekeeping power of the central office staff and strengthens its position as advisor to the board of education.

One measure of the potential importance of the central office staff is to determine how many members of the staff were hired from within the school system and how many were brought in from outside the system. One can also check on the training and expertise the person in question has brought to the position. This method will not provide an absolute determination of the power of the staff but will give some indication of how they were viewed as experts and advisers. The image of the staff as experts is very important in terms of their gatekeeping functions. If the board, the community, and the superintendent view the staff as being composed of educational experts, they are more likely to give close attention to the information, opinions, and advice coming from this group.

The importance and size of central office staffs in local school districts has increased in the last decade because of state and federal programs and increased regulation of the educational system for the courts. It is the central office staff that is responsible for applying for money from these programs and making sure the school system conforms to state and federal guidelines. Many members of these staffs have become educational entrepreneurs who frequently travel to their state capital and to Washington, D.C., in search of new funds and to attend workshops on how their school system can conform to new guidelines and regulations.

The next series of chapters discusses the increasing role in the control of local education by state and federal governments and other national organizations. One important thing to keep in mind when reading these chapters is that the increasing power of these groups in local education has had two important consequences. One is to decrease local control of education, and the other is to increase the size and importance of the central office staff. Or to state it another way, decreasing local control of education has been directly linked to increasing the importance of the local educational bureaucracy.

EXERCISES

1. Determine occupations of members of a local board of education and compare with distribution of local population in the different occupational categories in the U.S. census. Is the school board representative of the population of the community?

2. Using the methods of Nunnery and Kimbrough described in this chapter, determine the power structure of your local community. For practical reasons, one might want to limit interviews to a few leading members of the community.

3. Interview local board members to determine how one can get elected to the board. Remember it is important to find out about the local informal power structure and if the backing of certain groups is required for actual election.

4. Interview a local school superintendent about the amount of power this person feels he or she has in relationship to the central office staff, the school board, the state, and the federal government.

Suggested Readings and Works Cited in Chapter

Cronin, Joseph N. *The Control of Urban Schools: Perspective on the Power of Educational Reformers.* New York: Free Press, 1973.

This is a history of the control of American schools and an exploration of the major issues surrounding the relationship between the public, school board members, and professional staff.

Davis, Lee K. "The School Board's Struggle to Survive." *Educational Leadership,* November 1976, pp. 95–99.

This issue of *Educational Leadership* is devoted to the topic of the politics of education. Its articles range from the politics of education at the local level to the national level.

Gans, Herbert J. *Levittowners: Ways of Life and Politics in a New Suburban Community.* New York: Random House, 1969.
    This community study provides a good description of school board politics in a new suburban community.

Hansen, Lee H. "Political Reformation in Local Districts," *Educational Leadership,* November 1976, pp. 90–94.
    An associate superintendent's view of shifts in power in local school districts.

House, Ernest. *The Politics of Educational Innovation.* Berkeley, Calif.: McCutchan, 1974.
    The first four chapters of this book are excellent studies of the internal politics in local school systems.

Iannaccone, Lawrence, and Lutz, Frank. *Politics, Power and Policy: The Governing of Local School Districts.* Columbus, Ohio: Charles E. Merrill, 1970.
    A study that focuses on school board politics in a small community.

Koerner, James. *Who Controls American Education?* Boston: Beacon, 1968.
    Koerner argues that professional educators control American education.

McGivney, Joseph, and Haught, James. "The Politics of Education: A View from the Perspective of the Central Office Staff." *Educational Administration Quarterly,* Autumn 1972, pp. 18–38.
    Another good study of the internal politics within a local school system.

Nunnery, Michael Y., and Kimbrough, Ralph B. *Politics, Power, Polls, and School Elections.* Berkeley, Calif.: McCutchan, 1971.
    A guide to studying local politics of education and community power structures.

Zeigler, L. Harmon, and Jennings, M. Kent. *Governing American Schools: Political Interaction in Local School Districts.* North Scituate, Mass.: Duxbury, 1974.
    A major national study of local boards of education.

6

POWER AND CONTROL AT THE STATE LEVEL

IN 1968 A GROUP OF AMISH PARENTS IN Wisconsin was arrested for refusing to comply with the state compulsory education law, which required them to enroll their children in high school. The Amish in Ohio, Pennsylvania, Iowa, and Wisconsin had fought compulsory schooling laws for years because they believed that high schools taught values that undermined the religious and communal style of their way of life. The Amish eventually won their case (see chapter 10 for a detailed analysis of their suit) against state-imposed compulsory education.

The Amish case is only one of the many problems that occur as a result of state regulation and control of education. Another example is the situation of the Wichita Collegiate School, a private school in Kansas established in 1960, which existed without accreditation from the state because of its refusal to conform to state laws on teacher certification. These laws require that certified teachers have specified education courses as well as other academic courses. The parents of students at the Wichita Collegiate School were more concerned about teachers receiving training in a specific academic field rather than education courses in methods of teaching. The parents felt that education courses were a threat to academic quality. The accrediting division of the Kansas State Department of Public Instruction conceded that the school's faculty had better college grades and broader academic backgrounds than other teachers in Kansas, but the Collegiate teachers still did not meet state requirements because of the lack of education courses. When the parents refused to have their school accredited by the state, their children were excluded from a state law guaranteeing graduates of accredited Kansas schools admission to at least one semester at a state-supported university.

The Amish case and the Wichita Collegiate School situation highlight some central issues with regard to state involvement in education. One of these issues is the amount of regulation of education engaged in by state governments. Traditionally, both private and public schools have expressed some degree of displeasure with regard to the extent of state regulation of education. On the other hand, there are those who argue that education is as important as medicine and therefore requires state licensing and certification to avoid the establishment of schools that are unsafe and the hiring of incompetent teachers.

Another major issue is the extent of domination of state departments of education and state educational policy by groups of professional educators. In the previous chapter this issue was discussed at the local level in terms of the school staff versus the community power structure. At the state level the issue exists in terms of competing lobbying groups, many of them representing organizations of educators, promoting their particular goals and policies before members of the state legislature and state department of education. Also involved in the issue is the question of domination of state departments of education by professional educators and their actual power over state educational policy.

To understand these issues one must first understand the extent of state authority over education and the variety of ways states have organized to exercise this authority. After presenting descriptions of state authority and educational organization, this chapter deals with the issue of professional domination of education and the extent of state regulation of education.

State Authority over Education

The U.S. Constitution does not mention education; consequently, education is a power reserved to the states. Most state constitutions give legal responsibility for local education to the state. These two conditions, in theory at least, give state government the greatest authority over education of any government unit in the United States. A school district, in most cases, is legally an agent of the state. Local school boards have and can exercise only those powers that are granted explicitly by the state legislature.

In the early nineteenth century state governments exercised very little control over local education. In the 1830s Horace Mann in Massachusetts worked for increased state involvement in education through the establishment of teacher-training institutions and promoting good schools in local communities. Throughout the century, state departments of education remained relatively small and confined their activities to collecting educational statistics and promoting good schools and teacher training. In the late nineteenth and early twentieth centuries, the states began to expand their role in education with the passage of compulsory education laws and laws requiring specific curriculum content in the schools. Compulsory education laws required expanded staffs to ensure their enforcement. Early state curriculum requirements were often the result of state lobbying by "patriotic organizations" and groups concerned about the Americanization of immigrants. Over the years these curriculum requirements have expanded in many states to cover a great deal of the course content offered in local school districts. Teacher certification requirements have also increased and become more complex. As a result of the enforcement requirements of these laws, state educational bureaucracies have steadily grown in the twentieth century.

The increased involvement of the federal government in education in the 1960s further extended the importance of state departments of education. Federal money was provided for the expansion of state educational bureaucracies as a means of strengthening their role in funneling federal money and programs to local school districts. This widening of state educational power carried with it seeds of controversy. For some, an expanded state educational enterprise signaled the collapse of local control of education. For others, state control of education appeared to be lost as federal money increasingly determined the functions of state educational bureaucracies.

Today, most states exercise the following functions with regard to education. Most states set minimum standards for curriculum, pupil promotion, and graduation and for specific educational programs such as kindergarten, vocational education, and high school. Some states have detailed courses of study for specific subjects such as social studies and math and adopt textbooks that are distributed to local schools. Most states have detailed regulations with regard to the physical features of school buildings and the size of school libraries. States define the length of the school day and year. State regulations are very detailed with respect to requirements for the certification of teachers.

States increasingly are having a major role in the financing of local schools. In some states, tax limits are set for local districts and requirements are made for certain local budget breakdowns. State financial support has varied greatly from state to state. For instance, in 1969–70 the New Hampshire state government provided 8.5 percent of the total school expenditures, while the state government of Hawaii provided 87 percent. States will probably assume greater shares of educational expenses as state courts rule that existing systems of financial support provide unequal educational opportunities. These court cases are discussed in more detail in chapter 10 when we examine the involvement of the courts in education.

The Organization of State Systems of Education

The broad authority that states have over education is usually exercised through a governmental system that includes the governor's office, the state legislature, a state superintendent of education, a state department of education, and a state board of education. The actual arrangement and relationship of these groups varies from state to state.

Only Wisconsin and Illinois do not have state boards of education. In the other forty-eight states there are three differing methods of selecting members of the state board of education: (1) election by the people or representatives of the people, (2) appointment by the governor, or (3) automatic appointment as a result of holding another state office.

The selection of the state superintendent or chief state school officer also varies from state to state. In some states the superintendent is elected; in other states the person is appointed by the governor or state board of education. Table 4 classifies states according to their method of selecting state school board members and chief state school officer.

The state department of education is the administrative staff of the chief state school officer or superintendent and the state board of education. The staff of the state department of education is mainly composed of professional educators, who do most of the administration and regulation of state educational laws and programs. Some of the major activities of state departments of education include the actual operation of state schools for the handicapped and involvement in the operation of vocational programs and teachers' colleges. The

TABLE 4

Classification of States According to Method of Selecting State School Boards and Chief State School Officers, 1969

METHOD OF SELECTION	STATES
1. State school board members	
a. Ex officio	Florida, Mississippi
b. Appointed by governor	Alabama, Alaska, Arizona, Arkansas, California, Connecticut, Delaware, Georgia, Idaho, Indiana, Iowa, Kentucky, Maine, Maryland, Massachusetts, Minnesota, Missouri, Montana, New Hampshire, New Jersey, North Carolina, North Dakota, Oklahoma, Oregon, Pennsylvania, Rhode Island, South Carolina, South Dakota, Tennessee, Vermont, Virginia, West Virginia, Wyoming
c. Elected by the people or representatives of the people	Colorado, Hawaii, Kansas, Louisiana, Michigan, Nebraska, Nevada, New Mexico, New York, Ohio, Texas, Utah, Washington
2. Chief state school officer	
a. Appointed by governor	New Jersey, Pennsylvania, Tennessee, Virginia
b. Elected by popular vote	Alabama, Arizona, California, Florida, Georgia, Idaho, Illinois, Indiana, Kentucky, Louisiana, Mississippi, Montana, North Carolina, North Dakota, Oklahoma, Oregon, South Carolina, South Dakota, Washington, Wisconsin, Wyoming
c. Appointed by state board of education	Alaska, Arkansas, Colorado, Connecticut, Delaware, Hawaii, Iowa, Kansas, Maine, Maryland, Massachusetts, Minnesota, Michigan, Missouri, Nebraska, Nevada, New Hampshire, New Mexico, New York, Ohio, Rhode Island, Texas, Utah, Vermont

SOURCE: From John Thomas Thompson, *Policymaking in American Public Education* (Englewood Cliffs, N.J.: Prentice-Hall, 1976), p. 127.

regulatory activities of state departments of education can include such areas as curriculum and teaching standards, school construction, school buses, civil defense and fire drills, and other items specified in the state code or constitution.

In addition, most state departments of education provide consulting service to each local school district and conduct development and research activities. Members of the state department of education consult and advise groups and individuals working on educational projects. They often provide in-service education for teachers or establish programs through universities to provide further training for teachers. State departments of education usually publish and distribute information to local school districts on educational research and teaching aids. On top of all these activities, state departments of education administer and regulate federal programs, which are funneled through the state governments.

The sources of most of the responsibilities and power of state boards of education, departments of education, and superintendents are the state constitution and the state legislature. Most state constitutions specify the general organizational features and methods of selection of the state superintendent and board of education and define their general responsibilities. The laws passed by the state legislature provide the more detailed and specific responsibilities of the state educational agencies.

Most state legislatures have a specific legislative committee that is responsible for proposing educational legislation, conducting hearings on proposed legislation, and recommending to the legislature the passage or defeat of specific laws affecting education. Sometimes educational legislation is initiated by the governor's office and is reviewed and placed before public hearings by the education committee of the state legislature. Legislation is often proposed by the state department of education and outside lobbying groups representing professional educators. In fact, the major role of these two groups in proposing and campaigning for specific legislation has often led to the charge that professional educators dominate state educational politics.

The Structure of Power in State Education

A majority of the work and initiative in state educational policy takes place within the ranks of professional educators in the state department of education and among lobbyists for educational associations. The reasons for this are the relative lack of political value of education issues for the governor and state legislators, and the lack of activity and involvement of state boards of education.

Gerald Sroufe has argued, in research findings presented at the 1969 meeting of the American Educational Research Association, that state boards of education primarily function as a legitimating agency for broad educational policies. The overwhelming majority of state board members in Sroufe's survey were professionals earning high salaries. This means that, like local boards of education, the social composition of state boards of education is not representative of the total population.

Whether the state board is elected or appointed by the governor has little effect upon its social composition or its involvement in educational issues. In those states where the board is appointed, Sroufe found that at the time of appointment, board members did not have highly specific educational goals or to evidence concern about particular educational issues.

Most elections to state boards of education can be described as nonevents. Over half the elected members in a survey reported that they did not campaign. Most candidates issue a single press release and do little to interest the public in state educational issues. Public interest in the election is minimal, and candidates receive a minimum of publicity. Sroufe argues that the "reason board members are so much alike is that no one expects the board to be very influential in formulation or implementation of state educational policy."

The reader will note the similarity between state boards of education and local boards of education in terms of involvement in educational policy. In fact, from the evidence it would appear that local boards are more active and turn less decision-making power over to the professional staff than do state boards of education. The minimal role of state boards of education results in increased authority being given to state superintendents of education and the staff of state departments of education.

It can also be argued that state boards of education merely legitimate the actions of the department of education as long as the actions of the professional staff within that agency conform to the ideological outlook of the members of the board. This contention is based on the fact that the majority of board members are from one particular (upper) social class in the United States. The board approves the actions of educational bureaucrats as long as they reflect the members' views about education. If this is true, state board members exert influence and give approval through silence and lack of activity. Most gubernatorial candidates avoid educational issues unless there is some specific educational crisis within their state, such as public protest over busing, sex education, or student discipline. When this occurs, the candidate for the governor's office must be very careful about speaking on these issues so as not to offend too many voters. What this means is that important educational issues such as curriculum organization, teaching standards, and other less emotional issues do not become part of the campaign. Like campaigns for state and local boards of education, most gubernatorial campaigns do not provide a platform for educational issues except those that are highly controversial and emotional.

Once in office, most governors continue to avoid educational issues because of the lack of agreement within the educational establishment about what should be done and because there is no apparent political payoff in future elections. Some governors do attempt to build their political careers on educational issues. This was particularly true in the South during periods of desegregation, when governors like George Wallace of Alabama used opposition to school integration to gain political support.

In most states, the governor's office is hindered in its involvement in education by the lack of an educational staff. In some states the state superintendent or chief state school officer is a member of the governor's cabinet. Some governors have a one- or two-person educational staff while others have none. Thus, in most states, the governor must rely on the advice and work of the state department of education. Like the state board of education's lack of public discussion of educational issues and active involvement in educational work, the governor's benign neglect of educational issues results in the strengthening of the authority of the professionals in the state department of education.

A major change might be taking place in the governor's role in education with the increased political activity of teachers' associations. In the presidential election of 1976 the National Education Association supported Jimmy Carter and claimed that the votes of its members provided the crucial votes for winning the election. During the same campaign, local chapters of the National Education Association worked for candidates for the governor's office and state legislature that they felt would support the National Education Association's platform on education. Sometimes this effort was directed toward electing a state legislature that could overcome what they felt were anti-education actions of the governor. For instance, I heard a member of the Ohio Education Association declare publicly after the 1976 election that the association had the Ohio legislature in its back pocket and would be able to override any veto by the governor of any education bill the organization supported.

How well will teachers' organizations be able to deliver the vote to a particular candidate for governor or for the state legislature in the future? One of the problems in the past has been that the members of these organizations have not always acted in unison with regard to political matters. Very often, the leadership of these organizations is more politically liberal than the membership. But if these organizations are able to deliver votes in state elections, they will begin to exercise tremendous political power. Candidates for state offices will be forced to take positions on issues supported by the teachers' association. This might lead to a public debate of educational issues, which might lead to greater voter involvement. It will also strengthen the authority of the professional educators in these organizations over educational policy.

Like the governor's office, the weaknesses of state legislatures have contributed to the authority of bureaucrats in state departments of education. Some of the weaknesses faced by most state legislatures are low salaries, rapid turnover in composition of the legislature, and lack of professional staffs to assist legislators and legislative committees. These factors contribute to a general lack of expertise and ability to formulate policy. Without a professional staff to aid in the formulation of public policy, it is very difficult for a legislator or committee singlehandedly to gather all the information needed and organize it into a rational policy statement. As a consequence, state legislators and legislative committees must rely heavily upon lobbying groups and state administrative agencies for information and policy proposals. It is currently argued that the authority of state legislatures has declined as the authority of state bureaucratic agencies and the governor's office has increased.

Lobbyists and the State Legislature

Of fundamental importance for understanding the actions of state legislatures with regard to educational policy is an understanding of the organization of educational lobbying groups and their influence on the state legislature.

The relationship between educational lobbyists and the state legislature varies from state to state. Laurence Iannaccone in his *Poli-*

tics in Education has classified the differences in relationships into four major types. He calls his first type pattern "local-based disparate." Within this pattern, which he describes as characteristic of Vermont, New Hampshire, and Massachusetts, state educational associations are unable to reach agreement on educational issues or present a unified set of proposals to the state legislature. The main points of contact within this pattern are between local school administrators and local state legislators who seek their advice on educational issues.

Iannaccone's second type pattern, which he calls "monolithic," is the most common among states and can be found in New York, Missouri, New Jersey, and Rhode Island. Unlike the local-based disparate pattern, the monolithic pattern has all state educational associations plus the state department of education working together to develop a legislative program and influence the state legislature. Conflicting ideas are worked out between these groups and a unified front is presented to the state legislature. The leadership of this educational monolith is usually dominated by school administrators. Education experts from universities are used to help formulate legislative proposals. These groups usually maintain close contact with certain state legislators and supply them with information. Lobbyists for these groups appear before state legislative committees to build a case for their proposals. Since this pattern contains most of the educational expertise within a state, it has a virtual monopoly over information about education received in the state legislature. Without a doubt this monolithic structure gives the greatest political influence to state educational associations.

With the third type, called the "disparate" pattern, educational associations are not united and there is a great deal of conflict. This pattern, according to Iannaccone, can be found in California and Michigan. When this pattern appears, state legislators become very aware of the issues dividing the groups and are often forced to take sides. For instance, the Michigan Association of School Administrators is often in conflict with the National Education Association; the NEA is viewed by the state legislature as primarily a bargaining agent for teacher-welfare issues while the administrative organization concentrates on local tax issues.

The fourth pattern is characteristic only of Illinois and is called by Iannaccone a "statewide syndical" system. Illinois has a School Problems Committee that functions like a legislative council and is composed of representatives from government and major groups having interests in educational decisions. This group has become the center of educational decision making, and most of its proposals are passed by the state legislature with a minimum of debate.

It must be remembered that Iannaccone's framework was developed in the 1960s and that patterns have changed in many states. The financial crisis in education in the 1970s probably resulted in the educational associations in many states working together for particular legislation. This would mean a broader development in most states of the monolithic pattern and the strengthening of the power of educational lobbyists and state departments of education over legislative action. These patterns vary from state to state; each state must be analyzed separately to determine its particular pattern at a particular time.

The educational groups that have statewide lobbyists include state teachers' associations and unions, state school administrators' associations, state school board associations, and parent organizations such as the PTA. In most areas the strongest lobbying group is the state teachers' association, which in many states is a state affiliate of the National Education Association. In some states, such as New York, the American Federation of Teachers has gained considerable statewide influence. (These two teachers' associations are discussed in greater detail in chapter 8.) Paid lobbyists of state teachers' associations usually attempt to maintain close contact with the head of the legislative committee on education and members of the state department of education. The directors of these state associations work to mobilize support within their own organizations and from the general public through the publication of newsletters and monthly journals. A study by Nicholas Masters in *State Politics and the Public Schools* found in the three states in his sample that legislators considered the state teachers' associations the most powerful interest groups in the state.

Increasingly throughout the states school administrators are forming their own organizations. Administrators traditionally belong to state teachers' associations, but with the increasing militancy of teachers, administrators have been forced to seek their own organizations. Although these organizations are small in size when compared to teachers' organizations, their influence has sometimes been strong because of local contact between superintendents and locally elected state legislators. Also, many superintendents of large urban areas have governmental relations officers on their staffs to work with state and federal political and administrative personnel.

Also having great influence on state educational policies are state school board associations. These organizations are composed of representatives from local school boards and are often in conflict with teachers' associations and associations of state administrators. Because they usually have the support of the power structure in their local community, they have easy access to state politicians. The National School Board Association and state school board associations have both traditionally fought to maintain local control of the schools. Another statewide educational lobbying group is the PTA. For many years the PTA primarily existed to provide community support for local superintendents and principals. Increasingly, members of this group have become more militant and have been placing pressure on state legislatures for support of particular educational programs.

Other state lobbying groups from time to time have had considerable influence on particular features of state educational policy. Patriotic organizations such as the American Legion have often campaigned for increased emphasis on patriotism in the schools. Farm groups have worked hard for greater support of agricultural education programs. Labor organizations have been interested in ridding the schools of anti-union bias and making sure that vocational education is not used to undermine union apprenticeship programs. Business groups such as the chamber of commerce have sought legislative support in some states for proposals that would require the teaching of a particular type of economics. One could construct an almost endless list of people and organizations that would like certain subjects and ideas made mandatory in the schools by state legislative action.

One of the major weaknesses of the lobbying activities of state educational associations is their lack of unified effort. As stated earlier, Iannaccone found that a monolithic structure of educational groups was most effective for lobbying. If the state teachers' associations, administrators' associations, school board associations, the PTA, and the state department of education are able to unite around educational programs, they can exert considerable influence on the state legislature.

While these educational lobbying groups have had considerable influence over the details of educational policy because of their frequent monopoly of information, their greatest area of weakness is in gaining financial support for school programs from state legislatures. Nothing shows more clearly that these educational groups do not have complete control of educational policy than the financial crisis of the schools in the early 1970s, when many state legislatures refused to increase state school support. The reason was the greater influence of other lobbying groups in the areas of state expenditures and tax policies. These lobbying groups include taxpayers' associations and research leagues created by various economic groups within the state and organizations such as the chamber of commerce. These groups do not usually attack educational spending directly but call for decreased taxes and fiscal responsibility, which usually means less money for social programs such as education.

In summary, one can make the following generalizations about the interactions between educational lobbyists and state legislators. In most states, because of the lack of large professional staffs to help state legislators and committees, legislators tend to rely on state administrative agencies and lobbying groups for information and expertise. In terms of educational policy, this means educational associations and the state department of education have considerable influence over state policy. The degree of influence on state legislative action by educational associations depends on the degree of cooperation existing between the various educational groups. The more unity of action there is, the greater the influence on the state legislature. In the area of educational finance, educational lobbyists do not seem to have as much influence as economic lobbying groups.

The Role of the Professional Educator

One of the major complaints leveled against American education, a complaint that first surfaced in the early 1950s, was that the schools were dominated and controlled by professional educators who had received most of their training in colleges of education in methods of teaching and school administration. The concern was that the professional educator was primarily educated in process and methodology and not in academic content. This resulted, the critics believed, in the public schools being anti-intellectual because of the stranglehold of the professional educator. For instance, the Council for Basic Education was established by a private group of scholars to attempt to wrest control of the curriculum from professional educators. The Council for Basic Education argued that the public schools had become a threat to democracy because they did not provide students with an equal opportunity for an academic education. They believed that scholars in the different university disciplines—history, English, and science—should determine the curricula in their respective areas in the public schools rather than educators from the college of education.

Other Americans, especially those concerned about the Cold War with the Soviet Union, argued that the public schools were the weakest link in national defense because they did not produce enough scientists and engineers to win the technological race with our rivals. The problem, as it was stated by military leaders such as Hyman Rickover, was that the schools were controlled by professional educators who had no respect for the life of the mind and had produced an anti-intellectual climate in the United States. Government organizations such as the National Science Foundation tried to correct this situation by enlisting scientists and engineers into the business of creating new mathematics and science programs for the public schools.

The concern about the domination of education by professional educators can best be understood by looking at the interlinkages between educational policy-making groups at the state level. As discussed in earlier sections of this chapter, educational policy at the state level tends to be dominated by the state department of education and educational lobbying groups. The positions within these organizations are primarily held by professional educators who move from one organizational setting to another. In other words, a member of an educational lobbying group one year might be on the staff of the state department of education the next year. In fact, many members of state departments of education hold membership in state educational associations that have lobbyists at the state capital.

To understand how this process works, one must understand the following circumstances. To become a teacher, an individual must take courses that meet state requirements for teacher certification. After becoming a teacher, the individual usually joins a local teachers' association that is affilated with a statewide organization. Anyone who wants to become a public school administrator has to meet state certification requirements, which in most states necessitates a certain number of years of teaching experience and a certain number of courses in public school administration. After becoming an administrator, an individual usually joins a statewide association of school administrators.

Now the professional staff of the state department of education is usually drawn from the ranks of teachers, school administrators, and executives in educational associations and from the faculties of schools of education. It is the combination of these groups working in state departments of education and in state educational associations that has the major power over educational policy and certification requirements. Of course, tight control of state educational policy occurs only when the state department of education and educational organizations work together.

The faculties of colleges of education are in a unique position in this process. In the first place, their very jobs often depend on state certification requirements. If certain courses are required for teaching or public school administration, then the education faculties will be guaranteed that students must take their courses. Second, it is important for faculties of education to maintain good working relationships with local school districts because the cooperation of these districts is necessary in placing teachers for student teaching and in faculty research. In addition, many faculty members supplement their incomes as paid consultants at local schools. In turn, local school administrators often use the prestige and expertise of the university consultant to strengthen their own political position.

Because of these relationships, faculties of colleges of education tend not to be highly critical of the educational establishment, but to join it as professionals. This often means membership in state educational associations and close cooperation with state departments of education. In many cases, faculties of education come from the ranks of public school teachers. In some states, public school teaching and certification is a requirement before teaching on a faculty of education.

The close connections between these different educational groups and the movement of the same people through their ranks, combined with their strong influence over state educational policy, is what is meant by professional domination of education. The domination of policy is of course not complete, particularly in states where educational groups fight among themselves. It is also limited by the activities of other state groups that have greater influence over financial policies. But in terms of teacher certification, educational standards, curriculum requirements, and general educational policy, this interlocking group of professional educators tends to have the greatest power at the state level.

It can be argued that this is the ideal model for governing education, with professionals making the major decisions. Doctors and lawyers govern their professions by controlling entrance and standards; therefore, in the equally important area of educating children, professionals who are most knowledgeable about education problems should govern. One fault with this argument has always been the fact that public schools are supposed to be controlled by the public. The tension between public and professional control will continue to be one of the continuing problems in American education.

Should the State Regulate Public and Private Schools?

This chapter began with two examples of protests against state regulation of public and private schools. With the rapid growth of small alternative private schools in the 1960s and the expansion of religious schools in the 1970s, this issue has become a center of major debate. Many of these schools encountered difficulty with their particular state governments because they did not meet some state standard, or they refuse to comply because of their own particular desires or needs.

The major authority states have had for exercising regulation over public and private schools has been compulsory education laws. In most states parents can be arrested if they do not send their children to school. The state usually defines a "school" as *an educational institution that conforms to state standards and regulations, including curriculum and teacher certification requirements.* This means that if an educational institution is not accredited by the state as complying with all state school requirements, its pupils are technically truant and their parents are liable for criminal prosecution. Without compulsory school laws, parents would be free to send their children to educational institutions that do not conform to state regulations.

Compulsory school attendance laws vary from state to state in their actual form and interpretation by state courts. Robert P. Baker, a lawyer, has reviewed judicial interpretations of compulsory school laws in an article titled "Statute Law and Judicial Interpretations" in *The Twelve Year Sentence,* edited by William F. Rickenbacker. Baker divides compulsory schooling laws into what he calls the "other guy type" and the "cookie cutter type." The argument given for the "other guy type" of law is that while most people would educate their children without compulsory schooling laws, there is somebody somewhere who would not educate his children. Compulsory school laws in this case are designed to protect children from parents who are not willing to educate them. Where adopted, the "other guy type" of interpretation results in a compulsory schooling law requiring no more than what most parents would do anyway.

The "cookie cutter type" of law is one based on the idea that all children should have the same type of experience within the same type of institution. The most extreme example of a "cookie cutter type" of law was a 1920 Oregon statute that required all children to attend public schools. One purpose of the law was to close Catholic schools. The U.S. Supreme Court ruled in 1925 that the law was not constitutional. The Court stated, "The fundamental theory of liberty upon which all governments in this Union repose excludes any general power of the state to standardize its children by forcing them to accept instruction from public teachers only." But the ruling also upheld the right of the state to regulate private schools, which continued its right to enforce some form of standardization.

The differences between the "other guy" and the "cookie cutter" laws are best exemplified in judicial interpretations. For instance, in New Jersey in 1937 a Mr. and Ms. Bongart were accused of being disorderly persons because they themselves were educating their children in their homes. The New Jersey compulsory schooling law required attendance at school or equivalent instruction. Education in the home was not considered equivalent instruction by the trial judge because, in his words, "I cannot conceive how a child can receive instruction and experiences in group activity and in social outlook in any manner or form comparable to that provided in the public school." This is what Baker would call a "cookie cutter" interpretation of the law. In a similar case a young girl in Washington state was considered a delinquent and made a ward of the court for not attending school. The trial court found that the instruction being given to the girl in her home was at least the academic equivalent of that available in the public schools. Despite this finding, the Washington Supreme Court ruled against the child and her parents with the argument that no school existed unless instruction was being given by a teacher certified by the state of Washington.

On the other hand, the "other guy" type of judicial interpretation can result in more flexible application of compulsory schooling law. The most famous case was in Illinois in the 1950s in *People* v. *Levisen*, in which the parents, who were Seventh-day Adventists, believed that educating their daughter in a public school would create an un-Christian character. The parents argued, "For the first eight or ten years of a child's life, the field or garden is the best school room, the mother the best teacher, and nature the best lesson book." Education in the parents' home was considered adequate: the father was a college graduate and the mother had received training in pedagogy and educational psychology. Unlike the New Jersey and Washington courts, the Illinois courts formulated the "other guy" philosophy in their ruling that "the law is not made to punish parents who provide their children with instruction equal or superior to that obtainable in the public schools. It is made for the parent who fails or refuses to properly educate his child."

The interpretation and application of state compulsory schooling laws and educational regulations will vary from state to state between the "cookie cutter" and the "other guy" interpretations. In recent years all states have been limited in their application of the law as interpreted by the U.S. Supreme Court in the 1972 Amish case, *State of Wisconsin, Petitioner,* v. *Jonas Yoder et al.,* mentioned at the beginning of the chapter. In this situation the Court argued that religious freedom was more important than state compulsory schooling laws and that state law could not abridge the practice of religion. This meant that if parents could prove in court that attending public school would interfere with the practice of their religion, they could not be forced to conform to state compulsory schooling laws. Thus the Supreme Court recognized that public schools were not in all cases neutral in terms of religion. The social life, curriculm, and educational goals of the public schools could be in conflict with some religious customs and practices.

One of the most thorough criticisms of state regulation of education has been made by one of the participants in the Amish case. Professor Donald Erickson provided expert educational testimony defending the right of the Amish to maintain their own educational practices. Erickson summarized some of his views in the *Super-Parent: An Analysis of State Educational Controls,* written for the Illinois Advisory Committee on Nonpublic Schools.

In his critique Erickson argues that there are two major reasons given for state programmatic control of education. One reason is to ensure that all children have a reasonable chance to pursue happiness as free individuals. Education might be able to provide the individual with some of the intellectual tools required for autonomous behavior. The second major reason given for state control of the schools is the protection of society from unemployment, indigence, crime, juvenile delinquency, mental illness, and political strife. This reason encompasses the social purposes of education discussed in the first chapter of this book.

In response to the first reason, that state-controlled education ensures autonomous individuals, Erickson points out that state-prescribed education is in direct conflict with the autonomy of all parents and does not provide the child with a model of a society of freely acting individuals. Erickson states, "In complex societies all over the world, however, state-controlled education arouses parental resistance. The reason is that child-rearing practices sponsored or required by the state in pluralistic societies are at odds with many parental views of the good life and how to prepare for it."

Erickson argues that what is essential for the development of the autonomous individual in modern society is to learn reading, writing, arithmetic, and the fundamental workings of society's political, legal, and economic institutions. But even if we agree that knowledge of these is essential for autonomous action, it does not, according to Erickson, justify the maintenance of the current system of compulsory school attendance and regulations. Parents and children could be given complete freedom to decide how the specified competencies were to be learned, and the child could be required to demonstrate through a national system of tests that progress is being made. This system would require compulsory education, but not compulsory school attendance.

The distinction between compulsory education and school attendance is very important for Erickson's argument. Compulsory education without compulsory school attendance would allow for the protection of those children suffering from parental neglect without burdening all children with attendance at a state-regulated school. If during the course of examinations the state found that a child was not learning the basics, it could prescribe some form of remedial action like required attendance at a state school.

With regard to education beyond elementary school, Erickson argues, there is no agreement among scholars about what knowledge is of most worth and what is essential for autonomous growth. This being the case, he feels that parents and children can make their own determination of what they should know and how they should learn it. Even if state officials can identify indispensable understandings and skills beyond the elementary ones described above, this does not require programmatic state regulation of schools. State intervention could be limited to those cases in which it is shown by tests that children are not making satisfactory progress toward the acquisition of those competencies.

Erickson rejects the second major reason given for state regulation of schools, which is protection of society from crime, unemployment, political strife, and other social problems. First, Erickson argues that no one knows what attitudes, understandings, and skills are truly necessary for the survival of a society. Second, no one knows how much consensus about social and political beliefs is required before that same consensus actually becomes harmful to a society by limiting the freedom to find new ideas and adapt to new situations. The reader should remember from the first chapter that the argument for the achievement of the social and political purposes of schooling centered around the development of a consensus of political and social beliefs. Erickson rejects state involvement in this process with the argument that "state officials are probably the last group we should trust to decide how much commonality is essential to the general weal. It is in the interest of these officials to discourage the dissension and diversity that may jeopardize their positions, subject them to challenge, and make public institutions more difficult to govern smoothly."

In addition, it has never been proved that a relationship exists between the amount and quality of education available in a society and a decrease in crime, unemployment, and other social, economic, and political problems. In the twentieth century the amount of education received by each person in society has steadily increased. At the same time crime has either remained the same or increased; unemployment has fluctuated with changes in the economy and labor market; indigence continues; and mental illness seems unaffected by the quantity of education. The nineteenth-century dream of schooling as a panacea for social problems does not seem to have been justified by the events of the twentieth century.

Conclusion

The questioning of the degree of state regulation of the schools is occurring at the same time that state responsibility for education is increasing. School desegregation is resulting in the development of larger school districts and more state involvement in the regulation of programs. The crisis in school finance and court decisions are resulting in state governments assuming more and more of the burden for financing the schools. Probably the issue of school finances will be the most important reason for the expansion of state regulation of educaion.

Because of the nature of state government, and because of greater voter interest and involvement in local and national politics, the responsibility and burden of state regulation will likely continue to be mainly in the hands of the professional educator within state departments of education. For many years, state governments have been neglected as public interest has been directed to the more dramatic actions of the federal government. If greater public control of education is desired, this trend must be reversed and greater attention focused on events at the state level. The other alternative is to end or limit state regulation of the schools.

EXERCISES

1. Interview a local representative to the state legislature about the political process with regard to educational legislation. Inquire about the important lobbying organizations and the role of the state department of education.

2. In a discussion group or in an essay discuss whether there should be complete professional control of education.

3. In a discussion group or in an essay discuss what areas of education you think the state should regulate.

4. Contact your state department of education and find out the extent of regulation of schools in your state.

5. In a discussion group or in an essay discuss whether there should be compulsory education laws.

Suggested Readings and Works Cited in Chapter

Erickson, Donald. *Super-Parent: An Analysis of State Educational Controls.* Written for the Illinois Advisory Committee on Nonpublic Schools. Ms., n.d.
   An important critique of the concept and practice of state regulation of the schools.

Iannaccone, Laurence. *Politics in Education.* New York: Center for Applied Research in Education, 1967.
   This book classifies the major types of state lobbying groups.

Keim, Albert. *Compulsory Education and the Amish.* Boston: Beacon 1975.
   This book provides the background and discussions of the important U.S. Supreme Court decision regarding compulsory education.

Masters, Nicholas, et al. *State Politics and the Public Schools: An Exploratory Analysis.* New York: Alfred A. Knopf, 1964.
   An early and important work about state educational politics.

Rickenbacker, William, ed. *The Twelve Year Sentence.* Chicago: Open Court, 1974.

Essays in this book discuss legal, historical, and philosophical arguments about compulsory education.

Sroufe, Gerald, "Recruitment Processes and Composition of State Boards of Education." Paper presented at the American Educational Research Association meeting in 1969.

This paper has provided general information about the background of members of state boards of education.

Thompson, John Thomas. *Policymaking in American Public Education.* Englewood Cliffs, N.J.: Prentice-Hall, 1976.

Chapters 6, 7, and 8 are good summaries of current knowledge about state politics of education.

Wirt, Frederick, and Kirst, Michael. *Political and Social Foundations of Education.* Berkeley, Calif.: McCutchan, 1975.

Chapter 7 provides a good introduction to state politics of education.

7

POWER AND CONTROL AT THE FEDERAL LEVEL

THE MAJOR DEBATE ABOUT FEDERAL INVOLVEMENT IN EDUCATION has centered around general versus categorical funding. General funding of American education by the federal government involves the distribution of monies to the state or local level for the paying of teachers' salaries, building costs, and the purchase of supplies and equipment. Within broad guidelines established by the government, the decisions about how this money would be spent takes place at the state and local levels. Traditionally, professional educators have favored this form of federal involvement in education because it leaves most decision-making power at the local level.

Categorical aid, on the other hand, involves the distribution of federal money for the support of specific programs, materials, and curricula. This form of federal aid removes a great deal of the decision-making power from the local level and places it in the hands of Congress and bureaucrats in the Office of Education and other federal agencies. Categorical aid has been the major form of federal spending in education. As a result, the role of the federal government in controlling the curriculum and in regulating the schools has greatly increased in the last twenty years.

One of the reasons for the greater use of categorical aid at the federal level has been a basic distrust of the types of decisions made by the professional educators at the local level. Major federal involvement in the schools did not occur until the 1950s, when the schools faced strong criticism for failure to produce large numbers of scientists and engineers. The popular press and national leaders blamed the professional educator for the supposed anti-intellectual and non-academic stress of the public schools. It was in this atmosphere of distrust of the educator that major federal involvement in education began.

Prior to the 1950s the federal role in education was very limited. The Department of Education was established in 1867 (changed to Office of Education in 1869) to collect statistics and promote the cause of education. In its early years it did assume some responsibility for administering government legislation; for instance, it administered the Morrill Land-Grants of 1862 and 1890 and the educational system in the Territory of Alaska. In the latter part of the nineteenth century and early twentieth century, the Office of Education published bulletins of information about research in education and ideas for school curricula and solving educational problems. The dissemination of educational information has continued to be one of its major functions.

A major effort by the National Education Association and the American Federation of Teachers to secure general federal aid to the schools occurred after World War II. All these attempts to obtain general aid were doomed to failure. The NEA and the AFT sponsored two major federal aid bills in 1945, which after many amendments and lengthy debate in Congress were defeated in 1948. Attempts to provide general aid for school construction were defeated in Congress in 1956. The only general federal aid bill to survive was one that provided aid to schools affected by federal activities such as military installations and research centers.

There were three major reasons for the difficulties encountered in gaining general federal aid for the schools. One issue, still a major one in any federal debate about educational spending, was how the money was to be distributed. With general aid to the schools the issue has been that of flat grants versus some form of equalization formula. Under flat grants a fixed sum per pupil is distributed to each state, whereas under equalization formulas money is distributed on the basis of need. In general, congressional representatives divided on this issue according to how much benefit their own state would receive under either method. Representatives of wealthy states prefer flat grants because an equalization formula would mean less federal income even though those states would have been paying a higher percentage of federal taxes. Poorer states, of course, favor some form of equalization.

Another reason for the difficulties in achieving general federal aid was, and continues to be, the demands of private schools. Catholic education groups and other private school groups tend to seek categorical aid for nonreligious textbooks, health services, and transportation rather than general aid for school operating expenses and salaries. Because of the constitutional issue of federal involvement in religion, general aid could not be provided to private religious schools. Another stumbling block to general federal aid, which no longer exists, was fear by some states in the 1950s that general federal aid would result in forced racial integration of the schools.

The event that signaled defeat of attempts to achieve general aid was the passage in 1958 of the National Defense Education Act, which provided money for specific educational categories. The legislation was the product of a major concern about the technological and military race with the Soviet Union and the launching by the Soviet Union of Sputnik I. The National Defense Education Act provided money for improving science, mathematics, and foreign-language curricula and for counseling and testing programs in the schools. Also included were a fellowship and loan program for college students and money for the expansion of the work of the Office of Education.

The National Education Association opposed the passage of the National Defense Education Act because it did not provide general aid to the schools. When William Carr, the executive secretary of the association, testified before Congress against the legislation and in favor of general aid, he encountered major hostility against professional educators, who were blamed for America's failures in technological competition with the Soviet Union. The executive secretary did not want money specifically designated for mathematics, science, and foreign languages, but wanted decisions about money distribution to be made at the local level. Carr argued before a congressional committee, "I believe that one thing that will draw the underdeveloped nations of the world into the democratic rather than the totalitarian camp might well be our free and versatile system of public education."

The significance of the National Defense Education Act was the categorical nature of its aid and the fact that it was designed to change public schools throughout the United States. This meant that the federal government would not be a passive supplier of money but would attempt to influence the curriculum and organization of schools directly. For instance, one result of the National Defense Education Act and other government activity was the creation of new curricula in mathematics and the sciences, which were distributed to the schools through government effort and persuasion. In the 1960s and 1970s federal influence over local schools expanded further into areas like civil rights and the actual support of specific programs.

The next sections of this chapter deal with three major areas of expanding federal involvement and regulation of education. These areas include the regulation of civil rights in the schools, the development of school curricula by the federal government, and the attempts to solve major social problems such as poverty and unemployment through federal educational programs. The National Defense Education Act and the reliance upon categorical aid, as opposed to general aid, set the stage for these developments.

Expansion of Federal Control and Protection of Civil Rights

Title VI of the 1964 Civil Rights Act established the method and means by which the federal government could regulate education and protect civil rights in the schools. Title VI established the precedent for using the disbursal of government money as a means of controlling educational policy. It required the mandatory withholding of federal funds to institutions practicing racial, religious, or ethnic discrimination. Title VI stated that no person, because of race, color, or national origin, could be excluded from or denied the benefits of any program receiving federal financial assistance. It required all federal agencies to establish guidelines to implement this policy. Refusal by institutions or projects to follow these guidelines was to result in the "termination or refusal to grant or to continue assistance under such program or activity."

The strength of Title VI was in the fact that the government had already extended its activities into many educational institutions around the country. Federal spending had spread into most of the educational institutions in the United States through the activities of the National Science Foundation and the National Defense Education Act. In addition, research money funds flowed into universities from other government agencies, including the Department of Defense. Many institutions received funds for the Reserve Officers Training Program. Federal spending continued to increase in the 1960s, particularly after the passage in 1965 of the Elementary and Secondary Education Act. Title VI announced that all aid to institutions and school districts that failed to comply with federal guidelines would end. This was certainly a powerful government weapon. The most extreme concern about Title VI was voiced by Senator Sam Ervin of North Carolina, who claimed, "No dictator could ask for more power than Title VI confers on the President."

The justification for using the spending of federal money in this manner was given by Senator Hubert Humphrey during the Senate floor debate over the Civil Rights bill. The major concern at the time was the extent of racial segregation in educational institutions. Humphrey argued that Title VI was not designed to be punitive but was designed to make sure that funds were not used to support segregated programs. He also claimed that Title VI did not create any new government authority. "Most agencies," he stated, "now have authority to refuse or terminate assistance for failure to comply with a variety of requirements imposed by statute or by administrative action." While Title VI represented an unquestioned power of the federal government to establish the terms under which funds shall be disbursed, Humphrey made the point that "no recipient is required to accept Federal aid."

Title VI completely reversed the relationship that had existed between the Office of Education and local and state school districts. The Office of Education had traditionally defined its constituency as local and state school officials. The doctrine of local control and opposition to federal control had resulted in most money being disbursed by the Office of Education with minimum requirements and regulation. The Office of Education was viewed as a public servant of each local and state educational system.

With Title VI, the Office of Education was forced to embark upon a path that put it in an adversary position in relation to many school systems. School systems would now be required to show proof of compliance with civil rights guidelines, and the Office of Education would be placed in the position of judging the adequacy of the actions of local school systems. The Office of Education was also given the responsibility of drafting the guidelines that would be used in enforcing the provisions of Title VI in government educational programs. This meant the Office of Education was placed in the position of being both interpreter and enforcer of the law. An agency that had always avoided any hint of federal control was suddenly handed the problem of protecting the constitutional rights of children around the country.

The precedent for using the threat of withholding federal money as a means of protecting civil rights with respect to racial segregation also provided the basis for government attempts to end sex discrimination in the schools. Title IX of the 1972 amendments to the Higher Education Act stated, "No person in the United States shall, on the basis of sex, be excluded from partipation in, be denied the benefits of, or be subjected to discrimination under any education program or activity receiving Federal Assistance. . . ."

The passage of Title IX reflected over a century of struggle by women to attain equal rights in the United States. Women had traditionally been discriminated against in specific educational programs and in hiring practices in colleges and universities. In the public schools, male athletic programs often received more funding and were more varied than those provided for females. Girls were often excluded from certain types of vocational programs. A federal task force stated, "We believe it is not the case that opportunities exist for women which they simply decline to exercise. Rather, we find there are specific barriers which block their progress and which will not disappear without conscious effort."

Title IX expanded the activities of the Office of Education to include the writing of guidelines and the establishment of methods to determine the possible existence of sex discrimination. Women's organizations stepped up their efforts to end sex discrimination by filing complaints against educational institutions. In 1972 alone, the year of the passage of Title IX, formal charges of sex discrimination were filed against 360 institutions of higher learning.

In 1974 federal protection of civil rights in the schools was again expanded with the passage of what was known as the "Buckley Amendment," named after its sponsor, James Buckley of New York. The "Buckley Amendment" was a rider to the Educational Amendments of 1974, which stated that educational institutions would lose federal funds unless they gave parents the right to examine and challenge school records. Senator Buckley stated in an interview in the January 1975 issue of the *Nation's Schools and Colleges* that the idea for the amendment came from an article he read in a Sunday supplement in a newspaper. The concern was that teachers and school officials often put damaging statements into student files and never provide the opportunity for children or parents to see these statements. A careless comment by a third-grade teacher calling a student a "born liar" might follow the pupil through school and affect the attitudes of other teachers and the pupil's whole educational career. Moreover, student files remain with the individual through college and are sometimes used when seeking employment. Senator Buckley stated in the magazine interview, "When you're talking about records that affect the life of an individual, that affect decisions that are being made about him, then he has a right to see them and to determine their accuracy."

The "Buckley Amendment" gives parents the right to examine school records and challenge the items they feel are inaccurate and to have misleading records changed. Parents must also give their consent before any records are shown to any individuals or groups outside the school. The same rights of inspection and challenge are given to any student eighteen and over attending institutions of higher learning. Specifically, parents and older students are allowed to inspect and review at will "official records, files and data, including all material that is incorporated into each student's cumulative record folder." These records include, in the words of the legislation:

---

identifying data; academic work completed; level of achievement (grades, test scores); attendance data; scores on standardized intelligence, aptitude; and psychological tests; interest inventory results; health data; family background information; teacher or counselor ratings and observations; and verified reports of serious behavior patterns.

The expansion of federal control initiated by the passage of the 1964 Civil Rights Act will probably continue in future years. The major consequence of Title VI of the Civil Rights Act was the breaching of the barriers against federal control of education. The government, of course, had always had the power to tax and the power to spend. Implied in this right was the power to determine how money would be spent. In the area of education this right had been exercised primarily in terms of categorical appropriations, where money was appropriated to be used for specific programs. Institutions or school districts were required to use this money for designated programs, but this had no direct effect on other policies and programs except where they might be influenced by the federally funded programs. Title VI reversed this situation by establishing the precedent that all programs and policies of an educational institution or school system had to meet federal requirements before the institution or system could receive funds for a specific program.

The Federal Government and a National Curriculum

Beginning in the late 1950s, the federal government became involved in the development and sponsorship of new curricula for the public schools. Prior to that time, with respect to curricula, the Office of Education had printed and distributed information about new curricula and had organized national and regional conferences on them. What happened in the late 1950s was that the federal government provided actual financial support of groups to develop new curricula, as well as use of federal institutes to train teachers and distribute the new school materials. Federal involvement in curriculum writing represented one more additional step in the establishment of national control of the educational system.

The late 1950s' case of federal involvement in curriculum writing provides an example of how a national curriculum can come into existence without direct control being imposed over all schools in the United States. One of the key government agencies in this process was the National Science Foundation established by Congress in 1950. The foundation was a product of the dreams of government scientist Vannevar Bush. In a report written in the closing days of World War II, Bush had originally called for a National Science Foundation, which would have as its objective the increase in scientific capital in the United States. This was to be accomplished, according to Bush, by improving science education in the public schools, supporting basic research in science, and providing undergraduate and graduate fellowships in science. Bush felt that the improvement of science education in high schools was imperative if latent scientific talent was to be properly developed. There was a great danger, he felt, if high school science teaching failed to awaken interest or provided inadequate instruction. The goal of the National Science Foundation to improve science instruction in the public schools paved the way for federal support and introduction of new curricula in the public schools.

The major involvement of the National Science Foundation in curriculum writing began in 1958, when President Eisenhower, at the same time he proposed the National Defense Education Act (NDEA), also called for a fivefold increase in appropriations for the scientific education activities of the National Science Foundation. President Eisenhower claimed that the scientific education programs of the foundation "have come to be recognized by the education and scientific communities as among the most significant contributions currently being made to the improvement of science education in the United States."

This major increase in funding resulting from passage of the NDEA in 1958 went immediately to support and expand projects started earlier by the National Science Foundation. Two of the major groups involved were the Physical Science Study Committee organized in 1956 and the School Mathematics Study Group organized in 1958. The Physical Science Study Committee was the brainchild of physicist Jerrold Zacharias of the Massachusetts Institute of Technology. He decided in the mid-1950s that one way of getting around the shortage and mediocrity of high school physics courses was through the production of teaching films and classroom equipment. A statement of purpose given at the initial meeting of the Physical Science Study Committee called for changes in the content of courses in physical science as a means of finding "a way to make more understandable to all students the world in which we live and to prepare better those who will do advanced work. It is probably that such a presentation would also attract more students to careers in science."

The distribution of materials by the Physical Science Study Committee and other curriculum groups sponsored by the National Science Foundation provides an excellent illustration of the combination of methods available to the national government to influence public schooling. First, government money was channeled through the National Science Foundation to support curriculum writing groups. Second, money was provided in the NDEA for local school districts to purchase new equipment for science and mathematics programs. Third, local school systems were heavily influenced to purchase materials developed by the curriculum groups sponsored by the National Science Foundation because their science and mathematics teachers were being trained to use these materials in summer institutes funded by the foundation. The summer institutes were very attractive to teachers because they had to pay no tuition to attend and often received some form of monetary compensation for attending. In addition, many institutes gave academic credit for attendance. In the case of most teachers, this meant a movement upward on the pay scale of their local school district.

This whole process was aided by the development of a national textbook market. Certainly one of the most important influences on the content of teaching in the public schools is the textbook. By the late 1950s fewer than a hundred textbook companies dominated the public school textbook market. Approximately one-half of these companies concentrated on elementary school textbooks while the rest published high school texts. Almost all textbooks were distributed on a national basis and at the same time had to conform to state statutes that covered things like the physical appearance of the book and marketing procedures. Textbook prices were essentially nationalized in 1934 with the passage of an Ohio law which stated that the price for any textbook sold in Ohio could not exceed the lowest price for a particular textbook sold anywhere else in the country. A majority of states followed the example of Ohio with the result that textbook prices became a matter of nationwide competition. Added to these factors was the similarity of state and local study guides influencing the content of textbooks.

One result of the concentration of textbook publishing and the national market was the virtual creation of a national curriculum. A person could travel from Maine to California and find a similarity between what was taught in the schoolhouses across the nation. In other words, the textbook industry had the ability to influence curriculum nationally by changing the nature and content of textbooks.

Textbook companies have not been in the business of sponsoring curriculum development and have had to rely on outside groups for new ideas and materials. The curriculum study groups supported by the federal government provided new materials that could be incorporated into the textbooks in the national school market. The control of the textbook market became a very important strategy of the School Mathematics Study Group.

The School Mathematics Study Group combined influence over the textbook industry with federal funding and summer institutes from the National Science Foundation to spread the "new math" through the country like a rapidly burning brush fire. The initial writing session of the group began during the summer months of 1958 with twenty-one participants drawn from college departments of mathematics and twenty-one from high schools. During this writing session an outline was developed for a series of textbooks in mathematics for grades nine through twelve and for the writing of a series of units on specific topics for students in grades seven and eight. The goal of the second summer writing session in 1959 was to carry out the actual writing of six textbooks and six teachers' manuals in a nine-week period. At the close of the summer's work there was a complete set of textbooks covering grade levels seven through twelve. During the fall of 1959 the new textbooks were tested in experimental centers around the country. The final revision of the textbook series took place during the summer of 1960. During the 1960–61 academic year the Yale University Press printed and sold 130,000 of the textbooks, with sales increasing to 500,000 the following year. Within four years of the organization of the School Mathematics Study Group, its material was being used by 20 percent of its intended market.

The tremendous success of the School Mathematics Study Group in being able to develop and market a textbook series in such a short period of time was a result of both its high level of federal funding and its sophisticated dealings with book publishers. In terms of the publishing industry, a committee was established by the study group after the textbook series was completed which each year was to review all mathematics textbooks on the market to determine if texts comparable to those of the School Mathematics Study Group were available, and if so, to remove the study group's text that was in competition with the commercial publication. The procedure was designed to put competitive pressure on the textbook industry. This pressure forced publishers to begin marketing similar textbooks in 1961 and 1962.

In terms of federal funding, the School Mathematics Study Group began with an initial grant of $100,000 in 1958 and during the summer months received another $1.2 million. In 1960 it received another $2.8 million. During the late 1950s, given the value of the dollar, this was a considerable sum to finance a project of this type.

The Physical Science Study Committee and the School Mathematics Study Group were landmarks in new curriculum developments of the late 1950s and early 1960s. Their work became models in many other areas of the school curriculum. In 1959 the American Institute of Biological Sciences Curriculum Study received a grant from the National Science Foundation and began working on a new curriculum for the public schools. Between 1960 and 1963 the Chemical Education Material Study produced a text, a laboratory manual, a teachers' guide, a set of motion pictures, and supplementary equipment.

The science and mathematics curricula of the late 1950s and early 1960s represent one method the federal government has used to develop and distribute a national curriculum. Another method and example is the career education movement of the early 1970s. In this case the program was initiated and financed through the Office of Education. In 1971 and 1972, Commissioner of Education Sidney Marland began to earmark the discretionary funds provided by Congress to the Office of Education for the development of career education models. Projects using these funds were begun in Arizona,

California, Georgia, Michigan, and New Jersey. In addition, funds were made available through the Office of Education to states for the development and operation of career education programs. As money started to flow from the federal coffers, educators began to jump on the bandwagon of career education. During the first two years $100 million in discretionary funds went into the program. Commissioner Marland was able to announce that in 1972–73, one year after the beginning of the program, 750,000 young people had participated in career education demonstrations and models supported by funds from the U.S. Office of Education and that five state legislatures had been persuaded to approve funds to launch career education. He also reported that the Dallas public school system had been completely restructured around the concept of career education.

The power of the federal government to influence curriculum development and distribution of materials was fairly well established by the early 1970s. Its primary means of influence was the availability of money to finance these types of projects. Local and state governments provided either nothing or minimal amounts of money for new curriculum projects. Private foundations were sometimes a source of research and development funds. But none of these sources could really match the spending power of the federal government nor the contacts the Office of Education had with local school administrators.

In the middle of the 1970s a raging controversy broke out about a social studies curriculum called *Man: A Course of Study* (MACOS). This turbulence seemed to indicate that the federal government would in the future restrict its activities to noncontroversial areas. Developers of MACOS received $2,166,900 in grants from the National Science Foundation to write, promote, and market a course designed to introduce students to anthropology and cross-cultural studies. The course first presented animal behavior and then focused on a Canadian Eskimo group. In March 1975 the controversy exploded with members of Congress attacking the curriculum for presenting alleged "lurid examples of violence and sexual promiscuity." One unhappy congressman was critical that schoolchildren were being exposed to "human characteristics" such as adultery, cannibalism, incest, infanticide, murder, robbery, wife-swapping, and sexual promiscuity.

The MACOS controversy not only made federal agencies wary of getting involved in controversial areas of the curriculum, but also of distributing materials directly to the schools. It will be remembered that the National Science Foundation had used competitive techniques to influence publishers to produce similar materials for the schools or else turned the material over directly to the publishers. In the case of MACOS, the National Science Foundation funded the publication and marketing of the materials. Congressman Albert H. Quie in an interview in the November 1976 issue of *Educational Leadership* stated that one of the major problems with MACOS was that the "National Science Foundation went contrary to its traditional manner. . . . It did not make MACOS available to publishing firms. It published the program and made it available to schools themselves. And, that is where NSF made the mistake."

Congressman Quie predicted in the interview that the federal government would probably continue federal development of curriculum, especially in vocational education and the physical sciences. "When you get into the social sciences, then I think we'll not see the federal government actually distributing curriculum (materials)." He went on to state that to "the extent that it finances the research, it will find some point short of directing the use of that 'curriculum' by school systems."

ESEA and the War on Poverty

The 1965 Elementary and Secondary Education Act (ESEA) was one of the major involvements of the federal government in public schools in the history of the nation. It was not designed to provide general aid to solve the financial problems of local schools, but was categorical aid given as part of a broader social policy to end poverty in the United States. Like the National Defense Education Act, the ESEA was part of a broader social policy in which schools were to be used as instruments to solve major social problems.

The 1965 ESEA must be understood as one piece of legislation in a total package of legislation which made up President Lyndon Johnson's War on Poverty. Another piece of legislation in the package was the Economic Opportunity Act of 1964, which included provisions for a Job Corps to train unemployed youth and provided the basis for the development of the early childhood education program Head Start. The Job Corps kept alive the tradition that had existed since the Civilian Conservation Corps of the 1930s of seeking a solution to the youth problems through some form of national youth service. Head Start was one of the most popular programs sponsored by the federal government and sparked public awareness and acceptance of the idea of early childhood education.

All of the above legislation was based on a particular philosophy about the nature of poverty in the United States and the methods by which it could be eliminated. Included in the philosophy were concepts about educational and cultural deprivation that were to influence educators around the country. In other words, the War on Poverty not only influenced local schools through direct funding of specific programs, but also by spreading a particular philosophy about poverty and the role education could play in eliminating poverty.

The document that gave full expression to the philosophy of the War on Poverty was a report compiled by the chairman of the Council of Economic Advisers and issued in 1964 as "The Problem of Poverty in America." This report was originally requested by President John F. Kennedy before his assassination and its analysis of poverty was accepted by President Johnson. Poverty, in the report, and in the thinking of many social scientists in the 1950s and early 1960s, continued in the United States as an interrelated set of causal factors that were mutually interdependent. For instance, a poor education restricted employment opportunities, which caused a low standard of living and consequently poor medical care, diet, housing, and education for the next generation. This model of poverty suggested that one could begin at any point in the set of causal relationships and move around the circle of poverty. In other words, improving medical care for the poor would mean more days of employment and consequently more money for better housing, diet, and education. Theoretically, the same chain reaction would occur if you improved any of the interrelated causal factors.

As was briefly mentioned in chapter 1 of this text, this circle of poverty was believed to be developing into a culture of poverty that would divide America into two parts because of its increased insulation of the poor from the rest of society. The rise of suburbia had reduced the contact between the poor, who increasingly inhabited the inner city, and the middle and upper classes. The poor were also becoming politically invisible because they lacked representation in unions, fraternal organizations, or political parties. It was argued that the family structure among the poor was different from the rest of society and was characterized by more homes without fathers, early pregnancy, different attitudes toward sex, and less marriage. The culture of poverty, it was felt, was beginning to perpetuate itself under the pressures of modern technology.

One of the important emphases in the "The Problem of Poverty in America" report of the Council of Economic Advisers was the role of education in uprooting the culture of poverty. The report proclaimed in its opening section: "Equality of opportunity is the American dream, and universal education our noblest pledge to realize it." The high incidence of poverty caused by low incomes was thus directly linked to education. The report claimed that the chief reason for low rates of pay was low productivity, which in turn reflected a lack of education. The report went on to state that the "incidence of poverty drops as educational attainments rise for nonwhites as well as white families at all ages." The assumption was that increased educational opportunity would eliminate poverty in the United States.

It was this belief in the relationship between education and poverty that provided the backdrop for both the Economic Opportunity Act of 1964 and the Elementary and Secondary Education Act of 1965. Part A of Title I of the Economic Opportunity Act established the Job Corps (the basic outline of this part of the legislation is described in chapter 4 of this text). Title II of the legislation provided for Urban and Rural Community Action Programs. Head Start was the first and probably the most popular of the community-action programs funded under Title II. The Head Start program (as the name suggests) was to give the children of the poor a "head start" in the educational race so that they might compete on equal terms with other children. What was supposedly unique about Head Start was its five components of action. The first of these was provision for medical and dental services for impoverished children. The second component was social services for the child's home environment and education of parents. Third and fourth components of the program were psychological services for the child and school-readiness programs with emphasis on preparing the child to enter school on equal terms with children of more-privileged members of society. The fifth component was the utilization of volunteer help.

The Elementary and Secondary Education Act of 1965, however, was the main part of the educational attack upon poverty. One of the important features of the legislation was the development of an aid formula that overcame the traditional obstacles to federal aid to education. Traditionally, the major obstacles to federal aid had been the issue of segregated schools, the problem of church-state relations, and fears of federal control. Essentially the issue of segregated schools had been taken care of in 1965 by Title VI of the 1964 Civil Rights Act. The issue of church-state relations had been the major obstacle to attempts to get legislation enacted providing federal aid to education. Parochial school leaders, of course, wanted federal aid to provide their schools with some sort of benefits. The solution to the problem was found in the funding formula of $A/2 \times B = P$. Within this formula, A represented a state's average expenditure per pupil and B represented the number of poor children in a school district. In addition, it was proposed to include special services and library support in the legislation that would go to both public and private schools. It was felt this could be done without raising the problem of church-state relations because of a Supreme Court ruling in 1947 that busing of parochial school students was aid to the pupils and not to the Catholic church. When the church-state issue was raised in legislative hearings, the problem was resolved under this child-benefit theory.

The most important section of the Elementary and Secondary Education Act was Title I, which received approximately 78 percent of the $1.25 billion initially appropriated for the legislation. The purpose of Title I was to provide improved educational programs for children designated as educationally deprived. Title I specifically stated that "the Congress hereby declares it to be the policy of the United States to provide financial assistance . . . to expand and improve . . . educational programs by various means . . . which contribute particularly to meeting the special educational needs of educationally deprived children."

The other sections of the legislation covered a variety of special purposes, which in many cases were included to assure passage of Title I. Title II provided financial assistance for school library resources, textbooks, and other instructional materials. Title III provided funds for the establishment of supplementary educational centers to promote local educational innovations. Educators who had helped President Johnson draft the legislation hoped that this could be one method for stimulating creativity in local school systems. Title IV provided money for educational research and for the establishment of research and development centers at universities and in different regions of the country.

Funds for strengthening state departments of education were designated under Title V. The purposes of this title were to allay the fears of those concerned about federal control of education by giving direct support to the state and to provide the money by which the state departments of education could administer the funds provided in other sections of the legislation. Title VI provided a statement of definitions used in the act and contained a clause prohibiting federal control over the operations of local school systems.

At the time of its passage, the Elementary and Secondary Education Act was the most important piece of educational legislation ever passed by Congress. It strengthened the importance of Title VI of the 1964 Civil Rights Act by making available large sums of money to local schools that complied with desegregation orders. Noncompliance with desegregation orders, in other words, meant a loss of funds from the Elementary and Secondary Education Act. Desegregation of the schools in the South had been progressing at a very slow rate. With the passage of this new legislation, desegregation began to occur at a more rapid rate.

Because of the difficult financial situation of most public schools in the United States, there was a rush to get funds, particularly under Title I. This resulted in local schools expanding their administrative staff to be able to apply for the funds and fill out what in later years would seem like endless government forms. While the legislation claimed no federal control over local education, in reality local school administrators and boards gave up part of their local autonomy as they were forced to comply with federal standards in order to receive the funds.

As mentioned, most local school systems would have preferred general aid from the federal government. The Elementary and Secondary Education Act provided categorical aid only. Many school systems, however, needed money to support their total programs. Because of this situation, many of these school systems were forced to cheat and claim the existence of large numbers of poor students in their districts in order to get federal money to support their general programs. Money designated for these nonexistent disadvantaged students made it possible for many school systems to remain in operation.

The secretary of Health, Education, and Welfare, Elliot Richardson, testified before Congress in 1972 that the major problem with the 1965 Elementary and Secondary Education Act was the actual misuse of Title I funds. He told a congressional committee, "The most prevalent failing has been the use by local school districts of Title I funds as general revenue. Out of 40 states audited between 1966 and 1970, local school districts in 14 were found to have spent Title I funds as general revenue." In these cases the funds were diffused through the educational system and did not reach the educationally deprived child. He announced that the Office of Education had recently asked eight states to return $6,249,915 in misused funds and would shortly take action against approximately fifteen additional states for another $23 million.

Even though local schools needed general revenue funds in the 1960s and 1970s, Congress continued to pass legislation that designated money for specific categories of instruction. In 1966, Education of Handicapped Children, or Title VI, was added to the Elementary and Secondary Education Act. Bilingual Education Programs, or Title VII, were added in 1967 to provide financial assistance for local schools to design educational programs for children who came from environments where the dominant language was other than English. In 1972 a large number of what were called "education amendments" were passed by Congress. Included in these amendments were an Emergency School Aid Act to help local schools with desegregation plans and an Ethnic Heritage Act to plan, develop, establish, and operate ethnic-heritage studies programs. Also included in the 1972 amendments was an Indian Education Act to develop innovative and bilingual programs and to provide health and nutritional services for Indian children.

The pattern that emerged from the federal legislation of the 1960s and 1970s was for the federal government to provide money in areas that were apparently neglected by local and state educational systems. The role of the federal government was not to support all schooling, but only those parts that appeared not to be receiving support by the local governments. By the 1970s the American public school system was functioning under three levels of financing and control. State governments were providing regulations and requirements to local districts, which in turn were administering these regulations and requirements in terms of local needs. The federal government provided the source of money and planning for innovative programs like ESEA programs under Title I and later ESEA amendments like the Bilingual Education and Ethnic Heritage legislation. In addition, the federal government functioned as guardian of civil rights in the schools through Title VI of the 1964 Civil Rights Act. The result was the creation of one of the most complexly governed educational systems in the entire world.

Power and Control at the Federal Level

Power and control in federal educational policy must be viewed from two different but interrelated perspectives. First, there is the formal policy-making process, which includes the President, Congress and federal agencies that deal directly with educational matters. Second, there are lobbyists and other groups outside government that provide information and proposals in an effort to influence government educational policy. (These will be discussed in detail in the following two chapters.) In addition, there is an informal structure of power that operates through both these components of educational policy making.

A great deal of the activity of the federal government in education since the 1950s can be explained in terms of presidential politics. Traditionally, American Presidents have not given a great deal of attention to educational matters because education has been considered a state and local matter and because other domestic and foreign problems have taken precedence over educational issues. But beginning in the 1950s, American Presidents have been forced to confront educational problems directly because of national and international events. For instance, President Eisenhower during the early years of his administration did not make education one of the focuses of his administration. In fact, he refused to discuss the 1954 Supreme Court decision (*Brown* v. *Board of Education of Topeka*) with regard to school desegregation. In his autobiography, *Waging Peace, 1956–1961*, he stated that he felt the civil rights campaign was an attempt to cause him to lose political support in the presidential election of 1956.

All of this changed in the fall of 1957, when Governor Orval Faubus took action to block the integration of the schools in Little Rock, Arkansas, by ordering the National Guard into the area. When black students appeared to enroll in the previously all-white high school in Little Rock, they found the doors of the schoolhouse blocked by the National Guard and were informed the school was off limits to "colored" students. Such an open and flagrant violation of the Supreme Court decision forced President Eisenhower to take action. He federalized the Arkansas National Guard and sent regular federal troops into the city. He then went on national television to explain the involvement of the federal government in local desegregation matters.

During President Eisenhower's administration the civil rights movement and the National Defense Education Act of 1958 made education an important factor in presidential politics. During the 1960 presidential campaign, John F. Kennedy became the first President to make aid to education a major element in his domestic program and to give it vigorous personal support. President Johnson, under pressure from the civil rights movement, made education a central part of his War on Poverty. In many ways, President Johnson wanted to be known as the "education President." President Nixon made opposition to busing for desegregation an important item in his 1972 campaign. Both the 1968 and 1972 presidential campaigns included major discussions of school desegregation. During the 1976 campaign busing and school desegregation were not major items of discussion by either Gerald Ford or Jimmy Carter, one of the reasons being that school desegregation had become such an explosive issue that both candidates seemed to feel it was best avoided as a major issue.

One event that did take place during the 1976 campaign might force all future presidential campaigns to make education a central issue. The National Education Association declared for the first time that it would give open support and aid to the presidential candidate who was most willing to support the goals and objectives of the association. In 1976, the support of this large organization of school teachers and other educational professionals went to Jimmy Carter. How important this support will be in future campaigns is difficult to measure, but it might force future candidates to speak more directly to educational issues.

One of the important powers Presidents have had with respect to education has been proposing educational legislation, such as President Johnson's important Elementary and Secondary Education Act. Another and somewhat more negative power has been withholding money from the financing of educational legislation. This became one of the hallmarks of President Nixon's administration. The Nixon administration adopted a method of budgeting called the "full employment budget," in which the amount of federal spending is determined by economic conditions. James Guthrie argues (in an article on "The Flow of Federal Funds for Education" in Harry Summerfield's *Power and Process*) that under full employment budgeting, where federal expenditures are "speeded up, slowed down, delayed, or drawn out, education expenditures tend to be among the first affected. This is so because dollars for school-related programs represent one of the few places in the budget where the president has a degree of discretion." Still another important power of the President is to withhold money appropriated by Congress for particular legislation. This occurs when Presidents are not willing to veto entire appropriations bills, but object to parts of the legislation. President Richard Nixon used his executive prerogative freely against educational legislation. James Guthrie in the previously mentioned article claimed that "between 1969 and 1973, it is likely that the Nixon administration forestalled or forbade the spending of approximately $1 billion in education funds."

Presidential power is also exerted over the U.S. Office of Education (USOE), which is the major administrative agency responsible for federal educational programs. The USOE is part of the Department of Health, Education, and Welfare (HEW). The secretary of HEW is appointed by the President and is a member of the President's cabinet. The President is also responsible for appointing the commissioner of education, who heads USOE under the leadership of the secretary of HEW.

The President can exert direct pressure upon the policies and actions of HEW and USOE. A classic example of this was described by Gary Orfield in his study *The Reconstruction of Southern Education: The Schools and the 1964 Civil Rights Act*, when in 1965 USOE decided to apply Title VI of the 1964 Civil Rights Act to Northern school districts. The USOE first took action against Chicago and announced that $32 million was being withheld from the Chicago public school system pending investigation of alleged racial segregation. At the time, Chicago had one of the best-documented cases of racial discrimination in the North. Black students in Chicago attended segregated, overcrowded schools on a double-shift basis. As a result, black students spent less time in school than white students.

The attempt by USOE to withhold funds from Chicago was almost immediately stopped by President Lyndon Johnson because of pressure from Richard Daley and congressional leaders from Illinois. Johnson quickly let it be known that he wanted the funds to begin flowing to Chicago. After the Chicago incident, the major thrust of Title VI under the Johnson administration was directed at the South.

The above example demonstrates the way in which Presidents can use the regulatory power of the USOE and educational spending to improve their own political positions and pay off political debts. Obviously, Republican Presidents will tend to be more sympathetic toward Republican mayors and governor, and Democratic Presidents to members of their own party. For instance, under Republican administrations in the 1970s, the USOE did apply Title VI to Chicago, but not against notoriously segregated Cleveland, where the mayor was Republican.

As mentioned previously in the chapter, the functions of USOE have increased rapidly since the passage of the 1964 Civil Rights bill and the 1965 Elementary and Secondary Education Act. Activities of USOE include not only the regulatory powers of Title VI of the Civil Rights Act but also the determination of how federal money will be spent. Legislation passed by Congress is usually not self-explanatory nor self-executing in any detailed sense. It is the administrative agencies, such as USOE, which must interpret and determine the exact meaning of congressional legislation. The USOE must prepare guidelines and regulations based on what they determine the intentions of Congress to have been when Congress passed a particular piece of legislation. This interpretation of legislative intentions give bureaucrats in the Office of Education a great deal of discretionary power.

Local and state school officials feel this discretionary power of the USOE directly. After the passage of any federal legislation, they must wait until the USOE issues guidelines and regulations to find out what the legislation will mean for them. In many cases, the guidelines and regulations of the USOE can mean that local school officials will have to reorganize their school systems and fill out lengthy reports and forms for the federal government. The previously mentioned "Buckley Amendment" and Title IX against sex discrimination, for instance, have resulted in regulations and guidelines that have had tremendous effect upon local educational units.

In 1972, most of the research activities of the USOE were taken over by the newly created National Institute of Education (NIE). The Nixon administration had proposed the establishment of the NIE because of a feeling that a great deal of federal money for education was being wasted on programs and ideas that had never been scientifically proven or tested. The NIE is designed to support basic research in education by funding research proposals from outside agencies such as universities. The major and extremely important limitation upon this support is that certain areas of research are designated as major areas of support. The areas so designated can of course reflect the interests of those appointed to the NIE. This means that what are considered areas worthy of basic research can become a political issue.

Presidential power and the power of federal agencies such as USOE all function within the framework of legislation passed by Congress. When the President impounds money, it is money appropriated by congressional legislation. When the President pressures agencies to act in certain ways and appoints particular people to those agencies, it is mainly in terms of influencing how congressional legislation is interpreted and executed. The Constitution invests in Congress "all legislative powers." In addition, Congress participates in the overseeing of the administration of policies by administrative agencies.

The majority of congressional activity takes place within a committee system. Committees can propose, review, hold hearings, and recommend action on particular legislative items related to the work of a particular committee. The committee in the House of Representatives responsible for educational legislation is the Committee on Education and Labor; in the Senate it is the Committee on Labor and Public Welfare. Education is not the primary concern of either of these committees, however. The primary concern is usually legislation affecting labor, and selection to the committees is therefore usually based upon a member's attitude toward labor.

Membership on these two congressional committees is not highly prized because they deal with many highly emotional issues that have little payoff in terms of furthering political careers. Since membership on these committees is not considered as prestigious as other committee assignments, there tends to be a high rate of turnover. Because of the lack of stability of committee membership, plus the fact that the primary interest of the committees is labor, relatively little educational expertise is to be found among committee members.

The result of this relative lack of congressional expertise in education and the lack of major interest in educational legislation is a situation similar to state legislatures, where there is a heavy reliance upon expert knowledge and opinion from government agencies and outside lobbying groups. The one major difference between members of Congress and most state legislators is that members of the Senate and House all have staffs that can be used to investigate issues surrounding legislation. This reduces part of the dependence on outside groups.

There are a small number of members of Congress who do attempt to build their political reputation on educational issues. One example is given by Jack H. Schuster in his article "An 'Education Congressman' Seeks Reelection" in Harry L. Summerfield's *Power and Process*. The case described in the article concerned Congressional Representative John Brademas, who was seeking reelection in a highly contested congressional district that included South Bend, Indiana. An important part of Brademas's strategy was to win support from educational groups within the area, which included the faculty of Notre Dame University. Brademas had sponsored some education-related legislation and had won awards from educational groups.

Brademas attempted to use his involvement in education in a number of ways to win votes in the election. Five days before the election, a representative of the National Education Association gave Brademas a Distinguished Service Award. Brademas's staff arranged for this award to be presented at the Faculty Club of Notre Dame University and invited local school and university educators. A top-ranking official of the Department of Health, Education, and Welfare who was interested in Brademas's reelection was also on hand to make kind comments about Brademas. During the award presentation a letter was read from the Indiana affiliate of the National Education Association praising Brademas's work in Congress.

Teachers in South Bend were represented by the American Federation of Teachers. A telephone call from the national head of the organization stimulated the local organization into activity to support Brademas. A group of eighteen teachers volunteered to canvass for Brademas under the title "Teachers for Brademas." Brademas's staff helped to train the teachers for door-to-door campaigning.

Written support of Brademas's campaign was given by the Department of Audiovisual Instruction of the National Education Association in letters sent to members residing within the congressional district. Other aid came from two officials of the Department of Health, Education, and Welfare. One official made the kind remarks at the previously mentioned award ceremony and then attended a meeting of local workers and officials of the Democratic party to give a pep talk for Brademas's reelection. The other official wrote letters of solicitation to fifty or sixty possible contributors to Brademas's campaign. A "Dear Educator" letter was mailed to nine thousand school and college personnel within Brademas's congressional district. In this letter Brademas urged their support because of his sponsorship of educational legislation. In addition to all these activities, a group of faculty wives from Notre Dame contacted college teachers for contributions, and the use of their names in a newspaper advertisement which when it appeared proclaimed in banner headlines: *350 College and University Educators from the Third Congressional District Endorse Congressman John Brademas' Bid for Reelection.*

A national campaign to gain support for Brademas's reelection was organized under a committee named "National Friends of John Brademas," whose membership included a former dean of Harvard's Graduate School of Education and a former commissioner of education. This group issued under special letterhead twenty-five hundred letters praising Brademas's educational activities. A slightly different form of the letter was mailed to Americans who had attended Oxford University, where Brademas had been a Rhodes Scholar. These efforts were directed at gaining financial support for the campaign.

Shortly before the election, Brademas, in cooperation with the Department of Education at Notre Dame, organized a conference on "Major Tensions in American Education: Shaping Policies for the '70's." Attending the conference and providing support for Brademas were a former commissioner of education, the president of the Ford

Foundation, the director of the teacher corps, and the superintendent of the Cleveland public schools. Several thousand invitations to the meeting at Notre Dame were mailed to school administrators and teachers throughout northern Indiana.

How much did this effort to enlist the support of the education community contribute to Brademas's victory in the election? And, of even greater importance, can members of Congress build their political support on issues related to education? Schuster's study of the Brademas campaign is inconclusive with regard to these questions. Schuster states, "On balance, then, the efforts made to harness educators at the local and national levels yielded visible but modest results. A cost-benefit analysis might well indicate that Brademas should have invested much of that campaign energy in ways other than those calculated to win minds, money, and manpower from within the education community."

Conclusion

Some very important things can be learned from John Brademas's campaign. One is the close relationship that can exist between educational interest groups and politicians. This was an issue that was discussed in the last chapter with regard to the state legislatures and lobbyists. During his campaign, Brademas was able to use both national organizations of teachers, the National Education Association and the American Federation of Teachers, to support and participate in his campaign. Also participating in his support was the head of the Ford Foundation, one of the major private foundations in the United States.

Another important point is the use by Brademas of officials from the Department of Health, Education, and Welfare. As mentioned in the previous chapter with regard to state governments, educational agencies tend to be major lobbyists for particular educational programs. It should also be noted that there tends to be an easy movement between outside educational interests and government positions. For instance, Francis Keppel, who was one of the major leaders of "National Friends of John Brademas" and who participated in Brademas's conference at Notre Dame University, had been dean of Harvard's Graduate School of Education, U.S. commissioner of education, and chairman and president of the General Learning Corporation.

What all this suggests is that an understanding of the control of education in the United States requires an understanding of the functioning of these educational interest groups. This is particularly important at the national level because the origin of most federal programs can be traced to the work of groups outside government. The next chapter is devoted to exploring the nature of these interest groups and their relationship to government.

EXERCISES

1. Discuss whether the federal government should provide general or categorical aid to American public schools. Consider this issue in the framework of the issues discussed in this chapter.

2. Contact a local senator or member of the House of Representatives about his or her involvement in national educational issues.

3. Investigate the percentage of financial support of local schools received from the federal government.

4. Contact an official of a local school system about the current requirements and guidelines of the federal government for compliance with the demands of federal legislation.

5. Investigate the policies of a local school system with regard to compliance with the "Buckley Amendment."

Suggested Readings and Works Cited in Chapter

Lapati, Americo. *Education and the Federal Government.* New York: Mason/Charter, 1975.

This is an important guide to federal involvement in education. It discusses all the major federal education legislation and Supreme Court decisions.

Orfield, Gary. *The Reconstruction of Southern Education: The Schools and the 1964 Civil Rights Act.* New York: Wiley-Interscience, 1969.

A study of the power of federal legislation to change American education.

"The Problem of Poverty in America." *The Annual Report of the Council of Economic Advisers.* Washington, D.C.: Government Printing Office, 1964.

This influential report provided the ideological justification for the War on Poverty of the 1960s.

Spring, Joel. *The Sorting Machine: National Educational Policy Since 1945*. New York: David McKay, 1976.

A history of the development of federal educational policy including the new curricula, response to the civil rights movement, the War on Poverty, and the attempt to achieve equality of educational opportunity.

Summerfield, Harry. *Power and Process: The Formulation and Limits of Federal Educational Policy*. Berkeley, Calif.: McCutchan, 1974.

The major section of the book is devoted to an analysis of federal education policy. Separate essays in the book deal with the methods of funding and a case study of Congressman John Brademas.

Thomas, Norman. *Education in National Politics*. New York: David McKay, 1975.

A good study of the educational policy process in the federal government.

8

TEACHERS' ORGANIZATIONS AS INTEREST GROUPS

INTEREST GROUPS IN AMERICAN EDUCATION HAVE HAD IMPORTANT lobbying functions at state and national levels in terms of being sources of information and initiators of educational proposals. Programs appearing in educational legislation usually originate in the work of these educational interest groups. In addition, some interest groups attempt to influence legislation by providing political support for particular legislative candidates. The campaign of John Brademas discussed in the last chapter is an example of this type of activity. Some educational groups, particularly private foundations, also provide money for educational research and programs that often become sources of innovative ideas in education. The ability of these private foundations to determine what type of programs and research to support sometimes gives them powerful influence over educational policy.

Other private groups influence educational policy by the very nature of their activity. Educational Testing Service indirectly controls the admissions policies of many institutions of higher education through the administration of tests such as the Scholastic Aptitude Test and the College Entrance Examination Board. Educational Testing Service has developed a further major gatekeeping function through the administration of entrance examinations to many professional and graduate schools. Independent agencies that accredit secondary schools and institutions of higher education directly affect the curriculum and organization of those schools through their particular standards for accreditation.

The interest groups to be discussed in this chapter are the two largest teachers' organizations, National Education Association (NEA) and the American Federation of Teachers (AFT). The major difference between these two groups is the AFT's affiliation with an organized labor group, the AFL–CIO. The NEA claims that its strength is in its size and independence from organized labor. The *NEA Handbook 1975–76* listed its total membership at 1,733,415, while the September 1976 issue of the AFT publication *American Teacher* gave its membership as 470,491. It is in terms of its larger membership and professionalism that the NEA claims its superior ability to represent American teachers. On the other hand, the AFT claims that its affiliation with organized labor provides its members with a broad base of support in terms of people in the labor movement and the financial resources of organized labor.

The AFT's affiliation with organized labor has contributed to its image as the more militant of the two organizations. Today, some observers say that there is little difference between the two organizations. For instance, the AFT, taking its cue from organized labor, pioneered in the use of the strike and collective-bargaining techniques as ways of improving education and protecting teachers. During the 1960s, however, the NEA began to use similar tactics; and in the 1970s it became associated with the Coalition of American Public Employees (CAPE), which represents roughly four million public employees. Currently, the major objective of CAPE is to achieve collective-bargaining legislation for all public employees. Essentially in the 1970s the NEA became an organized professional union, but one without affiliation with the AFL–CIO.

Even though the NEA has become a public employee union, there is still a tendency for the AFT to place educational issues in a broader economic context than the NEA. For instance, the head of the AFT, Albert Shanker, stated in an article "Teachers in Politics" in the September 1976 issue of the *American Teacher*, "Not only is labor the most powerful ally the schools have, but teachers now know that unless we are in the labor movement helping to bring about full employment in the private sector, there can be no prosperity for the public sector either." This statement reflects the mutually supportive role between the AFT and AFL–CIO and the AFT's dedication to helping both the American worker and the schools. A clear understanding of these differences can be gained by comparing the history and goals of the two groups.

The National Education Association (NEA)

The NEA was formed in 1857 as part of an attempt to bring together a variety of educational associations that had developed in the United States. The original letter calling for the first meeting stated, "The eminent success which has attended the establishment and operations of the several teachers' associations in the state is the source of mutual congratulations among all friends of popular education." The letter went on to state the goal of nationalizing the effort of state associations: "Believing that what has been accomplished for the states by state associations may be done for the whole country by a National Association, we, the undersigned, invite our fellow-teachers throughout the United States to assemble in Philadelphia. . . ."

The 1857 meeting in Philadelphia gave birth to an organization that in the nineteenth and early twentieth centuries had major influence over the shaping of American schools and contributed to the nationalizing of the American school system. From the platform of its conventions and the work of its committees came curriculum proposals and policy statements that were adopted from coast to coast. Until the 1960s the work of the NEA tended to be dominated by school superintendents, college professors, and administrators. These educational leaders would take the proposals of the NEA back to their local communities for discussion and possible adoption. The NEA thus had an important nationalizing function through the sharing of information between school leaders from different parts of the country and through its recommendations and proposals.

Examples of the work of the NEA include its major role in the shaping of the modern high school. In 1892 the NEA formed the Committee of Ten on Secondary School Studies under the leadership of Charles Eliot, the president of Harvard University. The Committee of Ten appointed nine subcommittees with a total membership of one hundred to determine the future of the American high school. The membership of these committees reflected the domination of the organization by school administrators and representatives of higher education: fifty-three were college presidents or professors, twenty-three were headmasters of private schools, and the rest were superintendents and representatives from teacher-training institutions. The work of the Committee of Ten set the stage for the creation in 1913 of the NEA Commission on the Reorganization of Secondary Education, which issued its epoch-making report on *Cardinal Principles of Sec-*

ondary Education in 1918. This report urged the creation of comprehensive high schools offering a variety of curriculums, as opposed to the establishment of separate high schools offering single curriculums such as college preparatory, vocational, and commercial. It was this report that became the major formative document of the modern high school.

The NEA also had a major influence on the standardization of teacher training in the United States. The Normal Department of the NEA began surveying the status of institutions for teacher education in 1886, and debates began within the organization about the nature of teacher education. The official historian of the NEA, Edgar B. Wesley, stated in his *NEA: The First Hundred Years*: "By 1925 the training of teachers was rather systematically standardized." The work of the Normal Department of the NEA can claim a large share of the credit for this standardization.

NEA conventions and meetings also became a central arena for the discussion of curriculum changes in elementary and secondary schools. During the 1920s and 1930s large numbers of surveys, studies, yearbooks, and articles were issued. In 1924 the Department of Superintendence began issuing what were to be successive yearbooks on various aspects of the curriculum at various grade levels. In 1943 the Society for Curriculum Study merged with the NEA Department of Supervisors and Directors of Instruction to form an enlarged department called the Association for Supervision and Curriculum Development (ASCD). ASCD is still recognized as the major professional organization for the discussion of curriculum issues.

After the passage of the National Defense Education Act in 1958, the NEA's leadership role in the determination of national educational policy was greatly reduced as the federal government became the central focus for national policy. As we shall see later in the chapter, during the 1960s and 1970s the NEA has become an organization whose central focus is teacher welfare and government lobbying. This shift was a result of several developments: the emergence of the leadership role of the federal government, demands within the NEA for more emphasis on teacher welfare, greater democratic control of the organization, and the success of the AFT in winning collective bargaining for its members.

To appreciate these changes in the role of the NEA, one must understand some of the traditional criticisms of the organization. No one has denied the important leadership role of the NEA, but the organization has been attacked in previous years for its close association with the American Legion, its early bias against women, its lack of concern about teacher welfare, and its control by educational elites. Except for the NEA's continued association with the American Legion, these other problems are no longer major issues within the NEA. Understanding how these problem issues have evolved in the NEA helps in understanding the difference between the NEA and the AFT.

The NEA and the American Legion formed an alliance in 1921 around mutual interests in the Americanization of aliens and the teaching of history, citizenship, and patriotism. American Legion speakers began to appear on programs at NEA conventions, and both organizations sponsored teaching booklets and American Education Week. The right-wing bias of the American Legion and its concern about subversion of America by left-wing radicals resulted in conflict between the two organizations in the 1950s. In 1952 an article titled "Your Child Is Their Target" appeared in the June issue of the *American Legion Magazine*. The article claimed that a subversive movement had existed in the teaching profession for thirty years. Members of the NEA denounced the article as containing misinformation and being hostile to teachers and the schools. Some members of the NEA tried to get a resolution passed by the annual convention denouncing the American Legion. When the resolution failed, the next step by the NEA was to submit an answering article for publication in the *American Legion Magazine*. The Legion refused to publish the article but did agree to prepare a second article on the subject and submit it to the NEA for criticisms. This major confrontation between the two organizations did not result in the breakdown of their association. The American Legion and the NEA have continued to sponsor American Education Week.

An early criticism of the NEA concerned the second-class role of women within the organization. The original 1857 constitution of the NEA limited membership to "gentlemen." This wording was not changed until 1866, when women within the organization demanded that "gentlemen" be changed to "person." After 1866 women began to attain some offices within the organization, but never in proportion to their numbers within the profession. Although after the Civil War women outnumbered men in the teaching profession, men outnumbered women in terms of administrative positions and offices held in organizations such as the NEA. Not until 1910 was a woman, Ella Flagg Young, elected NEA president. Even though Young had been a teacher, principal, district superintendent, professor of education, and superintendent of the Chicago schools, it still required a great deal of struggle by her supporters to get her elected as president of the organization. After Young's election, a struggle continued within the organization for equal representation for women; it was resolved in 1917 with the beginning of a tradition of alternating between men and women in elections to the presidency.

The traditional image of the NEA as an organization dominated by school administrators and college professors is a product of its early organization. As mentioned, these groups did dominate the policy-making committees and offices within the organization. This situation began to change in the early part of the twentieth century as women more actively sought offices within the organization. Until 1921, control of the NEA was in the hands of the business meeting of members. What this did was to create a situation of local control, in which those in attendance at the national conventions composed the business meeting of members. When Ella Flagg Young won the presidency of the organization in 1910 in Boston, it was because numbers of women came for the sole purpose of voting for her. Again in 1912 large groups of women attended the convention in an effort to elect Grace Strachan. In reaction to the growing militancy of women and the ability of groups to capture national meetings, it was proposed that the NEA move to representative control. Under the representative plan, individuals would attend and vote at conventions as elected representatives of local and state education associations. When this organizational plan was adopted by the NEA in 1921, it was an attempt to curb the growing power of women and classroom teachers as against the traditional leaders of the NEA, but at the same time it reduced the power of national leadership by giving power to local and state groups to elect representatives.

The current organization and control of the NEA reflects the increased power gained by classroom teachers in the twentieth century, particularly during the militant years of the 1960s. According to the *NEA Handbook 1975–76*, the Representative Assembly consists of some nine thousand delegates of state and local affiliates, as well as representatives of retired teachers, Student NEA, and school nurses. The Representative Assembly is the primary legislative and policy-making body of the organization. The Board of Directors consists of one director from each state affiliate, plus an additional director for each twenty thousand active NEA members within that state affiliate.

The democratization of control of the NEA is reflected in the 1975–76 membership of the Board of Directors. Of the 116 members of the Board of Directors from state affiliates, 104 were classroom teachers, 8 were administrators, 1 was a school psychologist, 1 was a director of a school materials center, 1 was a school social worker, and 1 was a coordinator of community relations. All members of the Executive Committee—besides the full-time positions of president, vice-president, and secretary-treasurer—were also classroom teachers. The NEA can no longer be accused of being an organization dominated by administrators and college professors.

One of the things that accompanied the development of teacher control of the NEA was its increased concern about teacher welfare. It should be remembered that the NEA was originally organized to provide a national platform for developing ideas in education and not to concern itself with teacher welfare items such as salaries, working conditions, and rights. It was not until 1905 that the NEA conducted its first survey of teachers' salaries, and only in the 1920s did it begin advocating higher salaries and tenure laws. Teacher tenure became a major issue in the 1920s when, under the pressure of the Red Scare of the early years of that decade, many teachers lost their jobs because of their political beliefs. Tenure was considered a means of protecting the freedom of speech of teachers.

Wesley's *NEA: The First Hundred Years*, claims that the NEA's advocacy of teacher welfare resulted over the years in major improvements for teachers and administrators. The term "claim" is used because the NEA did not use any direct pressure such as the strike or collective bargaining before the 1960s. Whether the improvements were actually the result of the advocacy of the NEA is therefore difficult to determine. What the NEA claims to have achieved was the increase in average salaries of classroom teachers, the establishment of tenure laws in thirty-two states, and the establishment of teacher retirement plans. It is probably true that the lobbying activities of the state affiliates did contribute to the passage of both tenure and retirement laws.

In 1962, the activities of the NEA underwent a dramatic transformation when it launched a program for collective negotiations. This meant that local affiliates would attempt to achieve collective-bargaining agreements with local boards of education. This development completely changed the nature of local organizations and required a rewriting of local constitutions to include collective bargaining. Up to this point in time many local education associations had been controlled by the local administrators, who used the local organizations to convey policies determined by the board and administration. Collective bargaining reversed this situation and turned the local affiliates into organizations that told boards and administrators what teachers themselves wanted.

The NEA's early approach to collective bargaining differed from that of the union-oriented AFT, which had pioneered collective bargaining in education. The NEA claimed it was involved in professional negotiating and not in union collective bargaining. Professional negotiation, according to the NEA, would remove negotiation procedures from labor precedents and laws and would resort to state educational associations, rather than those of labor, to mediate or resolve conflicts that could not be settled locally.

All pretense of the NEA not being a union ended in the 1970s, when the NEA joined the Coalition of American Public Employees (CAPE). CAPE is a nonprofit corporation composed of the National Education Association; American Federation of State, County, and Municipal Employees, AFL–CIO; National Treasury Employees Union; Physicians National Housestaff Association; and American Nurses Association. As mentioned, these organizations represent about four million public employees. The stated purpose of CAPE "is to provide a means of marshalling and coordinating the legislative, legal, financial, and public relations resources of the member organizations in matters of common concern." The most important of these matters "is supporting legislation to provide collective bargaining rights to all public employees, including teachers."

In 1975–76 teacher welfare through collective bargaining was one of six major goals of the NEA. The statement of goals of the NEA argued that "the most effective vehicle to guarantee the economic and professional security of teachers within the capability of NEA is the collective bargaining process." The NEA stated that its objectives were the passage of federal collective-bargaining legislation, exclusive bargaining recognition for each local affiliate, and the development of collective-bargaining support systems. To support the collective-bargaining process the NEA called for a coordination of national bargaining priorities and a feasibility study for a nationwide computer system for processing an immediate retrieval of salary information, negotiated benefits, school finance data, and school budget analysis. If the NEA is successful in establishing such a computer system, it might contribute to the national standardization of teachers' salaries as computer information about salaries is used in local negotiations.

The next two of the other six goal areas of the NEA were related to teacher welfare issues. One such goal was the maintenance of an independent, united teaching organization as a means of achieving the objectives of the organization. In this case, "independent" means not being part of the AFL–CIO. The NEA hoped to achieve the goal of a strong organization by increasing its membership, organizing higher education bargaining units, and strengthening local and state affiliates through the training of leadership and staff. Achieving these objectives would strengthen the organization in the collective-bargaining process.

The other goal relating to teacher welfare and the general welfare of public education was for increased legislative support for education. The NEA had four specific objectives in this area, all of which were part of its attempt to increase its lobbying activities and its involvement in political activities. The first objective was to secure increased federal aid for current education programs and to progress toward one-third federal aid for education. The second objective was increased lobbying in Congress to ensure the passage of federal collective bargaining and other NEA-supported legislation and working with federal agencies "to ensure that NEA's interests are promoted as legislation and regulations are drafted."

The third and fourth objectives within this goal of greater legislative support were organizing members to elect pro-education officials at the federal level and coordinating plans for possible NEA endorsement of a presidential candidate. The latter objective became a reality when the NEA endorsed Jimmy Carter as a candidate in 1976. In terms of supporting what it calls "pro-education" candidates, the NEA claimed that of the 310 congressional candidates endorsed by the NEA in 1974, 81 percent were elected. The methods used by the NEA to support candidates include first identifying pro-education candidates by keeping a tally of their voting records in Congress and then distributing information about how candidates voted, maintaining state political-action committees, and maintaining liaison with major political parties to influence their actions with regard to educational issues.

In its discussion of increased lobbying in Congress, the NEA clearly outlined its lobbying tactics. As discussed in the previous chapter, these lobbying tactics include supplying legislators with information, maintaining personal contact with representatives and senators, and influencing the work of government educational agencies. Below is a clear description of these tactics quoted from pages 40 and 41 of the *NEA Handbook 1975–76*.

NEA works to persuade Members of Congress to support the Association's positions. NEA provides statistical information and statements of Association policy, drafts legislation, works with Congressional Committees as legislation is prepared for floor action, presents testimony, and maintains continuous contact with key legislators.

NEA coordinates the efforts of "Congressional contact teams," composed of NEA members who maintain direct, personal contact with their Representatives and Senators, to press for support on vital issues as they arise in Congress, and to apply back-home constituent pressure on national legislators.

NEA also influences legislation through regular consultation with federal agencies which administer programs. Once a law is passed, NEA assumes a "watchdog" role, working with agency personnel responsible for preparing regulations and guidelines and allocating funds. Further, NEA consults with the federal agencies prior to the development of administration policy and legislative proposals.

Another goal designed to strengthen the position of teachers was professional excellence, which means teachers should have major influence over preparation and licensing, in-service education, and the curriculum or what they teach. This goal is part of the traditional belief that a profession should have control over its own licensing and practices. It means that teachers would become central to the decision-making process. In the words of the NEA statement of goals for 1975–76, "Basic to the program for professional excellence is a national effort to ensure that teachers are central to the decision-making process as it relates to instruction and professional development."

The remaining two goals of the NEA in 1975–76 addressed more general social and educational problems. One of these remaining goals was to ensure human and civil rights in education. The NEA objectives in achieving this goal included rights enforcement, minority rights, desegregation and integration, antiracism and antisexism, and student rights and teacher responsibility. The rights-enforcement program involved protection and extension of the rights of teachers through support of a legal defense fund. Increased involvement by minority groups in the NEA was to be accomplished by assisting affiliates in developing programs and methods of attracting minority groups. The NEA also pledged to provide technical aid to help teachers in districts preparing to implement desegregation plans. The antiracism, antisexism, and student rights objectives were to be achieved through training programs and assistance provided to teachers.

The final NEA goal in 1975–76 was leadership in solving social problems. The limited objectives of this goal reflected NEA's traditional tendency to concentrate directly on educational issues and not become involved in broader social issues. For instance, one of AFT's goals has been ending unemployment and improving the economy. On the other hand, the NEA objectives with respect to achieving leadership in social problems involved only a needs assessment, affirmative action, and migrant education. The needs assessment was to determine the social concerns of the membership of the NEA and propose activities to deal with those concerns. Affirmative action involved training local affiliates to improve and increase minority involvement and hiring. The support of migrant education probably represented the boldest objective. It involved the development of educational programs for minority children and support of the negotiation rights of migrant workers.

The NEA's support of collective bargaining and political candidates represents a major break with its origins in the nineteenth century and reflects its current primary emphasis on teacher welfare. Its lobbying activities in Congress and in educational agencies continue to give it some influence over national educational policy but not the commanding authority it had in the late nineteenth and early twentieth century. The 1975–76 limitation of its general social objectives to internal needs assessment, affirmative action, and migrant education reflects the continued narrowness of NEA's social concerns and essential conservativeness of the organization. On the other hand, it can be argued that its limited social objectives are in keeping with its goal of maintaining a strong, united and independent teachers' organization, whose primary purpose is the welfare of teachers and American public schools.

The American Federation of Teachers (AFT)

Unlike the NEA's origins as a national policy-making organization, the American Federation of Teachers (AFT) began in the struggle by female grade school teachers for an adequate pension law in the state of Illinois. The first union local, the Chicago Teachers Federation, was formed in 1897 under the leadership of Catherine Goggin and Margaret Haley. Its early fights centered around pensions and teacher salaries, with its success in winning salary increases resulting in its membership increasing to twenty-five hundred by the end of its first year. In 1902, with the urging of famous social settlement reformer Jane Addams, the Chicago Teachers Federation joined the

Chicago Federation of Labor, which placed them under the broad umbrella of the American Federation of Labor.

From its beginnings the AFT placed teacher welfare issues and improving public education in the more general context of the labor movement in the United States. In an interview titled "The School-Teacher Unionized" in the November 1905 issue of the *Educational Review*, Margaret Haley declared, "We expect by affiliation with labor to arouse the workers and the whole people, thru the workers, to the dangers confronting the public schools from the same interests and tendencies that are undermining the foundations of our democratic republic." Those "same interests" referred to in Haley's speech were big business organizations, with whom Haley felt both labor and educators were struggling. The early union movement believed there was unity in the educator's struggle with big business to gain more financial support for the schools and labor's struggle with the same interests to win collective-bargaining rights. Haley went on to state, "It is necessary to make labor a constructive force in society, or it will be a destructive force. If the educational question could be understood by the labor men, and the labor question by the educators, both soon would see they are working to the same end, and should work together."

Margaret Haley's comments during the interview reflected ideas about what were to be mutually supportive roles between teachers and organized labor. On the one hand, teachers were to work for the interests of workers by fighting for better schools and working to remove antilabor material from the classroom. In other words, teachers would fight to provide the best education for workers' children. Organized labor, on the other hand, would provide the resources of its organization to support the teachers' struggle for improved working conditions and greater financial support for the schools. In addition, the type of education received by children in the schools would provide children with the economic and political knowledge needed to continue the work of the union movement, and teachers could also share their knowledge with the adult members of the labor movement. Teachers would also increase their political and economic knowledge through their association with the labor movement.

The early work of the Chicago Teachers Federation reflected its commitment to these ideals. It is credited with being an important force behind the passage in 1903 of the Illinois Child Labor Law. During the same period Margaret Haley found that one of the serious financial handicaps of the Chicago school district was caused by the failure of three large corporations to pay their taxes. With the cooperation of a former Illinois governor, John Altgeld, the Federation entered into litigation against People's Gas, Light and Coke Company, the Chicago Telephone Company, and Edison Electric Light Company and successfully forced these corporations to pay $249,554 in taxes due to the Board of Education.

Another of the early goals of the teachers' union was increased participation of teachers in the decision making of local school districts. Support for this issue came from Ella Flagg Young, who was appointed superintendent of Chicago's schools in 1909. She instituted a system of teachers' councils that allowed the teachers to assist in formulating educational policy. Ella Flagg Young's support of the early efforts by teachers for more democratic control of the schools is one reason why Margaret Haley provided support for her election to the presidency of the NEA. It should be noted that not until the 1920s did the AFT consider itself a rival of the NEA. During these early years it viewed itself as something of a radical segment of the NEA.

Concern about teacher participation in the control of the schools was one of the major elements in the organization of a teachers' union in New York City in 1912. The statement calling for the organization of teachers in New York declared: "Teachers should have a voice and a vote in the determination of educational policies. . . . We advocate the adoption of a plan that will permit all the teachers to have a share in the administration of the affairs of their own schools." It should be pointed out that the early demands by teachers' unions did not involve collective-bargaining rights but administrative rearrangements that would have allowed for greater teacher participation.

In December 1912 the newly established magazine of the union movement, the *American Teacher*, issued a statement of beliefs of the growing union movement in education. First, the statement argued that the improvement of American education depended on arousing teachers to realize that "their professional and social standing is far too low to enable them to produce effective results in teaching." Second, it was necessary for teachers to study the relation of education "to social progress, and to understand some of the important social and economic movements going on in the present-day world." Third, it was believed that teachers could use their experience in teaching to adjust education to the needs of modern living. Fourth, in one of the earliest declarations for the end of sexism in education, the statement called for high-quality teaching "without sex-antagonism."

In 1915 union locals in Chicago and Gary, Indiana, met and

officially formed the American Federation of Teachers. In 1916 this group, along with locals from New York, Pennsylvania, Oklahoma, and Washington, D.C., were accepted into the American Federation of Labor (AFL) as the American Federation of Teachers. At the presentation ceremony, the head of the AFL, Samuel Gompers, welcomed the AFT "to the fold and the bond of unity and fraternity of the organized labor movement of our Republic. We earnestly hope . . . that it may . . . give and receive mutual sympathy and support which can be properly exerted for the betterment of all who toil and give service—aye, for all humanity."

The platform of the newly organized AFT called for improved teacher welfare and security through a program of tenure, increased salaries, teacher exchange programs, and sabbatical leave plans. In addition, the AFT opposed overcrowding in the schools and called for a decrease in class size. The platform condemned the movement at that time toward compulsory military service. In terms of educational programs, the AFT called for special programs for the gifted child and the development of an experimental pedagogy and expressed hopes for a scientific basis for education. This platform remained relatively unchanged between 1916 and 1929.

The AFT did not grow at a rapid rate; in fact, it proved very difficult during the 1920s to organize new locals. One of the more interesting experiments of the AFT during the 1920s was the establishment of the Brookwood Labor College and the Manumit school for workers' children. Both were established in reaction to what was believed to be the conservative economic and political philosophies of American colleges and public schools. There was a particular concern about the domination by big business and professionals of boards of education and boards of trustees of colleges. The Manumit school was an experiment to see if the labor movement could establish its own system of schooling as an alternative to the public schools. The Manumit school was operated as an industrial democracy with students exercising control through democratically operated meetings. The attempt to develop Brookwood and Manumit as an alternative system of education for the labor movement ended in the later part of the 1920s when the AFL charged Brookwood with Communist leanings and expelled the school from the federation.

Activity within the AFT increased rapidly during the depression years of the 1930s with its cutbacks in teacher salaries and increased support for the public schools. At its annual convention in 1931, the AFT called for a replacement of the property tax with a graduated income tax, the establishment of federal unemployment compensation, government planning of public works, and a shorter workweek. In 1933 twenty-eight thousand teachers and their sympathizers marched through the streets of Chicago to protest being paid in script. The march tied up traffic in the downtown area for several hours while groups of teachers attacked local banks. It should be noted that none of the activities of the AFT up to this point in time involved the use of the strike or the development of a collective-bargaining agreement with a school system.

The major educational philosophy to dominate the AFT during the 1930s was called "social reconstructionism." Social reconstructionism called upon American education to create a new social order that would not allow for the occurrence of depressions such as that facing the 1930s. This new social order was to replace economic competition with cooperative and national economic planning. Teachers, through the AFT, were to use the schools as a means of spreading social reconstructionism. It was hoped that in this manner, teachers would be at the vanguard of social change.

The social reconstructionist philosophy of the AFT in the 1930s had little impact on the schools because teachers could not exercise any organizational control over local school systems. This situation began to change in 1944 when the American Federation of Teachers local of Cicero, Illinois, signed the first collective-bargaining contract with a board of education. The form of the contract was like a regular labor-union contract. It recognized the local as the sole bargaining agent of the teachers and listed pay schedules and grievance procedures. At the annual convention of the AFT in 1946 a committee was assigned to study collective bargaining and its application to school management. In addition, material was to be collected from trade unions on the education of shop stewards and union practices. With the introduction of collective bargaining, the AFT entered a new stage in its development.

The new involvement of the AFT in collective bargaining led naturally to the question of teacher strikes. Since its founding, the AFT had had a no-strike policy. In 1946, the use of the strike as a means of supporting teachers' demands became a major issue at the annual convention. Those supporting the use of the strike argued it was the only means available to arouse an apathetic citizenry to the problems in American education. It was also the only meaningful leverage teachers had against local school systems. Those AFT members who favored retention of the no-strike policy argued that teachers were in a public service profession and that work stoppage was a violation of public trust. In addition, it was argued that a strike deprived children of an education and was counter to the democratic ideal of a child's right to an education.

The AFT maintained its no-strike policy in the face of growing militancy by individual locals. In 1947 the Buffalo Teachers Federation declared a strike for higher salaries. The strike was considered at the time the worst teacher work stoppage in the history of the country. Other local unions supported the strikers, with coal drivers delivering only enough fuel to the schools to keep the pipes from freezing. The Buffalo strike was important because it served as a model for action by other teachers around the country. School superintendents, school board associations, and state superintendents of education condemned these actions by local teachers. The national AFT maintained its no-strike policy and adopted a posture of aid and comfort but not official sanction. As William Edward Eaton states in his *The American Federation of Teachers, 1916–1961*, "Even with a no-strike policy, the AFT had emerged as the leader in teacher work stoppages."

The event that sparked the rapid growth of teacher militancy in the 1960s, and contributed to the NEA's rapid acceptance of collective bargaining, was the formation of the New York City local of the AFT, the United Federation of Teachers (UFT). The formation of the UFT provided the opportunity for the rapid rise to prominence of Albert Shanker, who first served as the local's secretary and later as president of the organization. In the 1970s, Albert Shanker was to become president of the national AFT.

In the late 1950s, the AFT decided to concentrate on New York City and to provide special funds for organizing. After the organization of the UFT in 1960, there was a vote for a strike over a dues check-off plan, the conducting of a collective-bargaining election, sick pay for substitutes, fifty-minute lunch periods for teachers, and changes in the salary schedules. On November 7, 1960, the UFT officially went on strike against the New York City school system. The union declared the strike effective when 15,000 of the city's 39,000 teachers did not report to school and 7,500 teachers joined picket lines around the schools. In the spring of 1961, the UFT won a collective-bargaining agreement with the school system and became one of the largest and most influential locals within the AFT.

During the 1960s teachers increasingly accepted the idea of collective bargaining and the use of the strike. This was reflected in the rapid growth of membership in the AFT. In 1966 the membership of the AFT was 125,421. By 1976 the membership had increased almost fourfold to 470,491. This increased membership plus the increased militancy of the NEA heralded a new era in the relationship between American teachers' organizations and the managers of American education. With the coming of age of the strike and collective bargaining, teachers in the NEA and AFT proved themselves willing to fight for their own welfare and the welfare of American public schools.

In 1974, Albert Shanker, the leader of the New York UFT, became president of the AFT. Shanker's rise to power represented not only the strength of the New York local within the AFT, but also a certain acceptance of Shanker's concepts of what should be the goals of the teachers' union. Prominent among Shanker's goals for American education is what he calls "Educare." Educare and the other goals of the AFT represent concerns that go beyond salaries and working conditions to include shaping the basic structure of American education. The goals, current operation of the union, membership, and condition of the AFT are published in every September issue of the *American Teacher*. Any person interested in finding out about the current status of the union is advised to look at the most recent September issue. In the September 1976 issue the first goal listed was Albert Shanker's proposed Educare program, designed to establish lifelong learning opportunities and teacher internships, along with early childhood education.

Educare was made a national priority of the AFT at its 1975 national convention. As officially explained by the AFT, Educare's lifelong education program is based on the idea that education should not be limited to one period of life. The goal of Educare is to provide cradle-to-grave educational opportunities. This means expanded pre-school programs and increased support for elementary and secondary schools. In addition, the AFT has asked the federal government to fund a broad-scope program which would include: "(a) continued and increased support for higher education and implementation of open admission and free or low tuitions; (b) continued and increased support for adult and continuing education to be available through public and non-profit organizations." Among the expanded education services called for by the AFT are programs for "school dropouts; for senior citizens; for those in need of career training and retraining; for people undergoing long-term institutionalization in hospitals, nursing homes, and prisons; for workers who want to take a sabbatical to improve their skills; and for enrichment programs to pursue self-growth interests."

In 1976 the AFT Higher Education Commission claimed that the identified potential adult learning population over age twenty-five in the United States was 76 million persons. These people, it was suggested, could be served by existing colleges and Lifelong Learning Resource Centers. In addition to seeking increased government support, the AFT states it would be working through state and local affiliates to achieve and maintain lower and free tuitions in colleges and universities.

Another Educare component, teacher internships, is directed to the problem of a surplus of teachers. The AFT proposed internships "to aid in reducing the influx of new teacher graduates who displace more experienced teachers because of lower salary demands or who find themselves among the long lists of unemployed." The idea of teacher internships would thus ease the problem of teacher unemployment and at the same time provide increased training for new teachers. Teacher internships would be served in teacher-controlled teacher centers designed in cooperation with colleges of education.

One of the major concerns of the AFT with regard to the early childhood education component of the Educare program was who should administer the funds. The AFT called for a change in the wording of proposed federal legislation to designate the public schools as the prime sponsors of early childhood education. The use of the public schools as the prime sponsors was opposed, however, by the Day Care and Child Development Council of America and the Children's Defense Funds. From the point of view of these organizations, early childhood education should be kept out of the hands of public school administrators and personnel. Wanting the public schools to have the first option to administer early childhood programs, the AFT proposed that schools should either provide services themselves or contract to do so with other agencies. The AFT's position was designed to protect the interests of public schools, which represented the basis of their membership.

One of the major, and traditional, goals of the AFT is increased financial support to the public schools. In 1976 the AFT supported two major ways of making more money available to the public schools. One area of support was the federalization of welfare. What this meant was that the federal government would assume full cost of welfare payments, thus freeing local and state money for support of the public schools. The 1976 resolution of the AFT stated: "If the Federal Government assumed responsibility for welfare costs, considerable state and local funding would be freed up for use in the schools."

The other area of support was full employment and increased productivity of the private sector. The reasoning of the AFT was that with high unemployment reducing state and local tax revenues, there was a decreasing amount of funds to maintain and improve the schools and pay teachers' salaries. The AFT therefore supported the AFL–CIO's attempts to gain full-employment legislation in Congress. In addition, the AFT supported increased federal aid to local schools. The 1976 AFT's statement of goals declared, "While national economic planning offers the only lasting solution to the twin evils of unemployment and inflation, the crumbling economies of cities and school districts cry out for immediate federal help."

One of the major concerns of the AFT in the 1970s was the rapid changes taking place in the area of school finance and the impact of those changes on collective bargaining. During the 1970s, because of court cases against the use of local property taxes to support education, many states were converting their school finance systems to either full state funding of schools or some method of combining local and state revenues to equalize spending between school districts. Any changes in the method of funding could have a direct impact on collective bargaining because the source of money can determine the bargaining agent. For instance, if the state assumed the burden of full support of the schools, would this mean that teachers would have to enter into collective-bargaining agreements with the state and not with the local school district? To find out the answer to these types of questions, the AFT established a special task force in 1974 to study the relationship between different forms of school financing and collective bargaining.

While all the major goals of the AFT are linked to either general school policy issues or to the national economy, they are all designed to protect and improve teachers' salaries and welfare and to increase teacher control of education. The proposed Educare programs are designed to expand the market for teaching skills from the cradle to the grave. This would, of course, mean a larger union as well as a means of dealing with the surplus of teachers. Concern about methods of school financing and public school control of early childhood education are related to methods of collective bargaining and, in the case of early childhood education, assuring an easy method for including early childhood educators in local union groups. The concern about welfare and unemployment is directly related to assuring enough money for improving public schools and increasing teachers' salaries.

AFT goals when compared to those of the NEA appear to be broader and more inclusive. Part of the reason for this is AFT's affiliation with the AFL–CIO and the relatively small size of the AFT when compared to the membership of the NEA. The size and diversity of the NEA makes it difficult for that organization to achieve a consensus about political and economic issues. At present it is hard to imagine the NEA stating, as the AFT did, that national economic planning is the only solution to unemployment. When a teacher joins the AFT, that teacher is making a commitment to support the goals of the American labor movement. A political and social commitment of this type is not asked of the teacher joining the NEA. The AFT claims its strength grows out of its association with the American labor movement. The NEA claims its strength is a product of its size and union independence.

The Future of Teachers' Organizations

During the early 1970s negotiations were begun between the NEA and AFT about a possible merger of the two organizations. The one issue that has consistently hindered merger attempts has been the AFT's affiliation with the AFL–CIO. The NEA refuses to combine with the AFT as long as it is part of the AFL–CIO, and the AFT refuses to break its ties with organized labor. In New York the state education association and the union did unite into a single teachers' organization, but the continued affiliation of the two groups was in doubt by the middle of the 1970s. If the two groups were to merge nationally and continue their support for particular political candidates, the combined organizations would become a powerful force in American political life.

From the point of view of the 1970s it appeared that both the NEA and the AFT would continue to increase their memberships and to struggle for stronger and more inclusive collective-bargaining agreements. Major factors contributing to this continued trend are low teacher salaries and the financial difficulties of local school systems. The financial problems of American education not only affect salaries but also teaching conditions. Many school districts have been forced because of lack of money to increase class sizes. As teachers witness these changes and other cutbacks in education, they often seek some means of stopping the continued deterioration of the public schools. Collective bargaining is one method teachers have for pressuring school systems into maintaining and improving the quality of American education.

Another factor contributes to the rapid growth of teacher unionism and that is the growing sense of powerlessness among public-service employees. One of the main demands of the NEA and AFT is greater teacher control and participation in the decision-making process of local school systems. This desire for greater control is also characteristic of other areas of growing professional unionism, such as nurses and medical technicians. Stanley Aronowitz argues in his book *False Promises* that this is the result of a growing sense of powerlessness among professional groups. For teachers this sense of powerlessness is caused by more and more of the daily classroom decisions being made by curriculum specialists and by programmed and pre-packaged learning materials. In addition, the hierarchical control within school systems leaves many teachers with only the option of teacher unionism as a means of making sure they are not only listened to, but also have some meaningful impact on school policies.

The major problem with teacher unionism in terms of traditional American thought is that it might increase teacher control of school policy at the expense of parental control of education. In some ways this might be a meaningless issue, since in the last several chapters we have discovered very little parent control of the public schools. But if the NEA and AFT were to merge and increase their political activity and lobbying, they could gain major control over American public education. This would represent the triumph of professional control over popular and local control of the schools.

EXERCISES

1. Contact local members of the AFT and NEA about current goals and issues in local school districts. Inquire about the lobbying activities of both organizations at the state and national level. If possible, organize a class debate between representatives of both organizations.

2. In a group discussion or essay discuss the current goals of the AFT and NEA. These goals can be found in the current *NEA Handbook* and the most recent September issue of the AFT's *American Teacher*.

3. Contact local members of boards of education about their views with regard to collective bargaining with the NEA and AFT. Ask what they think should be the role of teachers' organizations in American education.

Suggested Readings and Works Cited in Chapter

The best sources of current information about the NEA and AFT are the *NEA Handbook* and the AFT's *American Teacher*. Also contact local offices of these organizations for more information.

Aronowitz, Stanley. *False Promises: The Shaping of American Working Class Consciousness.* New York: McGraw-Hill, 1973.

An important book for understanding why professionals, including teachers, are rapidly joining the union movement.

Cardinal Principles of Secondary Education. Washington, D.C.: Bureau of Education, 1918.

The major policy statement of the NEA about the goals of the comprehensive high school in the twentieth century. This policy statement had a major impact on shaping the modern high school.

Eaton, William. *The American Federation of Teachers, 1916–1961.* Carbondale, Ill.: Southern Illinois University Press, 1975.

A history of the AFT. Much of the information on the history of the AFT used in this chapter was taken from this study. Quotations from articles by Margaret Haley used in this text were taken from chapter 1 of Eaton's history of the AFT.

Wesley, Edgar. *NEA: The First Hundred Years.* New York: Harper & Brothers, 1957.

The main source of information, besides original sources, about the early years of the NEA. The controversy about the American Legion article is discussed on pages 316–18.

9

OTHER INTEREST GROUPS IN AMERICAN EDUCATION

THE PREVIOUS CHAPTER DEALT WITH THE DEVELOPMENT AND goals of the two major teachers' organizations and their potential impact on the control of American education. This chapter deals with other organizations that have both a direct and indirect influence on educational policy in the United States. It is difficult to measure the influence of particular interest groups and determine with any degree of certainty which group is the most influential. One problem, as we shall see, is the interrelatedness of groups in terms of personnel and mutual support. All groups to be described are part of the complex web of American education.

Private Foundations

Private foundations are established in the United States by possessors of great amounts of wealth as a means of expressing philanthropic interests. Some of the largest foundations include the Ford Foundation, the Rockefeller Foundation, the Lilly Endowment, the W. K. Kellogg Foundation, and the Carnegie Corporation of New York. The very names of the foundations indicate the sources of the large industrial fortunes that went into the establishment of these charitable organizations.

Because of their resources, these organizations have been able to provide large sums of money to support studies, research, and organizations. These foundations have had a major impact on American social policy in the United States. The broad scope and variety of activities sponsored by the foundations has led to their activities being attacked by both the political left and the political right in the United States. Right-wing groups have attacked foundations as instruments of large corporate wealth designed to promote a social policy that works against the interests of smaller industrial groups. In other words, right-wing groups see foundations restricting competition and supporting monopoly control of the marketplace through their funding of particular organizations and policy. In a similar fashion, left-wing political groups have been concerned about the foundations exerting control of American social policy.

The real power of foundations is in their choices of areas in which to spend money. Until the recent expansion of the federal government in the funding of research and social-action projects, the foundations were the main source of funds for these activities in the United States. In many ways the decisions of the boards of directors of these foundations about the type of research, social projects, and organizations to be funded have determined the evolution and direction of scientific and social research, as well as social policy in the United States.

The influence of foundation spending can most clearly be seen in the field of education. Foundations have supported particular projects that have influenced the basic structure of American education. Foundations have also funded research and studies that have had influence over major court decisions related to education and national educational policy decisions. Foundation funds have been used to support particular educational interest groups and thus directly influence the organizational control of American education. All these influences on American education can best be understood by specific examples of the means and types of influence foundations have had over American education.

A good example of how foundation support of particular projects has affected the basic structure of American education is to be seen in the rise of segregated, industrial education for blacks in the South after the Civil War. As Henry Bullock explains in his prize-winning book, *A History of Negro Education in the South*, money from large foundations made possible the implementation of segregated, industrial education designed to train a labor force for the emerging industrial South in the early part of the twentieth century. Money for the support of segregated education came from the Peabody Fund, the General Education Board of the Rockefeller Foundation, the Slater Fund, and the Rosenwald Fund. One of the concerns of this group of philanthropists was the development of a nonimmigrant and nonunion labor force for the new industrial South. It was believed that freed black people could provide this labor pool if given adequate industrial education.

Evaluating the deeds of philanthropy in the South reveals one of the basic dilemmas about the role of private foundations in a democratic society. On the one hand, the power of philanthropic aid can be criticized because it supported a segregationist educational structure and it reflected the self-interest of the donors in providing a controllable industrial work force. On the other hand, there might not have been any large-scale development of schools for blacks in the South if the money had not been given by these large foundations. In other words, the foundations can be praised for providing money that was not available from other sources. In either case, the private foundations had a tremendous influence on the development of segregated education in the South.

Another example of how foundation action resulted in shaping educational policy through particular projects was the Ford Foundation support of the Mobilization for Youth program in the late 1950s. As Peter Marris and Martin Rein describe it in their *Dilemmas of Social Reform*, the Ford Foundation had previously used two approaches in granting aid for city problems. One of these promoted the establishment of metropolitan governments that would reintegrate the central cities with the suburbs. The other promoted urban renewal, which was designed to attract prosperous residents and businesses back to the central city. Dissatisfied with both these approaches to reform, the Ford Foundation in the late 1950s backed Mobilization for Youth, which had community action as a central feature. The basic assumptions of community action were the existence of the poverty cycle and the lack of opportunity for the poor. It was believed that existing social service agencies, such as those for education, medical care, and welfare, were making the poor dependent rather than self-reliant. The goal of community action was to make the poor self-reliant by their participation in the management and policy decisions of these agencies. This idea was incorporated in the Economic Opportunity Act of 1964 as a requirement that all programs sponsored by the legislation have maximum feasible participation. Since the Head Start program in early childhood education resulted from this legislation, community participation became one of its features.

Community action resulted in a great deal of political controversy. Some people charged that it resulted in conflict between elected local officials and groups sponsored through community-action programs. Other groups charged the program with sponsoring local radicals who tried to take over special agencies. What it did accomplish in the 1960s was to increase community participation in the schools and establish school advisory committees.

Foundations have sponsored research projects and major social studies that have had a profound impact on American schools. One of the most famous and important studies sponsored by the Carnegie Corporation contributed to the U.S. Supreme Court decision ending school segregation in the South. The study was of American blacks and was begun in 1938 under the leadership of Swedish social scientist Gunnar Myrdal. World War II slowed down the work, and the final study was published in 1944 as *An American Dilemma*. It was this study, cited in the 1954 Supreme Court case ending school desegregation, that was a main part of the social science evidence demonstrating that segregated schools were inherently unequal.

During the 1950s, the Carnegie Corporation sponsored James Conant's influential study, *The American High School Today*. The study was conducted during a time when there was strong public criticism of the failure of the schools to produce enough scientists and engineers. One of the major recommendations of the Conant study was that high schools should consolidate so that a wider range of programs could be offered to students. It was believed that students could not be properly differentiated into programs geared toward their future social roles in small high schools. The Conant report's recommendations for larger high schools resulted in a national movement to consolidate high schools.

Foundations have also helped to strengthen and establish organizations that have had a direct influence on educational policy. Charles Biebel in a 1976 article in the *History of Education*, "Private Foundations and Public Policy: The Case of Secondary Education During the Great Depression," states that during the 1930s John D. Rockefeller's General Education Board reorganized and supported the American Council of Education as a vehicle for instituting the General Education Board's own plans to restructure American secondary education. In addition, the General Education Board established the American Youth Commission and provided money to the National Education Association to establish the Educational Policies Committee. All these groups were extremely influential in the formulation of secondary school policy.

An extremely important organization that the Carnegie Corporation helped to found in 1947 was the Educational Testing Service (ETS). Most college students and candidates for professional schools in recent times have taken some test administered by ETS. The two major testing enterprises originally brought together in ETS were the Scholastic Aptitude Test (SAT) and the College Entrance Examination Board (CEEB). Over the years ETS has expanded its testing activities to become one of the major gatekeepers to the professions and to institutions of higher learning. By the 1970s consumer advocate Ralph Nader criticized ETS for its almost monopolistic control of testing and for the high cost of taking their examinations.

Because of the controversial nature of foundation activity in the United States and the criticism of its activity from every part of the political spectrum, it is difficult to make any single general judgment about the role of foundations in American education. Any person interested in the workings of a particular foundation must ask the following types of questions. The most important question is about the social composition and political views of the members of the board of directors of the foundation. This is important because it is usually this group which establishes the guiding philosophy for determining the types of projects to be funded. It should be remembered that where the money is spent can have a tremendous influence over shaping educational institutions and policy. The next important question is about the type of relationships between foundation staff and the community. The informal activities of the staff can result in the solicitation of particular types of proposals for funding and certain types of information being received by the board of directors. Very often the major contact of staff members and boards of directors is with social elites within communities. This might not be true if the foundation aggressively pursues broader contacts within the community.

A third important question concerns whether or not the past record of foundation activity reflects any particular social or political philosophy. Sometimes the answer to this question is to be found in the type of things the foundation refused to support. If, for instance, a foundation has provided money to support particular organizations and not others, the question must be asked, why? The same question must be asked of research and projects funded by foundations. Very often a careful reading of statements by foundation officials about what they think is a good education or a good society will give clues to the general social and political philosophy behind foundation activity.

Foundations will continue to have an important impact on American society and education. It is only through regulatory legislation that the general public can directly control the activities of foundations. Local groups can indirectly place pressure on foundations by surveying their activities and writing letters of either praise or criticism to local newspapers and seeking other public forums for discussion of foundation influence over community life. A combination of these approaches should be used by those interested in public control of the influential power of these tremendous foundations of private wealth.

Washington Lobbyists

According to the estimates of Stephen K. Bailey, in his *Education Interest Groups in the Nation's Capital*, there are between 250 and 300 educational organizations located in or near Washington, D.C. All these organizations purport to speak for some interest group in American education. They vary in the scope of their concerns from general organizations, such as the American Council on Education, to more specific groups, such as the Music Educators' National Conference. Their activities range from organizing conferences and publishing research bulletins for their particular constituents, to organizing lobbying activities.

Bailey divided these education interest groups into ten categories. The first category he calls "umbrella" organizations, which are broad-based organizations with institutional and associational memberships. One organization in this category is the American Council of Education, which does not have persons as members but is a conglomerate of institutions and associations. For instance, the inner group of higher education members (group A) includes the American Association of Community and Junior Colleges, the American Association of State Colleges and Universities, the Association of American Universities, and five other major higher education associations. In addition, the American Council of Education has a group B membership of 60 associations, such as the American Association of Colleges for Teacher Education and the American Library Association. The American Council on Education claims a total membership of fourteen hundred institutions representing nearly all universities in the United States, most four-year colleges, and one-third of the accredited community and junior colleges.

The second category of interest groups includes institutional associations, many of whom are members of the American Council on Education. These are associations of institutions such as the American Association of Community and Junior Colleges and the Association of American Universities. The third category is made up of the teachers' organizations described in the previous chapter. Also included in this category with the NEA and the AFT is the American Association of University Professors (AAUP).

The fourth category of interest groups contains groups structured around a professional field or subject matter discipline, for instance, the National Council of Teachers of Mathematics, Journalism Education Association, and the Home Economics Education Association. Most of these organizations are affiliated with either the National Education Association or the American Council on Education.

Some of the most influential associations compose the fifth category of interest groups. These are the groups interested in books and supplying educational materials and technology. Many of these are private industrial groups and book publishers who have an economic stake in educational legislation. Book publishing and educational technology is big business in the United States. Two of the major interest groups in this category are the National Audio-Visual Association and the Association of American Publishers. The membership of the National Audio-Visual Association is primarily composed of private manufacturers and dealers who sell equipment to the schools. The Association of American Publishers represents about 275 publishing firms, with the major control of the organization in the hands of the large publishers that have substantial interests in text and reference works.

The sixth category includes organizations with a particular religious, racial, or sex interest in education. Religious organizations, such as the National Catholic Educational Association, represent powerful religious interests in educational affairs. The National Association for the Advancement of Colored People (NAACP) is an example of one group dedicated to ending racial discrimination in education. The American Association of University Women has for years worked for women's rights in education.

The seventh category includes what is called the "liberal-labor" lobby in education. The primary work done in this category is by the Legislative Department of the AFL–CIO. This work is of course done in cooperation with the AFT. The eighth category includes particular institutions and institutional systems such as Pennsylvania State University and the New York State Education Department. Increased federal funding in the 1950s and 1960s resulted in many institutions of higher education having their own representatives in Washington, D.C., to find out where money would be available and to lobby for research proposals and other funding proposals from their particular institutions.

The ninth category includes influential groups of educational administrators. There are four major associations of elementary and secondary school administrators: the Council of Chief State School Officers, representing superintendents and commissioners in the states and territories; the American Association of School Administrators, representing local and district school superintendents; the National Association of Elementary School Administrators; and the National Association of Secondary School Principals. There are also a variety of groups representing administration in higher education. Finally, there is the National School Boards Association, representing about 84,000 members of local school boards.

The tenth category is composed of miscellaneous educational interest groups. The National Committee for Citizens in Education are primarily concerned about the welfare and rights of students and parents. The Council for Basic Education has since the 1950s been concerned about scholars, as opposed to professional educators, gaining control of American education. In addition, there is a range of Washington attorneys who represent a variety of educational clients.

As the reader can imagine from this survey of the various types of educational interest groups, there is a certain amount of conflict between the groups, and they do not work in harmony for common goals. For instance, the NEA does not support the goals of the Council for Basic Education for reduced professional control of education. The American Library Association and the Association of American Publishers are not always in agreement over such issues as copyright laws. Each educational interest group has its own particular profession and goals to protect. Agreement often occurs between the groups, though, when it comes to the issue of increased funding for education.

The Committee for Full Funding of Education Programs is an umbrella organization of education interest groups bound together by a common concern for the level of federal appropriations for education. As Stephen Bailey describes its history in *Education Interest Groups in the Nation's Capital*, the organization was formed in 1969 by the NEA, AFL–CIO, and the National School Boards Association and now claims membership of from fifty to sixty associations and institutions. The committee was originally created in response to the growing difference between educational legislation and congressional appropriations to support that legislation. This problem increased during the Nixon and Ford administrations, when not enough money was appropriated by Congress and the administration moreover refused to spend all the money that was appropriated.

Besides time spent on this concern about increased educational funding, a great deal of the time of educational interest groups is spent protecting their own particular profession from possible harm from federal legislation. Very often harm occurs as an indirect and unforeseen consequence of legislation. Legislation affecting fiscal policy, military policy, manpower policy, and a score of other areas always has some potential consequence for education. The same thing is true of any changes in policies and regulations from federal agencies. Interest groups must keep a watchful eye on all government actions to protect their own interests.

For example, a 1973 price freeze issued as part of the President's anti-inflation program had the potential of creating chaos with summer school tuitions, which had been set by state legislatures only weeks earlier. In another case, the National Audio-Visual Association had to fight the concept of "central purchasing" of audio-visual equipment because of a fear that it would put its members out of business. The National Association of Elementary School Principals, the National Association of Secondary School Principals, the American Association of School Administrators, and the other major governing groups in education have resisted and protested for many years the requirements in federal legislation for local advisory groups and community-action groups because of the potential threat to their own ability to govern at the local level. The list of examples of what interest groups must watch for in agency and congressional action could take up several volumes. It seems likely that if government continues to expand and become more complex, this will continue to be a major function of these organizations.

To protect the interests of their members and help to shape legislation and agency regulations, interest groups rely upon control of information and a symbiotic relationship with government agencies. One of the problems in lobbying for educational groups is the Internal Revenue Code, which permits an organization to have a tax-exempt status if a substantial part of its activities are not devoted to propaganda or trying to influence legislation. Because of this code, most education associations attempt to influence without lobbying and to provide information without it being propaganda. The NEA has attempted to avoid these problems by registering as a "business league organization" and creating a foundation called the National Foundation for the Improvement of Education, which can accept tax-exempt gifts from other foundations. This allows the NEA to function openly as a lobbyist while maintaining part of its operation in a tax-exempt foundation. Most education associations attempt to avoid the problem by claiming they are providing Congress and agencies with "data" and not "propaganda." And they claim to provide information to their members but do not force their members to pressure their congressional representatives.

The major power of education associations is in their central location as intermediaries in an information network that provides federal agencies with feedback about their programs and about the profession, and provides members of the association with information about federal programs. Because of this information network, agencies and educational groups tend to need each other. Federal agencies need to get information about new programs and regulations to those who will be affected. Newspapers, radio, and television cannot possibly relay the constant flow of information emanating from federal offices. Newsletters from educational associations are the major channel of information about educational policies and programs. In turn, agencies often depend on associations for information to use as guides for implementing new programs. Associations also supply agencies with data about membership reaction to new programs and their apparent effectiveness.

If one were to evaluate the overall impact of these education interest groups, one would have to consider the relationship between these groups and federal agencies as the most important. As described in chapter 7 on the role of the federal government in education, in only a few cases in the past have educational groups had a significant impact in electing congressional representatives or Presidents. This, of course, might change in the future. Up to now, the significant role for educational interest groups has not been as great in influencing the passage of educational legislation as it has been in influencing the agencies which administer the legislation. Like the influence of private foundations, this influence and relationship exists outside the control of the general public.

Accrediting Associations

Accrediting associations are nongovernmental professional organizations that establish standards and criteria for educational institutions. Six major regional agencies accredit institutions of higher education and secondary schools. The six range in size from the North Central Association of Colleges and Secondary Schools, with five hundred institutions of higher education and nearly four thousand secondary schools on its accredited list, to the Northwest Association of Secondary and Higher Schools, with fewer than one hundred institutions on its list.

Accrediting agencies originally developed to deal with the problem of admission of students from high school into colleges. In the nineteenth century this was a major problem for many high schools because each college and university had its own admission examination and requirements. This sometimes meant that high schools would have to prepare students differently depending on the particular college they planned on attending. To deal with this problem two types of institutions developed. One was the testing organization, which developed common tests to be used for admission to a variety of colleges. The College Entrance Examination Board (CEEB) was established for this purpose. The other organization was the accrediting association, whose accreditation activities ensured that students would be admitted to college if they graduated from an accredited high school. This is still true in many states, where graduation from an accredited high school guarantees admission to a state university or college. Most institutions of higher education now use a combination of attendance at an accredited institution and test scores in their admissions requirements.

Accrediting agencies can exert a great deal of influence over secondary education. The standards of judgment established by these agencies touch almost every aspect of school life. They range from administration and relationships with the community to the curriculum and extracurricular activities. Periodic inspections by accrediting agencies require schools to compile answers to long lists of questions and several days of on-site inspection. Visiting accrediting teams usually conclude their visits with an evaluative statement about the school's performance and a list of recommendations for improvements and changes.

A major critic of accrediting is James Koerner, past president of the Council for Basic Education. One of Koerner's complaints is that accrediting groups have tended to perpetuate mediocrity in education. Since institutions are not rated in terms of one institution being superior to another, the only real function of accrediting is not to give accreditation to borderline institutions. This means that simply because an institution is accredited does not guarantee that the institution has a high quality program.

Koerner also criticizes accrediting practices because they destroy a certain amount of local control over education. This is one of Koerner's major concerns in his book *Who Controls American Education?* Koerner believes that local control of the schools has been replaced by the control of professional educators. From his perspective, accrediting associations are one more group of professional educators imposing outside standards over local schools. As he states in his book, "These agencies can therefore bring irresistible pressure to bear on institutions to force them to conform to what people outside the institutions think are desirable practices in matters of faculty, budget, instruction, facilities, or most other matters of moment in education."

Some of Koerner's major criticism is directed at the National Council for Accreditation of Teacher Education (NCATE), which accredits programs in professional education. NCATE is one of the largest and most powerful of the professional agencies that accredits particular subjects and degrees. One of the reasons for this is that teacher education is one of the larger areas of higher education in terms of numbers of undergraduates and graduate programs for teachers, school administrators, and future professors of education.

Koerner's concern about NCATE is "its monopolistic power and narrowness of its policies, but mostly because it was an organization of, by and for the professional establishment." In this statement from *Who Controls American Education?* we have the recurring argument that it is the professionals who control education and accrediting agencies are merely one part of the network of professional control. In addition, Koerner complains about the failure of NCATE to rate teacher education and provide some means of judging the superiority of one institution over another. As with the accrediting agencies for secondary schools, Koerner feels that NCATE contributes to maintaining a level of mediocrity in teacher education around the country.

Koerner does admit that there is a great deal of value in having accrediting associations to assure that some standard of education is maintained in secondary schools and institutions of higher education. There is also value in providing the general public with information about which institutions attain certain standards. The major issues with regard to accrediting agencies is who should control them and how extensive should be their rating of institutions. Should there be public control rather than professional control of accreditation?

Should accrediting institutions inform the public about which high schools are superior to other high schools? Should teacher education be rated? If in the future the answer to these questions is yes, it would mean more influence and power for accrediting associations.

A Theory of Conflict in American Education

The discussion in the last several chapters has been about the control of American education at the local, state, and national levels. There have been two theories about the control of American education that have woven their way through these discussions. One theory is that economic and political elites control education at the local, state, and national levels. The other theory is that professional educators have actual control at these levels.

The theory that is being proposed here is that no single group controls American education but that there is competition between these two major power groups. This competition does not always occur, however. At times, there is a harmony of interests between the two groups. For instance, at the local level, community elites often have a major role in the selection of local school administrators. Because these administrators act in accordance with the desires of the community power structure, they are allowed to exercise major control over the local educational system. The same argument can be made about the state and national level.

But this harmony of interests between elites and professional educators is not always constant. Educators develop their own sets of interests, which are sometimes in conflict with elite groups. Teachers, school administrators, college professors, and leaders of major educational interest groups have their own economic stake in education. Their economic stake includes job protection, higher salaries, and expansion of the educational system. This is not to imply that educators act primarily out of personal economic greed. Most teachers and school administrators believe in the importance of schooling for all people and devote a great deal of their lives to trying to improve educational institutions. Nevertheless, the combination of idealism and economic stake in education often results in conflict between the interests of professional educators and elite groups.

The major area of conflict is over school financing. Educators have a major economic and professional stake in obtaining more money for the schools. The NEA and the AFT have consistently fought at every level of government for increased spending for the schools. Often the major groups resisting increased spending for the schools are local industrialists and taxpayers' associations. But at the state and federal levels, professional educators exert little influence over appropriation committees. In fact, the major evidence that professional educators do not control the schools is the fact that American schools have consistently throughout the twentieth century lacked adequate financial support. If educators controlled the system, there would not be school closings and overcrowded classrooms in most of the school systems in the United States.

Also, professional educators do not seem to have major control over educational policy. As noted earlier in this chapter, private foundations have had an important influence over major educational policy in the twentieth century. In terms of the federal role in national educational policy since 1945, educators have consistently fought for general aid while the federal government has provided categorical aid. The types of categorical aid, moreover, have been primarily determined by groups other than professional educators. For instance, the National Defense Education Act received its major support from the military-industrial complex, while the basic philosophy of the Elementary and Secondary Education Act has grown out of the work of private foundations.

Where professional educators have the major power is in influencing the actions of state and federal educational agencies and in implementing policy. Now it should be recognized that average classroom teachers do not feel they have direct influence over the actions of state and federal agencies. It is their representatives in teachers' organizations and other educational associations who have this type of influence. The control of information, the network of personnel that move between educational groups and government agencies, the influence over the administration of legislation, and the administration of local school systems are the areas of major control by professional educators.

The increased political militancy of the NEA and the growth of the AFT might result in greater power for professional educators over school financing and educational policy. But this will not occur without increased and continued conflict with local and national power structures. In the interest of American education, the American teacher must not only labor in the classroom but must also struggle in the political arena.

EXERCISES

1. If a private foundation operates in your local area, investigate the social composition of its board of directors and the types of projects and organizations it sponsors. Try to determine what affect it might have over local social and educational policy.

2. Check with the research office of your university and find out what type of research projects at the university are being sponsored by private foundations.

3. Ask a university official about the types of lobbying activity and lobbying organizations the university sponsors.

4. As a way of understanding accreditation, ask to see the NCATE evaluation of your department or college of education.

Suggested Readings and Works Cited in Chapter

Bailey, Stephen. *Education Interest Groups in the Nation's Capital.* Washington, D.C.: American Council on Education, 1975.
 A survey of the educational lobbying groups in Washington.

Biebel, Charles. "Private Foundations and Public Policy: The Case of Secondary Education During the Depression," *History of Education Quarterly*, Spring 1976.
 Provides a good example of foundation influence over educational policy and organizations.

Bullock, Henry. *A History of Negro Education in the South.* New York: Praeger, 1970.
 Chapter 5, "Deeds of Philanthropy," shows the influence of foundations on Southern educational policy.

Conant, James B. *The American High School Today.* New York: McGraw-Hill, 1959.
 The Carnegie-funded study of the American high school. This study is discussed in more detail in chapter 1 of this text.

Koerner, James. *Who Controls American Education?* Boston: Beacon, 1968.

Koerner argues that professional educators control American education.

Marris, Peter, and Rein, Martin. *Dilemmas of Social Reform.* Chicago: Aldine, 1973.

A reading of this book will give a person an understanding of the influence of foundations over American social policy.

Myrdal, Gunnar. *An American Dilemma: The Negro Problem and Modern Democracy.* New York: Harper & Brothers, 1944.

Carnegie-sponsored study that has had a major influence on race relations in the United States.

Nielsen, Waldemar. *The Big Foundations.* New York: Columbia University Press, 1972.

A survey of the origins and activities of the major foundations in the United States.

10

THE
COURTS
AND
THE
SCHOOLS

THE COURTS HAVE PLAYED AN INCREASING ROLE IN protecting individual rights with regard to schooling. Chapter 3 discussed the important role of the courts with regard to school desegregation. This chapter discusses the role of the courts in protecting religious rights, academic freedom, due process for students, and inequalities in school financing.

Compulsion, Religion, and the Schools

One of the major areas of conflict in American education has been the relationship of the public schools to established religions. The First Amendment to the U.S. Constitution states that "Congress shall make no law respecting an establishment of religion, or prohibiting the free exercise thereof. . . ." The problem with this amendment in relationship to education is that many religions and individuals believe that education cannot be separated from religion. Both are concerned with the moral and social development of the individual. On the other hand, the U.S. Supreme Court has interpreted the First Amendment to mean that the government cannot support religious practices and cannot infringe upon the rights of individuals to practice religion.

Religion, education, and the First Amendment come into conflict when certain religious groups are forced to send their children to school and conform to the practices of the school, and when religious groups demand that the schools engage in certain religious practices, such as school prayers. In the first case, forced attendance and compliance with school regulations can be an infringement on an individual's right to practice religion if school practices are in conflict with religious beliefs. In the second case, religious activities in public schools can mean that the government is giving support to particular religious practices.

The first major U.S. Supreme Court case related to the conflict between compulsory schooling and religious freedom was *Pierce* v. *Society of Sisters* (1925). The case originated in 1922 when Oregon passed the Compulsory Education Act, which required every parent, guardian, or other person having control or charge or custody of a child between eight and sixteen years to send the child to a public school. The act was clearly an attempt to close parochial schools by forcing all children to attend public schools. Two private schools in Oregon immediately obtained injunctions against Governor Pierce and Oregon state officials.

The First Amendment was not directly involved in the case because the law affected both religious and nonreligious private schools. The Supreme Court did indirectly support the guarantee of religious liberty, however, by maintaining the right to choose a religious school in preference to a public school. The Court stated in its decision that the "fundamental theory of liberty upon which all governments in this Union repose excludes any general power of the State to standardize its children by forcing them to accept instruction from public teachers only."

The Supreme Court ruling in *Pierce* v. *Society of Sisters* was based on an earlier ruling that involved a Nebraska law requiring that all subjects in private and public schools be taught in the English language. The purpose of the law was to curb a feared growth of nationalism during World War I by limiting the use of foreign languages. The Court in its ruling *Meyer* v. *Nebraska* (1919), which declared the law unconstitutional, recognized the right of the teacher "to teach and the right of parents to engage him so to instruct their children." The importance of the *Meyer* decision was the recognition of the parental right to direct the upbringing of their children within the reasonable limitations of the law.

In *Pierce* v. *Society of Sisters* these rights were again confirmed in declaring the 1922 Oregon law unconstitutional. The Court stated, "Under the doctrine of *Meyer* v. *Nebraska* . . . we think it entirely plain that the Act of 1922 unreasonably interferes with the liberty of parents and guardians to direct the upbringing and education of children under their control." But the Court did not recognize the complete control of the parents and guardians over the education of their children. The Court very clearly defined the power of the states with regard to education.

Probably the most important part of the *Pierce* decision, besides declaring that children could not be forced to attend public schools, was the recognition of the power of the state to regulate education and compel students to attend school. The Court stated, "No question is raised concerning the power of the State reasonably to regulate all schools, to inspect, supervise and examine them, their teachers and pupils; to require that all children of proper age attend some school." Besides recognizing the right of regulation and requirements to attend, the Court also recognized the right of the state to certify teachers and regulate the curriculum with regard to citizenship studies. The Court stated that the state had the right to require "that teachers shall be of good moral character and patriotic disposition, that certain studies plainly essential to good citizenship must be taught, and that nothing be taught which is manifestly inimical to the public welfare."

These qualifications to the *Pierce* decision placed important limitations on the right of parents and guardians to direct the education of their children. The state had the right to force attendance at an educational institution that met state requirements with regard to teachers, curriculum, and other reasonable standards. The only right recognized for parents was the choice between public and private schools, and this right was limited by the ability to pay for private schooling. The unresolved issue was what would happen if the state standards used to regulate public and private schools were in conflict with religious practices and the state required attendance at a state-accredited school. This is the problem that occurred with regard to the Amish.

The Amish are a subgroup of the Anabaptist-Mennonite tradition who have refused to be assimilated into both the mainstream of American society and the modern urban and industrial world. They first came to America in the eighteenth century and settled in eastern Pennsylvania in compact communities. They retained in America their original European dress style of men wearing black clothes and wide-brimmed hats and women wearing capes and aprons. In areas of Pennsylvania, Ohio, Indiana, and Wisconsin, communities of Amish continue to exist with traditional religious practices, clothes, and community living. The Amish continue to use horse and buggies for transportation and avoid the use of electricity and telephones.

One of the major threats to the Amish way of life has been the public school and compulsory education. The public school threatens the destruction of the Amish community by the teaching of values contrary to its traditions and the introduction of the children into modern styles of life. For the Amish, this threat can occur in areas that might seem unimportant to other people. For instance, one objection of Amish parents to compulsory high school attendance is the requirement that girls wear shorts for physical education, which is in serious violation of Amish beliefs. In the nineteenth century the Amish began to object to the rise of public schools. Albert N. Keim in an article "From Erlanback to New Glarus" (in a book he edited titled *Compulsory Education and the Amish*) quotes a nineteenth-century Amish leader who stated, "The righteousness that counts before God is neither sought nor found in the public or free schools; they are interested only to impart worldly knowledge, to ensure earthly success and to make good citizens for the state."

The Amish particularly objected to the high school because of its broader curriculum and preparation for a vocation or college. The Amish do their own vocational training within their communities. In addition, the Amish objected to what was considered the modern education of the twentieth century. Amish education stresses following instructions, respecting authority, and mastering basic information. The Amish disapprove of education that stresses critical thinking and asking questions. Obedience to authority and tradition are considered essential for the survival of the community.

New Glarus, Wisconsin, was the scene of the final confrontation between the Amish and compulsory education laws. In 1968 public school authorities insisted that the Amish community comply with a Wisconsin law requiring school attendance until sixteen years of age. The county court upheld the school authorities. The Amish appealed the case to the Wisconsin Supreme Court, which rejected the lower court's decision and ruled that compulsory schooling of Amish children beyond the eighth grade was a violation of the free exercise of religious rights. In 1972 the U.S. Supreme Court in *State of Wisconsin, Petitioner*, v. *Jonas Yoder et al.* upheld the Wisconsin Supreme Court decision.

In the *Yoder* decision the U.S. Supreme Court placed some limitations upon the right of a state to compel school attendance, as recognized in *Pierce* v. *Society of Sisters*. The Court stated that in the

Pierce decision there was recognition given that the "values of parental direction of the religious upbringing and education of their children in their early and formative years have a high place in our society." In addition the Court argued that a state's interest in universal education should not be at the sacrifice of other rights, specifically those of the First Amendment. In the words of the Court, "We can accept it as settled, therefore, that however strong the State's interest in universal compulsory education, it is by no means absolute to the exclusion or subordination of all other interests."

The *Yoder* decision also placed limitations on state educational requirements. The Court stated that there were two primary arguments for maintaining a system of compulsory education. One argument was the necessity for citizens to be prepared to participate intelligently in an open political system. The other argument was that education was necessary to prepare people to be self-reliant and self-sufficient in society. The Court clearly stated with regard to these two arguments, "We accept these propositions." The Court then went on to argue that the requirement that Amish attend school beyond the eighth grade did not aid in the achievement of the above educational goals. The Court stated that the Amish community was a highly successful social unit and its members were productive and law-abiding. Education within the community therefore appeared to fulfill the state interests in education.

The importance of the 1972 *Yoder* decision is in the placing of First Amendment religious freedoms above those of the state's interest in education. This would mean that in the future any conflict between religious practices and compulsory schooling would be decided in favor of individual religious freedom. The decision also requires that in any future cases dealing with compulsory schooling the state must show some relationship between its educational requirements and standards and its interests in educating self-sufficient and intelligent citizens. State standards cannot be arbitrary and unrelated to these objectives.

The U.S. Supreme Court has also protected First Amendment rights when required practices in the schools come into conflict with religious beliefs. This decision was made with regard to the objections of the Jehovah's Witnesses to saluting and pledging allegiance to the flag. The case began in the early 1940s when the West Virginia Board of Education ordered that the flag salute become a regular part of the school program and that all teachers and pupils be required to salute the flag and say the pledge of allegiance. Refusal to participate was to be viewed as an act of insubordination, and pupils who failed to conform were to be expelled from school. Pupils expelled from school were considered delinquent and could possibly be sent to juvenile reformatories.

The Jehovah's Witnesses objected to the flag ceremony because they believed that the obligations imposed by the law of God were superior to the laws of government. One of the laws of God taken literally by Jehovah's Witnesses is, "Thou shall not make unto thee any graven image, or any likeness of anything that is in heaven above, or that is in the earth beneath, or that is in the water under the earth; thou shalt not bow down thyself to them nor serve them." Jehovah's Witnesses believe that the flag is an image and refuse to salute it for religious reasons.

The U.S. Supreme Court ruling in *West Virginia State Board of Education* v. *Barnette* declared the West Virginia School Board ruling unconstitutional because of its abridgment of First Amendment freedoms. In its decision the Court went beyond the issue of protection of religious practices to the issue of protection of all constitutional privileges within public schools. The Court argued, "That they are educating the young for citizenship is reason for scrupulous protection of Constitutional freedoms of the individual, if we are not to strangle the free mind at its source and teach youth to discount important principles of our government as mere platitudes." Within the same framework the Court emphasized that patriotic exercises should not be made compulsory. In the words of the Court, "To believe that patriotism will not flourish if patriotic ceremonies are voluntary and spontaneous instead of a compulsory routine is to make an unflattering estimate of the appeal of our institutions to free minds."

One of the other major areas of controversy has been the issue of religious practices in the schools. There has been a great deal of pressure to introduce religious practice onto the schools in the form of Bible reading, prayer, and released time from school classes for religious instruction. All three practices have become issues before the courts and have generated a great deal of public controversy.

The U.S. Supreme Court has ruled with regard to released time for religious instruction that this is permissible as long as the religious instruction does not take place within the public school building. The decision of the Court against allowing religious instruction within school buildings during released time from the regular school day was made in *Illinois ex rel. McCollum* v. *Board of Education* (1948). In this case the Champaign, Illinois, school system permitted religious teachers employed by private religious groups to come weekly into school buildings during regular school hours. For a period of thirty minutes they were allowed to teach their particular religious beliefs. These religious classes were composed of students whose parents had signed printed cards requesting that their children be permitted to attend. The classes were taught by Protestant teachers, Catholic priests, and a Jewish rabbi. Students who did not attend the religious classes were required to leave their classrooms and go to some other part of the building to study regular school subjects.

The Court ruled against the practices of the Champaign school system because the state's compulsory school system was being used to aid and promote the work of religious groups. The Court stated, "Pupils compelled by law to go to school for secular education are released in part from their legal duty upon the condition that they attend the religious classes. This is . . . a utilization of the . . . public school system to aid religious groups to spread their faith." The Court made it clear that it viewed the First Amendment as having "erected a wall between Church and State which must be kept high and impregnable."

A different plan for released time was developed by New York City, a plan that the U.S. Supreme Court in *Zorach* v. *Clauson* (1952) decided was constitutional and not in violation of the First Amendment. The New York City program released students during the school day and allowed them to leave school grounds to attend religious centers for instruction. Students were released only on written request from the parents. The religious centers made weekly attendance reports to the schools by sending a list of students who had been released from school but had not attended religious instruction. Students who were not released from school for religious instruction were required to remain in their classrooms.

The Court argued in its decision that the New York City released-time plan did not involve the violation of the free exercise of religion. The Court stated, "No one is forced to go to the religious classroom and no religious exercise or instruction is brought to the classrooms of the public schools. A student need not take religious instruction." The decision recognized the constitutional importance of maintaining separation of church and state but also argued that this did not mean that the state was to be hostile to religion. For instance, the Court stated that students might request permission from the school to attend religious ceremonies of their particular faith. If the school denied permission to attend, this would be interference with the free practice of religion. In the same manner, denying a student the right to attend religious instruction outside the school might be considered a denial of the right to practice religion. The government cannot, the Court declared, "coerce anyone to attend church, to observe a religious holiday, or to take religious instruction. But it can close its doors or suspend its operations as to those who want to repair to their religious sanctuary for worship or instruction."

The school prayer decision in *Engel* v. *Vitale* (1962) has been one of the most controversial religious rulings of the U.S. Supreme Court. The decision denied the right of a public school system to conduct prayer services within school buildings during regular school hours. Those groups of people who have been angered by the decision have argued that it has made education godless and have sought an amendment to the Constitution that would allow for prayer ceremonies in the school. The Court decision against school prayer was primarily based on the argument that school prayer involved the state in the establishment of religion. This was viewed as a violation of the First Amendment.

The school-prayer case began in New York when a local school system was granted the right by the New York Board of Regents to have a brief prayer be said by each class at the beginning of the school day. The prayer was considered to be denominationally neutral and it read: "Almighty God, we acknowledge our dependence upon Thee, and we beg Thy blessings upon us, our parents, our teachers and our country." The New York courts granted the right of local school systems to use this prayer. The one requirement was that a student could not be compelled to say the prayer if the student or parents objected.

It was the above decision of the New York courts that the U.S. Supreme Court ruled against in *Engel v. Vitale*. One of the major objections of the Court was the fact that government officials had written the prayer. This seemed to put the government directly in the business of establishing religion. The Court stated that "in this country it is not part of the business of government to compose official prayers for any group of the American people to recite as a part of the religious program carried on by government." The Court reviewed the early history of the United States and the struggle for religious freedom and the ending of government support of churches. The Court argued, "By the time of the adoption of the Constitution, our history shows that there was a widespread awareness among many Americans of the dangers of a union of Church and State." The writing of a prayer by government officials ran counter to this traditional struggle in the United States.

The Court rejected the argument that there was no violation of rights because all students did not have to recite the prayer and the prayer was nondenominational. The Court argued that this confused the right of free exercise of religion with the prohibition against the state establishing and supporting religion. Excusing students from reciting the prayer might protect their free exercise of religion, but the very existence of the prayer involved the establishment of religion. In the words of the Court, "The Establishment Clause, unlike the Free Exercise Clause, does not depend upon any showing of direct governmental compulsion and is violated by the enactment of laws which establish an official religion whether those laws operate directly to coerce nonobserving individuals or not."

The Court appealed the same reasoning to the issue of Bible reading in the public schools. One of the cases to come before the Court, *Abington School District* v. *Schempp* (1963), involved a Pennsylvania law that permitted the reading of ten verses from the Bible at the opening of each public school day. The verses were to be read without comment and any child could be excused from reading or attending the Bible reading upon the written request of the parents or guardians. Like the school-prayer issue, the Court felt that a Bible-reading service of this type involved the state in the establishment of religion. The Court made it clear that it did not reject the ideal of Bible reading as part of a study of comparative religion or the history of religion. Nor did the Court exclude the possibility of studying the Bible as a piece of literature. What the Court objected to was the reading of the Bible as part of a religious exercise.

The U.S. Supreme Court cases dealing with religion and the schools have touched upon one of the most difficult aspects of establishing a public school system in a country with a great deal of cultural diversity and a wide variety of religions. Most religious groups believe that religious instruction should be a part of the education of children and adolescents. But the public schools cannot open their doors to religious groups because not all religious groups are in agreement about basic beliefs and what should be taught. Besides the practical problem of antagonistic religious beliefs in the schoolhouse, there is the clear constitutional prohibition against state support of religion and interference of religious practices.

But recognizing the practical problems and the constitutional prohibitions does not solve the problem for those people who believe that religious instruction should be a part of education. The *Pierce* decision provides some relief from this situation by allowing parents to send their children to private schools. Private schools can conduct religious services and provide religious instruction. The major limitation on this right is that the family must be able to afford the cost of private schooling. If a family cannot afford private schooling and they believe their children should be given a particular type of religious instruction, then their rights are limited by the state providing the only free education in public schools. The state cannot provide support to private schools, particularly religious schools, because the financial support of religion would be a violation of the First Amendment.

Those who want religion to be a part of education have been put in a bind because of the constitutional prohibition against religious services and instruction in the public schools and the prohibition against state support of private religious schools. There have been several attempts to provide indirect means to support private schools. The one method of indirectly providing support for private school students has been through what is called the "child benefit theory."

The child-benefit theory was enunciated by the U.S. Supreme Court in *Cochran* v. *Louisiana State Board of Education* (1930). At issue in this case was a Louisiana law that permitted the purchase and distribution of textbooks to all schoolchildren. Under this law textbooks were provided to children attending private religious schools. The U.S. Supreme Court affirmed the Louisiana Supreme Court ruling that the law did not involve the support of religious schools. Taxpayers' money was spent to purchase books that went directly to schoolchildren. The law existed for the benefit of children and not for the support of religious institutions.

The same reasoning was involved in the U.S. Supreme Court decision *Everson* v. *Board of Education* (1947), which allowed public support of school transportation for parochial students. Again in this case the support went directly to the child and not to a religious institution. The Court stated, "we cannot say that the First Amendment prohibits . . . spending tax-raised funds to pay the bus fares of parochial school pupils as a part of a general program under which it pays fares of pupils attending public and other schools."

The child-benefit theory has never provided full support for parents wishing a religious education for their children. Given the limitations placed on the state by the First Amendment in terms of supporting religious practices and institutions, people desiring a religious education will probably continue to be frustrated at having to support public schooling while paying extra for their children to attend private schools. There is, of course, no relief for those who cannot afford private schooling.

The Academic Freedom of Teachers and Students

During the nineteenth and early twentieth centuries school teachers were expected to be models of community purity. Pressure was placed on teachers outside the schools with regard to dress, speech, religion, and types of friends. Within the school, a teacher's freedom of speech was abridged at the whim of the school administrator. Some school administrators allowed teachers to discuss controversial topics freely within the classrooms, while others fired teachers who spoke of things within the classroom that were not approved by the administration. Very often, teachers were fired for their political beliefs and activities.

During the last several decades court actions, the activities of teachers' associations, and state laws granting teachers' tenure have expanded academic freedom in the public schools and protected the free speech of teachers. The expansion of academic freedom in the United States took place first at the college level and later in elementary and secondary schools. The concept of academic freedom was brought to the United States in the latter part of the nineteenth century by scholars who received their training in Germany. The basic argument for academic freedom was that if scientific research were to advance civilization, scholars had to be free to do research and lecture on anything they felt was important. The advancement of science depended on free inquiry. In Germany this was accomplished by appointing individuals to professorships for life.

The concept of academic freedom was not immediately accepted in institutions of higher education in the United States. Many professors were fired in the late nineteenth and early twentieth centuries for investigating certain economic problems and backing things like child labor laws. College professors found it necessary to organize into the American Association of University Professors (AAUP) to fight for academic freedom. The major protection of academic freedom in American universities is tenure. The idea behind tenure is that after individuals prove they are competent as teachers and scholars, they are guaranteed a position until retirement as long as they do not commit some major act of misconduct.

The ideas of tenure and academic freedom have been promoted by the NEA and AFT as ways of protecting the free speech of public school teachers. Many states have adopted tenure laws for the express purpose of protecting the rights of teachers. Court decisions have also played an important role in extending academic freedom. But there have been major differences between the way academic freedom has functioned at the university level and how it functions at the secondary and elementary level. The age of the children and the organizational nature of public schools have placed some important limitations on the extent of academic freedom of teachers.

It is important for teachers to understand their rights and the limitations of their rights before they teach in the public schools. There are three major areas of rights about which teachers must be concerned. The first deals with the rights and limitations of speech and conduct of teachers in relationship to administrators and school boards. The second deals with rights and limitations of the speech of teachers in the classroom. And the third major area deals with the rights of teachers outside the school.

The most important U.S. Supreme Court decision dealing with the rights of teachers in relationship to school boards and administrators was *Pickering* v. *Board of Education of Township High School* (1967). The case involved an Illinois schoolteacher who was dismissed for writing a letter to the local school board criticizing the district superintendent and school board for the methods being used to raise money for the schools. The letter specifically attacked the way money was being allocated between academic and athletic programs, and stated that the superintendent was attempting to keep teachers from criticizing the proposed bond issue. In court it was proved that there were factually incorrect statements in the letter.

The U.S. Supreme Court ruled that teachers could not be dismissed for public criticism of their school system. In fact, they argued in *Pickering*, "Teachers are, as a class, the members of a community most likely to have informed and definite opinions as to how funds allotted to the operation of the schools should be spent. Accordingly, it is essential that they be able to speak out freely on such questions without fear of retaliatory dismissal." The participation of teachers in free and open debate in questions put to popular vote was in this case considered "vital to informed decision-making by the electorate."

The Court also did not consider the factual errors in the public criticism grounds for dismissal. The Court did not find that erroneous public statements in any way interfered with the teacher's performance of daily classroom activities nor hindered the regular operation of the school. "In these circumstances," the Court stated, "we conclude that the interest of the school administration in limiting teachers' opportunities to contribute to public debate is not significantly greater than its interest in limiting a similar contribution by any member of the general public."

The *Pickering* decision did place some important limitations on the rights of teachers to criticize their school system. The major limitation was on the right to criticize immediate superiors in the school system publicly. In the words of the Court, immediate superiors were those whom the teacher "would normally be in contact with in the course of his daily work." The Court did not consider the employment relationship to the board of education or superintendent to be a close working relationship, however. One could imply from the decision that teachers could be dismissed for public criticism of their immediate supervisor or building principal. But what was meant by "close working relationship" was not clearly defined in the decision. The Court stated in a footnote, "Positions in public employment in which the relationship between superior and subordinate is of such a personal and intimate nature that certain forms of public criticism of the superior by the subordinate would seriously undermine the effectiveness of the working relationship between them can also be imagined."

There is a possible procedural limitation on a teacher's right to criticize a school system if the school system has a grievance procedure. This issue is dealt with in a very important book on teachers' rights published under the sponsorship of the American Civil Liberties Union (ACLU). The question is asked in David Rubin's *The Rights of Teachers*, "Does a teacher have the right to complain publicly about the operation of his school system even if a grievance procedure exists for processing such complaints?" The answer of this ACLU handbook is, probably not. The handbook states that this issue has not been clarified by the courts but there have been suggestions in court decisions that if a formal grievance procedure exists within the school system, a teacher must exhaust these procedures before making any public statements.

The ACLU handbook, *The Rights of Teachers*, also argues that a teacher is protected by the Constitution against dismissal for bringing problems in the school system to the attention of superiors. But again the teacher must exhaust all grievance procedures. The example in the ACLU handbook was of a superintendent who dismissed a teacher because her second-grade class wrote a letter to the cafeteria supervisor asking that raw carrots be served rather than cooked carrots because of their higher nutritional value. In addition, when the drinking fountain went unrepaired in her classroom, her students drew pictures of wilted flowers and of children begging for water and presented them to the principal. The ACLU handbook states that the court decision found "the school policy was arbitrary and unreasonable and in violation of . . . First and Fourteenth Amendment rights of free speech and freedom peaceably to petition for redress of grievances."

The U.S. Supreme Court has not ruled directly on the issue of freedom of speech of teachers in public school classrooms. The Court has ruled with regard to academic freedom in colleges and universities in *Sweezy* v. *New Hampshire* (1957). In this case the attorney general of New Hampshire subpoenaed Sweezy and questioned him about lectures he had given at the state university. He refused to answer and was jailed for contempt. The Court stated in this case that the content of classroom lectures was shielded from legislative investigation. The Court agreed that the right to lecture was a constitutionally protected freedom. In its opinion, the Court proclaimed its support of the concept of academic freedom. The Court stated:

> To impose any strait jacket upon the intellectual leaders in our colleges and universities would imperil the future of our Nation. No field of education is so thoroughly comprehended by man that new discoveries cannot yet be made. Particularly is that true in the social sciences, where few, if any, principles are accepted as absolutes. Scholarship cannot flourish in an atmosphere of suspicion and distrust. Teachers and students must always remain free to inquire, to study and to evaluate. . . .

The *Sweezy* decision does not provide an exact guide for teachers in public elementary and secondary schools. The ACLU handbook on *The Rights of Teachers* argues that the decisions of lower courts have provided some guidelines with regard to public school teachers. These guidelines should not be considered law or as final interpretations of the Constitution. All the guidelines can do is to help teachers to understand what types of arguments might be used in court in cases involving free speech in the classrooms of public elementary and secondary schools.

One of the most important things for public elementary and secondary teachers to know is that the courts seem to recognize certain limitations to freedom of speech in the classroom. One of the things the courts appear to consider is whether or not the material used in the classroom and statements made by the teacher are appropriate for the age of the students.

An example given by the ACLU in *The Rights of Teachers* of the courts giving consideration to the age of the students was a case in Alabama where a high school teacher had been dismissed for assigning Kurt Vonnegut's "Welcome to the Monkey House" to her eleventh-grade English class. The principal and associate superintendent of the school called the story "literary garbage," and several disgruntled parents complained to the school. School officials told the teacher not to use the story in class. The teacher responded that she thought the story was a good literary work and felt she had a professional obligation to use the story in class. The school system dismissed her for insubordination. The first question asked by the court was whether the story was appropriate reading material for eleventh-grade students. In the final decision the court found that the teacher's dismissal was a denial of First Amendment rights, since it had not been proved that the material was inappropriate for the grade level and that the story disrupted the educational processes of the school.

Another important thing that the courts seem to consider is whether the classroom statements of a teacher are related to the subject matter being taught. One example given in *The Rights of Teachers* was of a teacher of a basic English class making statements about Vietnam and anti-Semitism when the lessons dealt with language instruction. The court found that his remarks had minimum relevance to the material being taught, but might have been appropriate in courses like current events and political science. What is important for teachers to know is that their freedom of speech in the classroom is limited by the curriculum and subject being taught.

Whether the method used by the teacher is considered appropriate by other members of the teaching profession appears to be another consideration of the courts. In a case in Massachusetts an eleventh-grade English teacher wrote an example of a taboo word on the board and asked the class for a socially acceptable definition. The teacher was dismissed for conduct unbecoming a teacher. The teacher went to court and argued that taboo words were an important topic in the curriculum and that eleventh-grade boys and girls were old enough to deal with the material. The ACLU handbook states that the court ruled that a teacher could be dismissed for using in good faith a teaching method "if he does not prove that it has the support of the preponderant opinion of the teaching profession or of the part of which he belongs."

In summary, one can say that teachers do not lose their constitutional rights when they enter the classroom, but their employment does put certain limitations on those rights. It would appear that before introducing material and speaking in the classroom, teachers must consider the ages of the student, the relevance to the prescribed curriculum and subject matter, and the opinion of other members of the profession.

The other major area of concern with regard to a teacher's rights is activity outside the school. One of the most controversial issues has been membership in a teacher's association with radical political organizations. The two most important U.S. Supreme Court decisions regarding this issue have both originated in cases resulting from New York's Feinberg Law. The Feinberg Law was adopted in New York in 1949 during a period of hysteria about possible communist infiltration of public schools. The law ordered the New York Board of Regents to compile a list of organizations that teach or advocate the overthrow of the U.S. government by force or violence. The law authorized the Board of Regents to give notice that membership in any organization on the list would disqualify any person from membership or retention in any office or position in the school system.

The first decision was given by the U.S. Supreme Court with regard to the Feinberg Law in *Adler* v. *Board of Education of New York* (1952). This ruling upheld the right of the state of New York to use membership in particular organizations as a basis for not hiring and dismissal. The Court argued that New York had the right to establish reasonable terms for employment in its school system. The Court also recognized the right of a school system carefully to screen its employees because, as stated by the Court, "A teacher works in a sensitive area in a schoolroom. There he shapes the attitude of young minds toward the society in which they live. In this, the state has a vital concern." The Court went on to state that not only did schools have the right to screen employees with regard to professional qualifications but also "the state may very properly inquire into the company they keep, and we know of no rule, constitutional or otherwise, that prevents the state, when determining the fitness and loyalty . . . from considering the organizations and persons with whom they associate."

The *Adler* decision underwent major modification when the Feinberg Law again came before the U.S. Supreme Court fifteen years later in *Keyishian* v. *Board of Regents of New York* (1967). In this case a teacher at the State University of New York at Buffalo refused to state in writing that he was not a communist. This time the Court decision declared the Feinberg Law unconstitutional because mere membership in an organization "without a specific intent to further the unlawful aims of an organization is not a constitutionally adequate basis for exclusion from such positions as those held by appellants." The reasoning of the Court was that membership in an organization did not mean that an individual subscribed to all the goals of the organization. The Court stated, "A law which applies to membership, without the specific intent to further the illegal aims of the organization, infringes unnecessarily on protected freedoms. It rests on the doctrine of guilt by association which has no place here."

The *Keyishian* decision did not deny the right of school systems to screen employees nor to dismiss them if they personally advocated the overthrow of the U.S. government. What the *Keyishian* decision meant was that mere membership in an organization could not be the basis for denial of employment or dismissal.

Whether a teacher's private life can be a basis for dismissal from a school system has not been clearly defined by the U.S. Supreme Court. The American Civil Liberties Union in its *The Rights of Teachers* argues that courts have been increasingly reluctant to uphold the right of school authorities to dismiss teachers because they disapprove of a teacher's private life. Examples given by the ACLU include an Ohio court ruling that a teacher could not be dismissed for using offensive language in a confidential letter to a former student. The Ohio court ruled that a teacher's private actions were not the concern of school authorities unless they interfere with the ability to teach. The California Supreme Court ruled that a teacher could not be dismissed because of a homosexual relationship with another teacher. The court could not find that the relationship hindered the ability to teach.

It would appear that the major concern of the courts is with whether teachers' private lives interfere with their professional conduct as teachers. But the difficulty of establishing precise relationships between private actions and ability to teach allows for broad interpretation by different courts and school authorities. Teachers should be aware that there are no precise guidelines in this area. The best protection for teachers is to develop some form of agreement between their teachers' organization and school district with regard to the use of private actions as a basis for dismissal and evaluation.

One of the limiting conditions applied to the actions of teachers and students by the U.S. Supreme Court is whether the activity inter-feres with normal school activities. For instance, in *Board of Educa-tion* v. *James* (1972) the U.S. Supreme Court upheld a lower court ruling that a teacher could not be dismissed for wearing an armband in class as a protest against the Vietnam war. The lower court had reasoned that the wearing of the armband did not disrupt classroom activities and therefore there was no reason for school authorities to limit a teacher's freedom of expression. The reasoning in this case was similar to that in the landmark case dealing with the rights of stu-dents, *Tinker* v. *Des Moines Independent School District* (1969).

The *Tinker* decision is considered one of the most important cases in the area of students' rights. The case originated when a group of students decided to express their objections to the war in Vietnam by wearing black armbands. School authorities in Des Moines adopted a policy that any student wearing armbands would be suspended. When the case was decided by the U.S. Supreme Court, clear recogni-tion was given to the constitutional rights of students. The Court stated that a student "may express his opinions, even on controversial subjects like the conflict in Viet Nam. . . . Under our Constitution, free speech is not a right that is given only to be so circumscribed that it exists in principle but not in fact."

One extremely important condition was placed on the right of free speech of students and that was the possibility of disruption of the educational process. The Court did not provide any specific guide-lines for interpreting this condition and limitation. What it meant was that school authorities had both an obligation to protect the constitu-tional rights of students and at the same time assure that there was no interference with the normal activities of the school.

The *Tinker* decision was a major step in recognizing students' rights. Later court cases dealing with student rights were to be argued in terms of students having a property interest in public education and a right to attend public schools. A student's "property interest" in education is the result of a state statutory entitlement to a public education. The right to attend public schools is usually conferred on children by state law. This law, of course, can vary from state to state.

Property interest and right to an education were major considera-tions of the U.S. Supreme Court in dealing with due process and suspensions from school in *Goss* v. *Lopez* (1975). This case dealt with suspensions from school of junior and senior high school students. The Court ruled that due process "requires, in connection with a suspen-sion of 10 days or less, that the student be given oral or written notice of the charges against him and, if he denies them, an explanation of the evidence the authorities have and an opportunity to present his side of the story." The Court based its decision on "legitimate claims of entitlement to public education" as given in state law. What this meant was that a student's right to an education could not be taken away in an arbitrary manner.

The *Goss* decision requires that due process be a requisite before a school-dismissal decision. R. Lawrence Dessem in a 1976 article, "Student Due Process Rights in Academic Dismissals from the Public Schools," in the *Journal of Law and Education* argues that in the future the due-process requirement might be applied to cases involving dismissal from school for academic reasons. The *Goss* decision dealt with suspension for disciplinary reasons. In either case there seems to be a clear obligation upon school authorities to guarantee due process for all students.

Dessem in his article outlines the basic procedures that must take place to assure due process for students. First, there must be an attempt to make all decisions on the basis of fact. Second, there must be some provision to guarantee future review of any decisions. And third, just procedures must be followed in reaching any decisions.

In practice the above three procedures mean very specific things. A student must be provided with a notice detailing the charges, and it must be received in sufficient time for the student to prepare answers to the charges. A student must be given the chance to present answers to the charges in a hearing before an unbiased group. Dessem argues that schools cannot be required to have groups outside the school conduct the hearings because of the expense. Dessem states, "A hearing before a panel of disinterested teachers and school administrators would seem to strike an acceptable balance between the right of the student to an impartial arbitrator and the school's interest in keeping the expense and inconvenience of such hearings to a minimum." Students do have a right to have the decision based only on the evidence presented.

The U.S. Supreme Court in *Goss* did place a limit on the procedural elements of due process by refusing to require that students be given the right to call witnesses and have legal counsel. "The Supreme Court's rationale," states Dessem, "for refusing to mandate this and several other procedures was that since 'brief disciplinary suspensions are almost countless, to impose in each such case even truncated trial type procedures might well overwhelm administrative facilities in many places. . . .' "

The *Tinker* decision has provided some protection for the freedom of speech of students in public schools, and the *Goss* decision has provided protection from arbitrary dismissal from public schools. Both decisions represent the continuing expansion of civil liberties under the Constitution of the United States. Teachers and other school authorities have a duty and an obligation to assure that these rights are protected. Teachers also have an obligation to protect their own constitutional rights as models for students and to set an example for interpreting the meaning of civil liberties in the United States.

School Finances

The issue of racial segregation and equality of educational opportunity was discussed in chapter 3 of this text. The reader will recall that in terms of segregation, equality of educational opportunity means equal access to educational institutions without regard for race. In terms of school finance, equality of educational opportunity is provided if equal amounts of public money are spent upon each child's public schooling. The existing problem in many states is that the amount of money spent per public school student varies from school district to school district.

Resolving the problem of unequal financing of public schools will not necessarily provide complete equality of educational opportunity. As mentioned in chapter 3, with regard to racial segregation as a denial of equality of educational opportunity, there might be more important factors getting in the way of equality of opportunity, such as the quality of teachers, type of curriculum, and instructional materials.

While the above considerations are important in accessing the quality of schooling, one should not lose sight of the basic issue of justice. One can argue that it is unjust for the child of one taxpayer to have less public money spent on his or her education than the child of another taxpayer. It is unjust for the child of a taxpayer to be denied equal access to public institutions because of race. Like the issue of racial segregation, the issue of school financing is directly related to equality of educational opportunity.

There are several reasons why unequal amounts of public money will be spent on school children within a particular state. One reason is the reliance upon local property taxes to support public schools. The degree of reliance upon property taxes to support schools will vary from state to state. According to Charles Tesconi and Emanuel Hurwitz, in their book *Education for Whom?*, in the United States about

52 percent of the financial support of schools comes from local taxes.

Reliance upon local property taxes can result in unequal support of schools because of the differences between school districts in the value of the property to be taxed and the amount a community is willing to tax its property. For instance, some communities might have several large industries and expensive residential and commercial areas that can be taxed for support of schools. Other communities might be composed of modest residential areas and not have any large industries. Both types of communities might levy equal taxes. This would not result in equal revenue because of the unequal value of property in the two types of community. This could mean, for instance, that a homeowner in one community could pay the same amount of taxes on a $40,000 house as a homeowner with a house of the same value in another community, but have less spent on the education of the homeowner's child because of the difference in total value of property between the two communities. Examples of these disparities can be found in table 5, which covers school districts in Cuyahoga County, Ohio.

TABLE 5

Property Valuations in Cuyahoga School Districts

School Districts	Per Pupil Valuation 1974–75	Current Costs Per Pupil 1973–74	School Tax Rate, 1975 Collection
Cuyahoga Heights	$260,014	$2,067.76	12.0 M.
Independence	66,017	1,483.04	27.8
Beachwood	44,246	1,759.94	57.2
Cleveland	22,209	1,224.50	42.2
North Royalton	20,718	954.83	52.1
Olmsted Falls	14,404	886.34	49.0

SOURCE: *Government Facts, Number 274, May 2, 1975.* Published by the Governmental Research Institute, Cleveland, Ohio.

The table illustrates the differences that can exist within a single county between property values, school expenditures, and tax rates. Within this particular county, Cuyahoga Heights has the lowest tax rate but spends the most per pupil ($2,067.76). The reason it is able to have a minimum property tax but generate the most income per student is because of the high property values within the community. Cuyahoga Heights is a tax haven for industrial concerns within Cuyahoga County. It is primarily composed of major industries with only small residential areas. This is why it has a per pupil property valuation of $260,014. On the other hand, Olmsted Falls taxes itself at more than four times the rate of Cuyahoga Heights but spends less than half as much per pupil ($886.34).

If the amount of money spent per pupil is considered as one part of equality of educational opportunity, then the children of Olmsted Falls and other school districts in Cuyahoga County are receiving unequal educational opportunity when compared to the children of Cuyahoga Heights. Because the residential area of Cuyahoga Heights is limited, the problem cannot be resolved by everyone moving into that school district. In addition, the majority of workers in the industries in Cuyahoga Heights cannot live in the school district because of its small size and, therefore, their children cannot benefit from the high per-pupil expenditures. In other words, the industries in this community are able to pay low taxes without sharing equally the cost of education within the county with other industries and property owners.

The book that provided the basis for the original court cases against inequality of educational opportunity caused by the reliance upon property taxes to support education is *Private Wealth and Public Education*, written by John E. Coons, William H. Clune, and Stephen Sugarman. This is a masterful study of the growth of school financing in the United States and the various attempts to solve these problems. The first part of the book presents a critical treatment of existing state aid to education plans and persuasively argues that existing attempts to equalize educational expenditures either have failed or have actually created greater inequalities. As a substitute for existing educational financing plans, the book offers a power-equalization formula that would equalize spending between school districts and between states. The formula supposedly would end inequality of educational resources between school districts. The study also presents a plan for implementing the power-equalization formula through the judicial process by arguing in court that the education of children should be considered under the Equal Protection Clause of the Fourteenth Amendment. One of the judicial techniques that is suggested is to compare the inequality of educational spending with the reapportionment decisions of the Supreme Court that led to the one-man, one-vote doctrine. In the minds of the book's authors, schooling should be considered the equal of voting in importance to a democratic society.

The rationale given in the study for the need to support a power-equalization formula is directly related to equality of educational opportunity. The book argues that the United States is a competitive democracy in which a marketplace of talent is the prime determiner of individual success. Like other discussions about equality of opportunity, the primary concern is with assuring equal competition. The book states that "the sine qua non of a fair contest system . . . is equality of training. And that training is what public education is primarily about." The authors also recognize that the primary purpose of American education is preparation for a competitive job market. They state, "There are, we hope, loftier views of education that coexist, but in a competitive democracy those views represent dependent goals that can be realized only upon a foundation of training for basic competence in the market." Providing for equality in the financing of public education is to make the operations of the marketplace fair and provide for the social mobility of the poor. The authors restated their faith in American education: "Social mobility as a value plays a potent role here, and public education must be seen in its special relation of the underclasses to whom it is the strongest hope for rising in the social scale."

The first major judicial decision dealing with school finances was made by the California Supreme Court in *Serrano* v. *Priest* (1971). This case involved the two sons of John Serrano, who lived in a poor, mainly Mexican-American community in Los Angeles. The local school in the area had rapidly increasing class sizes and a consequent shortage of textbooks and supplies. Local school authorities told John Serrano that the financial situation in the schools would not improve. According to Charles Tesconi and Emanuel Hurwitz in their book *Education for Whom?*, the family was forced to mortgage their property and move to another community to provide a better education for the two sons.

The case presented before the California Supreme Court put the situation of the Serrano family in the following terms: "Plaintiffs contend that the school financing system classifies on the basis of wealth. We find this proposition irrefutable. . . ." The court went on to assert that this was a direct result of the method of financing the schools. The example given by the court was of "Baldwin Park citizens, who paid a school tax of $5.48 per $100 of assessed valuation, were able to spend less than half as much on education as Beverly Hills residents, who were taxed only $2.38 per $100."

The California Supreme Court ruled in the *Serrano* case that the California school financing system, with its dependence upon local property taxes, violated the Equal Protection Clause of the Fourteenth Amendment. The court stated, "We have determined that this funding scheme invidiously discriminates against the poor because it makes the quality of a child's education a function of the wealth of his parents and his neighbors."

Serrano was a landmark decision for action within state court systems. When the issue finally reached the U.S. Supreme Court, a major setback occurred in the legal struggles. In 1973 the Supreme Court ruled in one of the school financing cases, *Rodriguez v. San Antonio Independent School District*, that the right to an education was not implicitly protected by the Fourteenth Amendment and was not entitled to constitutional protection. The Court declared, "The consideration and initiation of fundamental reforms with respect to state taxation and education are matters reserved for the legislative processes of the various states."

The *Rodriguez* decision meant that school financing cases would have to be argued within the courts of each state in terms of state constitutions. This would mean a long struggle within each state to achieve a method of providing equal financial support to the schools. One cannot predict whether this will occur in all states in the country, but it is one important part of the attempt to achieve equality of educational opportunity in the United States.

The courts have played an essential role in protecting individual rights within the public schools. Because public schools attempt to educate a large population with a variety of backgrounds and beliefs, there is always the danger that minority rights will be lost or forgotten within the school. In addition, public schooling is a property right and in most states is compulsory. These conditions mean that some institution must exercise vigilance in the protection of rights in education. This is the important role that the courts have assumed and will continue to assume in American education.

EXERCISES

1. Check with a local school district about their grievance procedures for teachers and students.

2. What provision do local school districts in your area have for protecting teacher and student rights?

3. Ask the local American Civil Liberties Union to speak to the class on academic freedom and student rights.

4. Read through current issues of the *Journal of Law and Education* to find out recent court rulings regarding education. Each issue of the *Journal* contains a summary of recent court cases.

Suggested Readings and Works Cited in Chapter

Coons, John; Clune, William H.; and Sugarman, Stephen. *Private Wealth and Public Education.* Cambridge, Mass.: Harvard University Press, 1970.

This is the book that provided the basic arguments for the school finance cases.

Dessem, Lawrence. "Student Due Process Rights in Academic Dismissals from the Public Schools," *Journal of Law and Education* 5, no. 3 (July 1976).

This article provides a basic summary of student due-process rights.

Keim, Albert N., ed. *Compulsory Education and the Amish.* Boston: Beacon, 1972.

This book contains articles about the Amish and their struggle against compulsory education.

Lapati, Americo. *Education and the Federal Government.* New York: Mason/Charter, 1975.

The last section of this book reviews all the major U.S. Supreme Court cases regarding education.

Lehne, Richard. *The Quest for Justice: The Politics of School Finance Reform.* New York and London: Longman, 1978.

A recent but excellent analysis of the movement for equitably sharing the cost of school finances.

Rubin, David. *The Rights of Teachers.* New York: Avon, 1972.

This is the American Civil Liberties Union handbook of teachers' rights.

Tesconi, Charles, and Hurwitz, Emanuel. *Education for Whom?* New York: Dodd, Mead, 1974.

This book contains essays about the school finance cases.

INDEX